THE

EVERYTHING

GUIDE TO

WASHINGTON
D.C.

Monuments, museums, family attractions, hotels, restaurants and more

Lori Perkins

x

Adams Media Corporation
Holbrook, Massachusetts

An Everything Series Book.
"Everything" is a trademark of Adams Media Corporation.

Published by Adams Media Corporation
260 Center Street, Holbrook, MA 02343. U.S.A.

ISBN: 1-58062-313-1

Printed in the United States of America.

J I H G F E D C B

Library of Congress Cataloging-in-Publication Data
Perkins, Lori.
The everything guide to Washington, D.C./Lori Perkins.
p.   cm.
ISBN 1-58062-313-1
1. Washington (D.C.)—Guidebooks. I. Title.
F192.3.P47   2000
917.5304'41—dc21   99-088136

This publication is designed to provide accurate and authoritative information with regard to the subject matter covered. It is sold with the understanding that the publisher is not engaged in rendering legal, accounting, or other professional advice. If legal advice or other expert assistance is required, the services of a competent professional person should be sought.
— From a *Declaration of Principles* jointly adopted by a Committee of the American Bar Association and a Committee of Publishers and Associations

City maps by Jeffrey L. Ward
Illustrations by Barry Littmann
Metro map ©Washington Metropolitan Transit Authority. Reprinted with permission.

This book is available at quantity discounts for bulk purchases.
For information, call 1-800-872-5627.

Visit our home page at http://www.adamsmedia.com

Contents

Chapter 4:
Where to Stay 53

Chapter 5:
Dining in D.C. 85

Chapter 11:
Other Important
Attractions 209

Chapter 12:
Especially for Children . . . 219

Chapter 13:
Day and Side Trips Outside
Washington, D.C. 239

CONTENTS

Acknowledgments

So many people gave me so much of their time during my research on this book. I'd like to thank my editor, Pam Liflander, for giving me the opportunity to write a travel book that is so concentrated on art, and Sarah Larson, who helped me meet my deadline.

Anna Maria Gambino-Colombo was an invaluable source for the art gallery listings. Alan Simensky was also a great help and made sure that I visited the Kreeger Museum and the Pope-Leighey House, which are two of the highlights of this book. John Hinds, a childhood friend whom I hadn't seen in years, drove me around the city, for which I am eternally grateful.

Linda St. Thomas, the Director of Public Information for the Smithsonian, was extremely patient and helpful in answering all my arcane questions. Randall Krammer, Director of Public Information at the National Museum of American History, made sure that I saw the improvements in the museum's new cafeteria and the new IMAX theatre, which my son Max thought were high points of his trip.

Introduction

Washington, D.C. is the vacation destination for 20 million travelers every year. Because it is the nation's capital, most people come here for the government buildings, the rich American history legacy, and the fourteen free museums that comprise the Smithsonian Institution.

But Washington, D.C. is so much more than just a living history lesson. It is also one of the top art centers of the country and the world, with as many museums as New York City and some fascinating architecture. It is the premier city for African-American history and art, as well as one of the most fun and educational places you can visit with children, from toddlers to teen-agers. On top of that, it is a college town with eight universities.

Because there is so much to see and do (and so many new museums and attractions opening every year), many people make Washington, D.C. a rotating spot on a variable list of vacation places and see a different side of the city each time they visit.

For those interested in how our government works and American history, the city offers the White House, the Capitol, the Pentagon, the National Archives, the Supreme Court, the Jefferson, Lincoln, Roosevelt, and Vietnam and Korean War Memorials, as well as a treasure trove of historical homes and monuments.

The Smithsonian Institution itself is like an American theme park. Its most popular museums are the National Air and Space Museum (featuring the Wright brothers' 1903 Flyer and the Apollo 11 space capsule), the National Museum of Natural History (with the Hope diamond and the Dinosaur Hall), and the National Museum of American History (featuring the ruby slippers Judy Garland wore in *The Wizard of Oz* and the gowns worn by the First Ladies at their inaugural balls). The Smithsonian collection also features museums on arts and industries, African art, Asian art, decorative arts, American art, great portraits, and modern art. The Smithsonian also runs the National Zoo (where you can see a white tiger), the National Postal Museum (a surprisingly entertaining experience), and the Anacostia Museum, which highlights African-American art and culture.

For the art lover, there are countless private museums in Washington that tend to feature the works of nineteenth- and

twentieth-century artists of both Europe and America. The National Gallery of Art, which is not part of the Smithsonian, takes up an entire block and even has a new addition with a twentieth-century sculpture garden that is profoundly inspiring. The Corcoran Gallery features contemporary art and has one of the most substantial twentieth-century African-American collections in this country. The Phillips Collection has an Impressionist collection that rivals anything in Paris, and the National Museum of Women in the Arts has a permanent collection of paintings by women artists from the Renaissance to the present.

In addition to the art, D.C. has many well-preserved historic homes from Colonial times, through Victorian to the present. Some of these highlights include Mount Vernon, George Washington's estate; the Decatur House, which many consider the first "decent" house in D.C.; Woodrow Wilson's home; the Heurich Mansion, which is a unique Victorian example of the nouveau riche around the turn of the century; and the Kreeger Museum, which was designed by Philip Johnson in the '60s and houses a spectacular collection of nineteenth-and twentieth-century art. In addition to all that, there is a Frank Lloyd Wright house just a few miles from Mount Vernon, which is now run by the National Trust and open to the public!

No other city in the country has the concentration of homes, art, and history of African-American culture that Washington, D.C. has. You can visit the preserved homes of famous nineteenth-century abolitionist Frederick Douglass and activist Mary McLeod Bethune, see portraits of famous black Americans (including Langston Hughes, George Washington Carver, and Rosa Parks) in the National Portrait Gallery, and learn more about the African-American experience at the Anacostia Museum. The National Museum of American History features a replica of a slave ship. The Sumner Museum was the first school for black Americans and is now a museum and research center, as is the Martin Luther King Jr. Library. The library features a wonderful mural of King's life and legacy, which was designed by world-renowned architect Ludwig Mies van der Rohe.

For children, D.C. is an interactive history lesson and playground. Aside from the most obvious kid attractions (the National Zoo, The National Air and Space Museum, The National Museum of Natural History), other guaranteed kid pleasers are the U.S. Mint, where they can see money printed, and the FBI tour, where the ballistics demonstration always wows them. The new MCI National Sports Gallery at the center is a must for any sports fan, with interactive games and fabulous memorabilia, such as Muhammad Ali's boxing gloves and Mark McGwire and Sammy Sosa's baseball jerseys. The nearby Discovery Store has some fascinating interactive exhibits on astronomy, biology, and earth science, as well as a T-Rex model that kids can get much closer to than they could in a museum. The National Geographic Explorer's Hall has interactive exhibits and a truly amazing giant dinosaur egg fossil. The recently opened Newseum allows kids to make their own broadcast (Mom and Dad can pay for a video of it), and the one-hundred-year-old carousel outside of the Smithsonian Castle has timeless charm for parents and kids alike. And the Smithsonian's National Postal Museum is a wonderfully kid-friendly attraction that includes a flight simulator in which kids "fly air mail."

For the history buff, no trip to Washington, D.C. would be complete without a visit to Ford's Theatre, where President Lincoln was shot, and to the Peterson House across the street, where he died. Arlington National Cemetery is the site of J.F.K's grave, the Tomb of the Unknown Soldier, and General Robert E. Lee's home, which is part of one of the most fascinating Civil War stories in this historic town. (More on that later!)

The purpose of this guide is to give you a grand overview of all the wonderful things there are to do in Washington, D.C., and to help you decide what attractions you want to see and how to go about seeing them. Although Washington, D.C. is a fairly small city with excellent public transportation, it would take more than a month to see everything. This book will get you better acquainted with this great city so that you can identify your personal must-see sights and must-do adventures.

Once you know what sights you want to see, this guide will give you suggestions for the best times to see them, how to get tickets (if you need them), how to get there, any shortcuts there might be, and where to eat along the way.

Your travel planning is about to begin. Make your reservations, pack your bags, and get ready to go! Washington, D.C. will keep you fascinated from dawn till dusk, and then some—the more you learn about it ahead of time, the more fun you'll have once you get there.

Chapter One

Planning Your Vacation to Washington, D.C.

Washington, D.C. is a year-round city with many wonderful seasonal attractions such as the famous cherry blossom trees circling the Tidal Basin that bloom in the early spring or the candlelight tours of the White House during the holiday season. Many people come annually for the solemn and touching Memorial Day ceremonies at the Vietnam Veterans Memorial and Arlington National Cemetery or for the fabulous fireworks display over the National Mall for the Fourth of July.

Because the climate is relatively mild for three seasons out of four, there is never a bad time to visit the nation's capital, which means that it is a city that regularly receives and accommodates tourists. However, this also means that the many sites and attractions are often crowded, which can translate into long lines to get into popular sites or no entry at all.

Tickets and Tours

It is possible to visit Washington, D.C. and wing it, but there are so many must-see things to do that require tickets (both free and paid) that it is really in your interest to plan ahead, especially if you are going for a short visit or vacationing during the holidays or the peak travel season.

Almost all the government tours require tickets, and some of these tours have very limited windows of opportunity. For instance, the White House is only open to public touring from 10:00 A.M. till noon, Tuesday through Saturday, so public tickets become available that day at 7:00 A.M. and are usually gone in the summer months by 8:00 A.M.

However, there is a fabulous loophole for the traveler who plans ahead. If you give yourself four to six weeks, you can get all the tickets you want to all the government attractions from your representative or senator's office, and you won't have to wait in line for tickets.

You can call your representative or senator's local office by looking up the numbers in your local phone book or by calling information. You can also write to him/her at: Name of Representative, House of Representatives, Washington, D.C. 20515 or Name of Senator, U.S. Senate, Washington, D.C. 20510. I would write the

Senator Jane Smith
U.S. Senate
Washington DC. 20510
Att: Advance Tickets

words "Advance Tickets" on the envelope. If you're short on time, it might be worth your while to call the Washington office and fax your letter. Many senators and representatives are online now, so you can search for their names and e-mail your request.

Government tours and sites that require tickets are:

- the White House
- the Federal Bureau of Investigation
- the Bureau of Engraving and Printing
- the Capitol
- the Supreme Court
- the Kennedy Center

In addition, some of the more popular attractions require tickets, which can eat up a lot of your day waiting in line for a ticket for a 4:00 entry, but you can call a ticket service and get advance tickets for a small service charge. Protix (800-400-9373, 10 A.M. to 9 P.M.) will supply you with up to four tickets for a nominal service charge of $3 per ticket and a $1 free processing charge on the whole order. They offer tickets to:

- the Holocaust Museum—tickets will be waiting for you inside at the pass desk.
- Ford's Theatre tour—tickets can be picked up at the Will Call Desk.

Tickets for Events

Washington, D.C. has a number of terrific theatrical and musical venues, some of which are free.

Before your trip, it might be a good idea to find out what events and performances are coming up while you are in town. The *Washington Post* publishes an excellent weekend guide every Friday, so if you have a friend in the city, make sure s/he saves a copy for you. If you don't, visit the *Post* Web site at www.washingtonpost.com and go to the entertainment listings of your choice. (See "Researching Your Trip on the Internet.")

The major cultural venues in Washington are:

Learning the D.C. Lingo

The Beltway—the 66-mile highway that circles the city, composed of I-95 and I-495. It is always crowded during rush hour.

The Hill—Capitol Hill is the area immediately surrounding the U.S. Capitol.

The Mall—The National Mall is the downtown area where you will find most of the Smithsonian museums, and several of the city's major sightseeing attractions. It is a two-and-a-half-mile strip between Constitution and Independence Avenues that starts at the Lincoln Memorial and ends at the U.S. Capitol.

The Metro—This is what the city's underground mass transit system (for subway) is called in D.C.

- The John F. Kennedy Center for the Performing Arts—There are free concerts most evenings at 6:00, as well as paid performances of theater, dance, music, and more. Call (800) 444-1324 for information or visit the Web site at www.kennedy-center.org.
- The MCI Center—The venue for sports and concerts. Call (800) 551-SEAT or visit the Web site at www.mcicenter.com.
- Wolf Trap Theater—An outdoor venue for theater, call (703) 255-1868 or visit online at www.wolf-trap.org.
- The National Shakespeare Company—Call (202) 393-2700 or visit online at www.shakespearedc.org.
- Ford's Theatre—The theater where President Lincoln was assassinated is still an active theater. Call (202) 347-4833 for information about performances.

If you know you want to see a performance, you might be able to get half-price tickets for performances that day. You can call the night before or the day of the show at TICKETplace (202TICKETS). Tickets can be purchased over the phone or bought directly at the TICKETplace sales booth in the Old Post Office Pavilion. Full-price tickets to most D.C. events can be purchased over the phone through Ticketmaster by calling (202) 432-SEAT.

If there is a big concert, sports event, or hot performance that you are desperate to see, you can always call a ticket broker and pay a slightly higher price for the tickets.

Washington, D.C.'s Seasons

Winter and fall are the least crowded times of the year to visit D.C. (although Congress is in session, so hotel rates are higher than in the summer).

Fall in Washington, D.C. and the surrounding areas of Virginia and Maryland is beautiful as the city and countryside are filled with trees and park lands that offer a wonderful display of fall foliage. Mount Vernon is especially scenic this time of year. The tourist crowds are sparse, except on the big national holidays and their three-day weekends (Columbus Day, Veterans Day).

Winter is also a good time to visit the capital, as it's less crowded, there are many special events planned around the holidays, and most of the museums and historic houses offer special Christmas displays. While the winter is milder than in the Northeast, it still snows in the capital.

Spring in the capital city is spectacular. In addition to the cherry blossoms, Washington, D.C. has a wealth of public gardens and greenery (as well as the annual Easter egg roll on the White House lawn). As the weather grows warmer, more and more tourists arrive, as well as the annual school trips, so the city is crowded this time of year.

Summer is the city's busiest tourist season, with tourists outnumbering residents twelve to one. The National Air and Space Museum and the National Museum of Natural History receive at least 1 million visitors each during the months of July and August. From Memorial Day through Labor Day all the sites are crowded, and you will need tickets for all major attractions this time of year.

But the good news is that the city is well aware of the volume of visitors it receives, so many of the nation's leading attractions are open late during the summer. You can pack more into a summer visit than any other time of the year. There are also free concerts and outdoor activities throughout the city all summer long.

Summer in D.C. can be brutally hot, but everything is well air-conditioned, from the museums to the metro to the lobbies of buildings.

The two busiest tourist weekends in D.C. are the Fourth of July and Memorial Day, so if you are planning on visiting then, make your hotel, transportation, and touring arrangements as early as possible.

What to Pack

Washington, D.C. is a fairly laid-back city. If you plan on visiting the tourist sites, comfort should be your priority: jeans (or shorts in the summer) and sneakers or comfortable walking shoes. If you're visiting a lot of museums and plan to shop, bring an empty knapsack, or you'll be carrying around shopping bags loaded with souvenirs all day.

Washington Quotes

"Washington is a city of Southern efficiency and Northern charm."
—ARTHUR M. SCHLESINGER

Spring and late summer are often rainy, so pack a collapsible umbrella or a rain poncho and put it in that knapsack.

If you are planning on going to the theater, the Kennedy Center, or some of the better restaurants, plan to dress up a bit—jackets and ties for men, nice dresses for women. Some of the better restaurants will not allow men to dine without proper attire. Besides, dressing up is part of the fun of an elegant night on the town!

In the summer, pack a bathing suit. Many of the hotels have pools, and you'll want to cool off.

If you know you will be attending an arena event, an outdoor concert, or parade, you might want to pack binoculars. Also, don't forget your camera and/or video camera.

Washington's Annual Events

January

January 20 after a presidential election. Every four years there's a presidential inauguration, which is always a major production in D.C. The swearing-in ceremony takes place in front of the Capitol, and crowds line the sidewalks. Afterwards, the new president and his entourage head toward the White House on Pennsylvania Avenue. The entire day features free public events, such as concerts and parades, as well as many semi-private parties.

Martin Luther King, Jr. Day, third Monday of the month. The city hosts a variety of activities such as speeches by Civil Rights leaders, lectures, readings, theatrical performances, and concerts. There's also the laying of a wreath at the Lincoln Memorial and the playing of King's "I Have a Dream" speech. The Martin Luther King, Jr. Library usually hosts some commemorative events. Call (202) 727-1186.

February

Late January to early February, Chinese New Year celebrations. D.C.'s Chinese neighborhood is centered around 7th St. and H, marked by a brightly colored arch given to the city by its sister city of Beijing. From the day of the Chinese New Year and the ten days following there are parades, fireworks, and celebrations. Area restaurants feature special menus. Check the *Washington Post* for listings.

Black History Month. The city offers a wealth of special exhibits, concerts, and performances all month long. Call the Smithsonian's Anacostia Museum for their events (202-287-3382) as well as the Frederick Douglass Historic Site (202-426-5960), the Mary McLeod Bethune House (202-673-2402), and the Martin Luther King, Jr. Library (202-727-0321). Also, check the *Post's* listings.

February 12, Lincoln's Birthday. There is an annual laying of a wreath ceremony at the Lincoln Memorial and a reading of the Gettysburg address at noon. Call (202) 619-7222.

February 12, Frederick Douglass's Birthday. A wreath-laying ceremony, performances, and activities all day long at Cedar Hill, his historic home, 1411 W St. Call (202) 426-5961.

February 22, Washington's Birthday. The Washington Monument features similar events as above, as well as a parade. Mount Vernon celebrates Washington's Birthday with free admission all day, as well as activities and fanfare on the bowling green. Call (703) 780-2000.

Late February Carnival. A Black History Month Masquerade Ball at the Smithsonian Castle, 100 Jefferson Dr. Tickets are expensive. Call (202) 287-2061.

March

St. Patrick's Day, the Sunday before March 17. Parades in both D.C. (Constitution Ave., from 7th to 17th St.) and Alexandria's Old Town.

Annual Flower Show at the U.S. Botanic Garden. Call (202) 225-8333. The gardens are undergoing reconstruction and won't open to the public until 2001.

Ringling Brothers and Barnum & Bailey Circus at the D.C. Armory, 2001 E. Capital St., and the MCI Center. Through April, call (202) 432-7328 for tickets and dates.

National Cherry Blossom Festival, late March, early April. National news media monitor the cherry tree budding and the festivities are timed to coincide with the two weeks when the trees along the Tidal Basin are in bloom. Activities include a parade, which marks the end of the season. For parade information or

Getting Started: Researching Your Trip on the Internet

Even if you don't have a computer, you can visit any local public library where you can search the Internet for events and information on your visit before you leave.

Once you are on the World Wide Web, you can use a search engine such as Excite or Lycos to surf the Web by typing in the words "Washington, D.C." This will bring hundreds of listings, everything from event calendars to sports listings. Your search will be more successful if you know where to look.

tickets for seats along the parade route, call (202) 728-1137. The National Park Service offers guided tours of the trees in bloom leaving from the Jefferson Memorial.

Late March, Seal Days at the National Zoo, 3001 Connecticut Ave. There are seal feeding and performances, as well as face painting for children. Call (202) 673-4717.

Smithsonian Kite Festival, last weekend in March. Kite flyers and makers from all over the country descend upon the parkland around the Washington Monument to show off their stuff and compete for juried prizes and ribbons. For more information and rules call (202) 357-2700.

April

Easter in the capital is a special time. Events include sunrise services at Arlington National Cemetery at the Memorial Amphitheater, call (202) 789-7000, as well as various services at The National Cathedral, call (202) 537-6200.

Monday after Easter Sunday, White House Easter Egg Roll. A fantastic hunt for over 1,000 wooden Easter eggs for kids between the ages of three and six. Entertainment is also provided for the parents and siblings who accompany them. The hunt and entertainment takes place between 10:00 A.M. and 2:00 P.M., but entry is by timed tickets, which are issued at the National Parks Service Ellipse Visitor's Center (just behind the White House at 15th and E St.) beginning at 7:00 A.M. If you're planning on attending, this might be something you should ask your representative or senator to see about getting tickets way ahead of time.

Easter Monday, African-American Family Celebration. This annual festival of music, dance, and art is at the National Zoo, 3001 Connecticut Ave. Call (202) 673-4717.

Early April, Capital Classic. High-school basketball players from all over the country play in this all-star game at the MCI Center. Call (202) 432-7328 for tickets and dates.

April 13, Thomas Jefferson's Birthday. Wreath laying, speeches, and a military ceremony take place at the Jefferson Memorial. Call (202) 619-7222.

Mid-April, White House Garden Tours. The White House opens its beautiful gardens and terrific outdoor sculpture to the public for two days in the afternoon. Call (202) 456-2200. Again, this might be something you might ask your representative or senator to see about getting tickets for.

Mid-April, Shakespeare's Birthday at the Folger Shakespeare Library. An afternoon birthday party includes performances for both kids and adults, music, and food as a birthday celebration for the bard. Call (202) 544-7077.

Mid- to late-April for two weeks, Washington International Film Festival. Showing of international films at various locations including theaters, embassies, etc. Call (202) 628-FILM for schedule and location or visit the Web site at capacess.org/filmfestdc.

Late April, Taste of the Nation. As part of a national fund raiser to feed the hungry, nearly 100 D.C. restaurants offer tastings of their cuisines at Union Station. Tickets run about $75, and there is an auction afterward. Call (800) 955-8278 for information and tickets.

Late April, Smithsonian Craft Festival. A juried craft fair in the National Building Museum on the Mall features about 100 artists and artisans offering beautiful, one-of-a-kind crafts. There is an entry fee per person. Call (202) 357-2700.

May

May 1, Annual School Safety Patrol Parade. Local schools honor their safety patrol members with a parade of marching bands, cheerleaders, etc. on Constitution Ave. from 7th to 17th St. beginning at 10:00 A.M.

Second Saturday in May, Georgetown Garden Tour. This once-a-year tour offers a glimpse into the private gardens of Washington, D.C.'s oldest homes. Light fare is usually provided with the cost of the ticket (about $20). Call (202) 333-6896.

Second Saturday in May, Annual Goodwill Embassy Tour. As you drive around Cleveland Park on your way to and from the National Cathedral, you will pass nearly two hundred embassy buildings and the residences of the ambassadors. This tour is your chance to see the inside of these fabulous old homes, now the property of other countries, as well the incredible art that hangs on many of the embassy walls. For a $30 fee, you board a bus that stops at ten or so embassies where there will be a tour guide, as

Other Great D.C. Web Sites

In addition, there are specialized Web sites that will give you opinionated reviews of niche cultural events, such as geocities.com/Paris/musee, which is a site run by Anna Maria Gambino-Colombo, a lawyer with an art history background who offers a comprehensive guide to the art galleries of Washington, D.C. as well as her personal list of the top ten galleries and why. A little creative searching will yield you plenty of interesting results about your personal area of interest in Washington, D.C.

well as music or performances from that country. Tours run from 10:00 A.M. to 5:00 P.M. Call (202) 636-4225 for information and tickets.

First Friday and Saturday in May, National Cathedral Annual Flower Mart. This May festival and flower sale also has activities for children and adults, as well as food. Call (202) 537-6200.

Sunday before Memorial Day, Welcome Summer Concert. The National Symphony Orchestra performs a free concert to welcome summer on the West Lawn of the Capitol. Call (202) 619-7222.

Mid-May, Candlelight Vigil. This memorial service honors the nation's law enforcement personnel who have died in the line of duty. Services begin at 8:00 P.M. at the National Law Enforcement Officers Memorial, 4th and E St. Call (202) 737-3400.

Mid-May, Annual Mount Vernon Wine Festival. Wines of Virginia and modern-day versions of those made at the Washington estate are presented, as well as arts and crafts of the Colonial period. Call (703) 799-8604 for more information and tickets.

Mid-May, Andrews Air Force Base Annual Air Show. Take in flying feats, parachute jumps, and an open house at the Air Force base, Rt. 5 and Allentown Rd. This is a crowded (and free) event, so get there early. Call (301) 981-1110.

Memorial Day, last Monday in May. A wreath-laying ceremony at the Tomb of the Unknown Soldier in Arlington National Cemetery is followed by a service and speeches by officials (sometimes the president), as well as a performance by a military band. Call (202) 685-2851 for information.

Wreath-laying ceremony, speeches, and the playing of taps takes place at the Vietnam Veterans' Memorial at 1:00 P.M.

U.S. Navy Memorial (701 Penn. Ave. NW) commemorates the Navy veterans with performances and speeches all day. Call (202) 619-7222.

June

Early June, Annual Dupont-Kalorama Museum Walk. An all-day event along Dupont Circle and the Kalorama district includes open houses of six museums and historic sites featuring food and performances. Call (202) 667-0441.

Mid-June, Shakespeare Theater Free for All. A two-week run of evening performances of a free Shakespearian play at the Carter Barton Amphitheater. Call (202) 547-3230 for information and dates.

June 19, Juneteenth. The Anacostia Museum (1901 Ft. Pl. SE) celebrates Juneteenth, a celebration of the day when Texas slaves learned of their freedom, with music, food, and performances, from noon to 6:00 P.M. Call (202) 287-2061.

Late June, through July Fourth Weekend, Smithsonian American Folklife Festival. This ten-day event features crafts, performances, music, and food from all fifty states, highlighting one region or state in particular. Most performances and demonstrations are free, but food must be paid for, on the Mall in tents. Call (202) 357-2700 for dates and featured states.

Late June, National Barbecue Battle. This national barbecue championship has food from local restaurants, Pennsylvania Ave. between 9th and 13th St. Call (703) 319-4040 for tickets.

July

Fourth of July Weekend. Millions visit D.C. for the Fourth of July, and the city hosts a number of free family activities.

There is a huge Independence Day parade down Constitution Avenue, with floats and 100 marching bands at noon.

At the National Archives, there is a morning reading of the Declaration of Independence, as well as performances by military bands.

The National Symphony holds an annual free evening concert on the west steps of the Capitol building at 8:00.

Fireworks over the Washington Monument begin at sunset (9:20 P.M.), while all day long there is free entertainment at the Sylvan Theater on the grounds of the Washington Monument.

July 9, Mary McLeod Bethune Annual Celebration. Gospel choirs, guest speakers, and a wreath-laying at the Bethune statue in Lincoln Park, 11th and East Capital Street NW, mark this ceremony.

July 10, Annual Soap Box Derby. Homemade and professional soap box cars drive down Constitution Ave., between New Jersey and Louisiana Aves. from 10:00 A.M. to 6:00 P.M. Call (301) 670-1110 for more information and entry rules.

July 14, Bastille Day. Hosted by the French restaurant Les Halles (1201 Constitution Ave.), this celebration of French Independence Day features a tray-balancing competition by the establishment's waitstaff from the restaurant to the U.S. Capitol and back, as well as live entertainment. Call (202) 347-8648.

Late July, Latino Festival. Latin bands from all over the United States play music on Pennsylvania Ave. between 9th and 14th Streets. Food is available for purchase.

Monday nights during July and August, Screen on the Green. See free showings of American movie classics on a 20-by 40-foot screen on the grounds around the Washington Monument. Past films include *The Wizard of Oz,* and *King Kong.* Bring a blanket to sit on. Films start at dusk. Call (202) 619-7222 for schedule.

August/September

First Monday of September, Labor Day Concert by the National Symphony Orchestra. The concert begins at 8:00 P.M. on the West Lawn of the Capitol.

Labor Day Weekend, National Frisbee Festival. An annual gathering for Frisbee lovers (and their dogs) is held on the grounds of the Washington Monument. Call (301) 645-5043.

Mid-September, National Black Family Reunion. This national celebration of black families in America features performances, food, and entertainment on the grounds of the Washington Monument. Call (202) 737-0120 for more information.

Mid-September, Kalorama House and Embassy Tour. All-day tour of the historic homes and embassies, call (202) 387-4062.

Mid-September, Kennedy Center Open House. A free concert and performances throughout the Kennedy Center from noon to 6:00 P.M. Call (202) 467-4600 for information.

Mid-September, Annual Children's Festival at the Wolf Trap Theater in Vienna. Featured are paid performances, as well as clowns and puppet shows. Call (703) 642-0862 for information on performers.

Helpful Web Sites

www.washingtonpost.com—Your first stop should be the *Washington Post*'s Web site. It covers just about everything you need to orient yourself to the city, from news highlights and a neighborhood guide to a yearlong calendar of events and even a tourism site where a *Post* reporter plays tourist for your benefit. The site also offers a trip planner: type in the days you will be visiting, and it gives you a listing of what will be taking place while you're there. The site also provides a weather forecast, tours of the town, metro maps, restaurant listings, Weekend Best Bets, and an archive.

www.dcpages.com—This site offers a fairly comprehensive overview of Washington, D.C. with weather forecasts, events listings, and a search of entertainment topics.

www.washington.org—This Web site, posted by the Washington, D.C. Convention and Visitor's Association, will give you an overview of the city that includes hotels, restaurants, and sight-seeing.

www.washingtonian.com—The *Washingtonian* is the regional magazine for the city, sold on newsstands. Their Web site will give you sample articles about the city from the recent issue, as well as listings for 100 Cheap Eats and the top 100 restaurants in the city.

www.washingtoncitypaper.org—This is the Web site for the capital's alternative newspaper, which is published free on Wednesdays and is available at most coffee shops and book stores. It features a lively and opinionated listing of events, as well as an archive of past articles.

Mid-September, Heurich House Octoberfest. This fabulous historic home in Dupont Circle hosts its annual celebration of turn-of-the-century brewer Christian Heurich with beers and German food for $3 per person. Call (202) 785-2068.

Mid-September, Wildlife Art Festival at the Smithsonian National Zoo. This two-day art festival and fair features eighty artists, craftpersons, and photographers, with art and animal demonstrations and a kid's creation station. The art festival is free but there is a patron preview party for $25. Call (202) 673-4613 for more information and tickets.

Late September Fiesta Festival. This two-day celebration of Hispanic Heritage is at the National Zoo, 3001 Connecticut Ave. Call (202) 673-4717 for information.

Late September, National Cathedral Open House. There are demonstrations by master stone carvers, activities, and food from 10:00 A.M. to 5:00 P.M. The *Washington Post* claims that this is the only opportunity to climb the central tower stairway and see the bells and a spectacular view. Call (202) 537-6200.

October

Mid-October, Dupont Circle Historic Homes Tour. From noon to 5:00 P.M., call (202) 265-3222 for tickets and information.

Mid-October, Goodwill's Giant Used Book Sale. Everything but the kitchen sink is on sale for five days, from books, CDs and artwork, at the Washington Convention Center, 9th and H St. Call (202) 636-4225, ext. 1257.

Mid-October, White House Fall Garden Tours. The White House opens its private gardens to visitors for two days, with musical entertainment. Call (202) 456-2200.

Columbus Day Weekend, Taste of D.C. Festival. Many of Washington's best restaurants (along Pennsylvania Ave. from 9th to 14th St.) offer samples of their fare for this three-day weekend, as well as performances and entertainment. The festival is free but tasting requires tickets. Call (202) 724-5430.

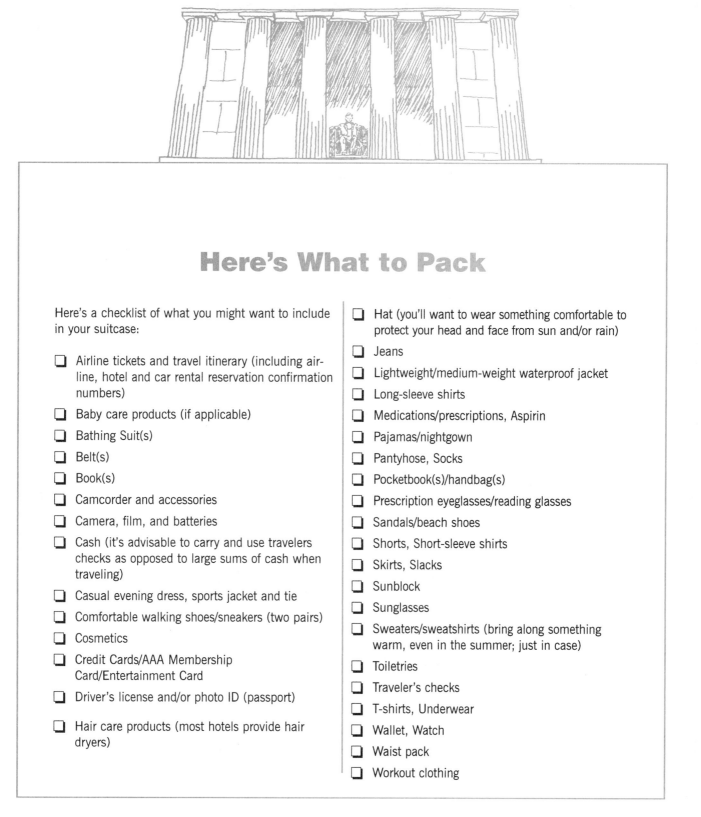

Here's What to Pack

Here's a checklist of what you might want to include in your suitcase:

- ❏ Airline tickets and travel itinerary (including airline, hotel and car rental reservation confirmation numbers)
- ❏ Baby care products (if applicable)
- ❏ Bathing Suit(s)
- ❏ Belt(s)
- ❏ Book(s)
- ❏ Camcorder and accessories
- ❏ Camera, film, and batteries
- ❏ Cash (it's advisable to carry and use travelers checks as opposed to large sums of cash when traveling)
- ❏ Casual evening dress, sports jacket and tie
- ❏ Comfortable walking shoes/sneakers (two pairs)
- ❏ Cosmetics
- ❏ Credit Cards/AAA Membership Card/Entertainment Card
- ❏ Driver's license and/or photo ID (passport)
- ❏ Hair care products (most hotels provide hair dryers)

- ❏ Hat (you'll want to wear something comfortable to protect your head and face from sun and/or rain)
- ❏ Jeans
- ❏ Lightweight/medium-weight waterproof jacket
- ❏ Long-sleeve shirts
- ❏ Medications/prescriptions, Aspirin
- ❏ Pajamas/nightgown
- ❏ Pantyhose, Socks
- ❏ Pocketbook(s)/handbag(s)
- ❏ Prescription eyeglasses/reading glasses
- ❏ Sandals/beach shoes
- ❏ Shorts, Short-sleeve shirts
- ❏ Skirts, Slacks
- ❏ Sunblock
- ❏ Sunglasses
- ❏ Sweaters/sweatshirts (bring along something warm, even in the summer; just in case)
- ❏ Toiletries
- ❏ Traveler's checks
- ❏ T-shirts, Underwear
- ❏ Wallet, Watch
- ❏ Waist pack
- ❏ Workout clothing

Late October, Marine Corps Marathon. Thousands of runners race from the Iwo Jima Memorial in Arlington through the city and end at the Mall. The race starts at 8:30 A.M. Call (703) 784-2225.

Halloween Weekend, usually the Friday and Saturday before Halloween, The Annual Boo at the Zoo. The National Zoo stays open late with night tours of the bat cave, haunted trails, and trick-or-treat stations for kids where costumed volunteers hand out treats. There's also a goodie bag for all grown-ups, from 5:30 P.M. to 8:30 P.M. Children under two free, members $6, nonmembers $12. Call (202) 673-4717 for more information.

November

Veterans Day. Memorial ceremonies are held at Arlington National Cemetery at the Tomb of the Unknown Soldier at 11:00 A.M. and at the Vietnam Veteran's memorial at 1:00 P.M.

Late November through New Year's Eve. There are free performances and holiday concerts at the Kennedy Center. Call (202) 467-4600.

December

Early December on a Wednesday or Thursday, Pageant of Peace. The lighting of the national Christmas tree on the Ellipse south of the White House by the president begins a three-week Pageant of Peace, with seasonal music, carolling, a Nativity, and a display of fifty state trees. Call (202) 619-7222.

Early December Tree Lighting Ceremony at the National Museum of Women in the Arts (1250 New York Ave.) from 11:30 A.M. to 2:00 P.M. The tree remains on display all month, with handmade ornaments by women artists. Call (202) 783-5000 for information on submitting ornaments for display.

Late December. Charles Dickens's *A Christmas Carol* has a two-week run at Ford's Theatre. Call (202) 347-4833 for tickets and information.

December 26–28, White House Candlelight Tours. Evening viewing of the decorated interior of the White House by candlelight

More Helpful Web Sites

United States Holocaust Memorial Museum—*www.ushmm.org*
Capital Children's Museum—*www.ccm.org*
White House—*www.whitehouse.gov*
Mount Vernon—*www.mountvernon.org*
Supreme Court Historical Society—*www.supremecourthistory.org*
National Gallery of Art—*www.nga.gov*
Corcoran Gallery of Art—*www.corcoran.org*
Phillips Collection—*www.phillipscollection.org*
Washington National Cathedral—*www.cathedral.org*
Folger Shakespeare Library—*www.folger.edu*
Library of Congress—*www.lcweb.loc.gov*
National Archives—*www.nara.gov*
National Geographic Explorer's Hall—
   www.nationalgeographic.com/explorer/
Newseum—*www.newseum.org*

For general touring information, you can use a search engine to find the tour guides available in the city by typing in the words "Washington D.C. tours" in your search engine. If there is a specific kind of tour you are interested in, you can refine your search even further, such as "Washington D.C. night tours."

To find what you are looking for, go to your favorite search engine and type in the words "Washington D.C. shopping" (or cafés, or music, whatever interests you) and a fairly good list of sites that apply to your interest will come up.

is available from 5:00 to 7:00 P.M. Lines are long for this special holiday event, so get there early or ask your representative or senator to put you on the list. Call (202) 456-2200.

All Month Long, A Frank Lloyd Wright Christmas at the Pope-Leighy House on the grounds of Woodlawn Plantation near Mount Vernon. Decorations from the 1940s, when the house was built, adorn the Christmas tree. Call (202) 703-4000.

All Month Long, Trees of Christmas Exhibition at the Smithsonian's National Museum of Natural History. A number of Christmas trees and their decorations are on view in the museum.

New Year's Eve, the Old Post Office Pavilion (1100 Pennsylvania Ave.). The Postal Service's giant "LOVE" stamp is lowered to ring in the New Year. Call (202) 289-4224.

Chapter Two

Getting to Washington, D.C.

Washington, D.C. is a full-access city, with many alternate routes of transportation available. It has three airports, a remodeled and very comfortable and safe train and bus station, and highways that are fairly easy to navigate.

One thing to keep in mind when planning a vacation to Washington, D.C. is that because the city's metro system is so good and taxis are affordable, you really don't need a car when you get to the city. Parking in the city itself is very expensive and often quite hard to come by because of all the political activities and tour buses. Most visitors park their cars in the hotels' parking lots, for an additional fee of up to $20 a day, and take the Metro to see the sites.

Getting There by Plane

The three airports serving Washington, D.C. have all been recently modernized and two of them are accessible by Metro, making it very easy and affordable to get from the airport to your hotel.

Ronald Reagan Washington National Airport

Formerly National Airport (the name was changed in 1998), this is the airport closest to downtown Washington. Situated just across the Potomac river, it is a short cab ride (about twenty minutes) or an easy Metro ride from the heart of the city. It is served by eleven airlines, none of which fly international flights (except Canada), as it is required by law that no flight can exceed 12,500 miles. Even with this restriction, it is one of the busiest airports in the nation.

With the name change came a rehab and a new terminal, where there is some fabulous artwork. The various concourses also feature a Smithsonian shop (just in case you forgot to buy something during your stay), a National Zoo store, a National Geographic store, and a selection of fast and slower food establishments as well as coffee shops.

Reagan National is served by the Metro system's blue and yellow lines.

Washington Dulles International Airport

One of two international airports serving the city, Dulles is twenty-six miles from downtown in Chantilly, Virginia. By car, it is a thirty-five to forty minute ride without rush-hour traffic. The airport is undergoing a ten-year expansion that will double its capacity by the year 2010.

Most travelers take a cab from the airport, which runs about $35 to $45. However, there is a Metro bus that serves the airport, which will connect you with the orange line of the Metro system. The bus ride is thirty minutes and then it's another ten to twenty minutes by subway.

The various concourses feature a wealth of news and book-stores, as well as coffee shops, gift shops, and restaurants.

Baltimore-Washington International Airport (BWIA)

This is a smaller airport than either Reagan National or Dulles. It is easier to book, because most people go for the large airports. It is forty-five minutes from downtown by car, just a few miles out-side of Baltimore.

Its main terminal also sports a Smithsonian shop, as well as the ubiquitous Starbucks. There is also a full-service cafe and a kids playground.

Almost every major airline flies into Washington, D.C. The cap-ital is served by thirteen domestic airlines and twenty-three foreign ones. They are:

Domestic Carriers
- American Airlines—(800) 433-7300 (RNA, Dulles, BWI)
- America West—(800) 235-9292 (Dulles, BWI)
- Continental—(800) 525-0280 (RNA, Dulles, BWI)
- Delta—(800) 241-1212 (RNA, Dulles, BWI)
- Frontier Airlines—(800) 432-1359 (BWI)
- Midway Airlines—(800) 446-4392 (RNA, BWI)
- Midwest Express—(800) 452-2022 (RNA)
- Northwest—(800) 225-2525 (RNA, Dulles, BWI)

Priceline

If you're looking to save money on your airfare and have some flexibility in your travel schedule, contact Priceline at 800-PRICELINE or www.priceline.com. Priceline works with the major airlines to sell unsold seats. What's great about this service is that you decide how much you want to pay for your tickets and Priceline will locate an air-line that has seats available and that will accept your offer. There are some restrictions, but the goal of Priceline is to provide trav-elers with the airline tickets they want at the price they want to pay. Tickets can be purchased hours, days, weeks, or even months in advance.

- Pro Air (800) 939-9551 (BWI)
- Southwest Airlines (800) 435-9792 (BWI)
- TWA—(800) 221-2000 (RNA, Dulles, BWI)
- United—(800) 241-6522 (RNA, Dulles, BWI)
- U.S. Airways—(800) 428-4322 (RNA, Dulles, BWI)

International Carriers
- Aeroflot—(800) 955-5555 (Dulles)
- Air Aruba—(800) 822-7822 (BWI)
- Air Canada—(800) 776-3000 (RNA, Dulles, BWI)
- Air France—(800) 237-2747 (Dulles)
- Air India (800) 255-3191 (Dulles)
- Air Jamaica—(800) 523-5585 (BWI)
- AirTran Airlines (800) 247-8726 (Dulles)
- All Nippon Airways—(800) 235-9262 (Dulles)
- Austrian Airlines—(800) 843-0002 (Dulles)
- British Airways—(800) 247-9297 (Dulles, BWI)
- El Al Israel Airlines—(800) 223-6700 (BWI)
- Ethiopian Air—(800) 445-2733 (Dulles)
- Icelandair—(800) 223-5500 (BWI)
- KLM—(800) 374-7747 (Dulles)
- Korean Airlines—(800) 438-5000 (Dulles)
- Lufthansa—(800) 645-3880 (Dulles)
- Quantas—(800) 227-4500 (Dulles)
- SAS Scandinavian Airlines—(800) 221-2350 (Dulles)
- Saudi Arabian Airlines—(800) 472-8342 (Dulles)
- Spanair—(888) 545- 5757 (Dulles)
- Swissair—(800) 221-4750 (Dulles)
- TACA International Airlines—(800) 535-8780 (Dulles)
- Virgin Atlantic (800) 862-8621 (Dulles)

The Delta Shuttle (N.Y.)

Delta runs an hourly shuttle flight between New York's LaGuardia Airport and Reagan National Airport on the half-hour from 6:30 A.M. until 8:30 P.M. on weeknights and a last flight at 9:00 P.M. The shuttle flies from 7:30 A.M. to 8:30 P.M. on Saturday and from 8:30 till 9:00 P.M. on Sunday.

Safety Tips for Travelling with Kids

Before You Go . . .

- Deal with reputable, well-known travel agents.
- Call for airfares ahead of time. Then you'll have a frame of reference for comparing prices to make sure you're getting a good deal.
- Don't be talked into something you do not feel comfortable about—after all, it's you who will be taking the flight and staying in the room, not the travel agent.

In the Airport . . .

- Do not leave baggage unattended.
- Do not leave your wallet (or important papers) in one of your carry-on bags. Have it on your person, in a deep front pocket or a closed handbag (the bag's clasp facing you).
- If you use a cash machine or make a phone call with a calling card, do not let others see what numbers you are pressing.
- Do not engage in conversation with strangers. Do not tell anyone where you are staying or that you are from "Out of Town."

In the City . . .

- Busses and subways can be crowded—so can the sidewalks for that matter. If you are in a tight squeeze with people all around you, keep a hand in your pocket on your wallet. Crowds are where pickpockets work best. And always hold hands with young children.
- Keep very young babies and toddlers strapped securely in strollers or baby backpacks.

U.S. Airways Shuttle (N.Y.)

U.S. Airways' shuttle service also flies from N.Y.'s LaGuardia Airport to Reagan National, with hourly flights from 7:00 A.M. to 9:00 P.M. on weekdays and Saturday, and service from 9:00 A.M. to 9:00 P.M. on Sunday.

Getting to and from the Airport

From Reagan National Airport: If you arrive at the Ronald Reagan National Airport and you don't have a lot of luggage, the fastest and cheapest way to get to your hotel is the Metro system. Reagan National Airport connects directly with the blue line. The cost of a ride is $1.10 during non-rush hours and $1.40 during rush hour (if you arrive during rush hours, you might want to take an alternate method of transportation because the trains are crowded at this time). You can also take a Metrobus from the airport.

A taxi from Reagan National Airport to downtown should cost you between $10 and $12. Washington, D.C.'s cabs are run on a zone and passenger number system, so it should be fairly straightforward and affordable, but some cab drivers do try to gouge tourists (especially if they think you don't know the city), so ask the price before you get going.

There are also two private transportation services that will pick you up and drive you to your hotel (and vice versa on the way back). They are the SuperShuttle, which is a shared-ride van, and the Washington Flyer Express bus. (See listing below for further information and rates).

From Washington Dulles International Airport: A Metrobus takes passengers to the orange line Metro station (with a bus transfer, the two rides cost only an additional twenty-five cents). It takes about an hour to get downtown. The Washington Flyer bus will take you to the Metro station for $8.00.

Both the SuperShuttle and the Washington Flyer Express Bus serve Dulles International Airport.

A cab ride from Dulles to downtown Washington will run between $35 and $45, and $45 from BWIA.

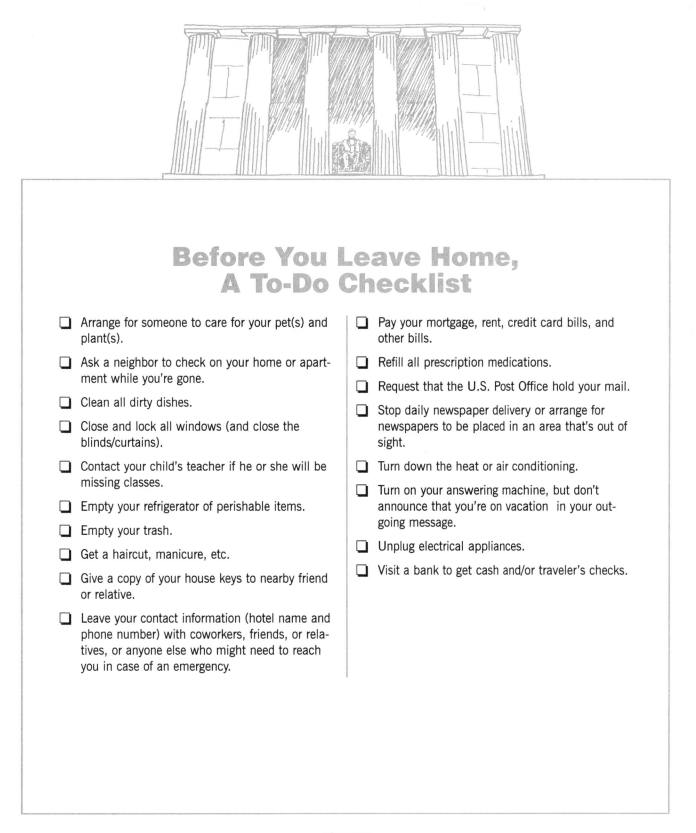

Before You Leave Home, A To-Do Checklist

- ❏ Arrange for someone to care for your pet(s) and plant(s).
- ❏ Ask a neighbor to check on your home or apartment while you're gone.
- ❏ Clean all dirty dishes.
- ❏ Close and lock all windows (and close the blinds/curtains).
- ❏ Contact your child's teacher if he or she will be missing classes.
- ❏ Empty your refrigerator of perishable items.
- ❏ Empty your trash.
- ❏ Get a haircut, manicure, etc.
- ❏ Give a copy of your house keys to nearby friend or relative.
- ❏ Leave your contact information (hotel name and phone number) with coworkers, friends, or relatives, or anyone else who might need to reach you in case of an emergency.

- ❏ Pay your mortgage, rent, credit card bills, and other bills.
- ❏ Refill all prescription medications.
- ❏ Request that the U.S. Post Office hold your mail.
- ❏ Stop daily newspaper delivery or arrange for newspapers to be placed in an area that's out of sight.
- ❏ Turn down the heat or air conditioning.
- ❏ Turn on your answering machine, but don't announce that you're on vacation in your outgoing message.
- ❏ Unplug electrical appliances.
- ❏ Visit a bank to get cash and/or traveler's checks.

From Baltimore-Washington International Airport: There are two shuttle-type services from BWIA. The Montgomery Airport Shuttle goes to Union Station and other locations, and the Airport Connection II will take you downtown in a shared van. Amtrak also runs train service to Union Station from BWIA.

SuperShuttle (800) 258-3826: This is a seven-passenger shared-ride van service that is easily recognizable by its blue color. It provides service from 5:30 A.M. to 12:30 P.M. and serves all three airports. Fares are based on zip code. A ride from Reagan National runs about $9, from Dulles about $22, and from BWIA about $30. There are reduced rates for an additional person traveling to the same destination.

Washington Flyer (888) WASHFLY: This bus service runs between Dulles and Reagan National airports, as well as to Union Station downtown and to the Metro station at West Church Falls. The ride to the Metro station is $8 to Reagan National or Union Station $16, and there is a discount for a roundtrip fare as well as a family fare for up to three members. Children under six ride free.

Washington Flyer Limousine (703) 685-1400: Stretch limos and sedans are available from Dulles to downtown Washington, D.C., with prices starting at $42.

The Montgomery Airport Shuttle (301) 990-6000: This twenty-four-hour shuttle service serves all three airports and runs to Union Station and a number of other locations. Fares start at $16, with a reduced price for the second person traveling to the same destination. Reservations are strongly recommended. Credit cards accepted.

The Airport Connection II (800) 284-6066: This is a shared-ride van service between BWIA and downtown D.C., with fares running between $20 and $30, depending upon your destination.

World Airport Shuttle: This shuttle offers van service from BWIA and Dulles. Sample fares are $29 from BWIA to downtown, $25 from Dulles to downtown. Call (800) 734-5566.

Amtrak: There is regular train service between BWIA and Union Station for $13 per person. You can pay on the train.

Maryland Rural Commuter System (MARC): During the week, commuter trains will take you from the BWIA train station to Union Station for $5 per person.

Getting to Washington by Train

Amtrak (800-USA-RAIL, www.amtrak.com) goes directly into Washington, D.C.'s remodeled Union Station with daily service from Boston, Chicago, New York, and Los Angeles, and many stops in between. From New York to Washington, D.C. there are Metroliner trains that make the trip in under three hours, which competes with the airline shuttle services because you now have to get to the airport earlier due to security measures.

Union Station is a pleasure to disembark into. It has three levels of shops, good upscale restaurants, and an entire food court offering a wide variety of fast food from sushi to saurbratten. It also features a nine-screen movie theater, which means it is bustling with locals, as well as travelers, at all times.

Union Station is a stop on the Metro system, so if you pack light, this is a quick and convenient way to get to your hotel. Outside the station is a taxi stand where you will never have to wait for a cab. Most cab rides to downtown hotels cost only $4 (one zone fare).

There are many different prices for fares to the same destination, depending on what day and what time of the day you leave. There are American Automobile Associates (AAA) discounts, as well as student and senior citizen discounts. Children between the ages of two and twelve are half-price.

Washington by Bus

Greyhound (800-231-2222) serves Washington, D.C. from almost anywhere in the country. Buses arrive at a station four blocks from Union Station (which is the closest Metro station), so if you arrive after dark, take a cab to your destination because the neighborhood often is desolate. There is a student and senior citizen discount club, and children between the ages of three and eleven ride for half-price.

Getting There by Car

Washington, D.C. is accessible from a number of major highways, and the ride is straightforward. From the north you can take I-270, I-95, and I-295; from the south you can take Route 1 and Route 301; from the east you can take Route

50/301 and Route 450; and from the west you can take Route 50/I-66, and Route 29/211.

Once you hit the city proper, you will have to navigate the fabled beltway (I-95 and I-495), which is a sixty-six-mile highway that circles the city and is usually crowded, especially during the morning and evening rush hours. Signage is not perfect in the city, so make sure you consult your map and know exactly where you are going.

Renting a Car

Although you don't need a car in D.C. itself, if you have business or vacation plans in the surrounding areas of Virginia and Maryland, a car is your best bet (for visiting Mount Vernon, for instance).

Car rentals are available at all three airports, as well as at Union Station. If you are flying or taking Amtrak, inquire about fly/drive packages with your airline at the time of your plane ticket purchase because often they can give you a good package deal.

Car rentals at the airports are often more expensive than at other locations, so be sure you price your package. Also ask about local taxes and surcharges.

The Car Rental Companies

- Alamo (800) 354-2322
- Avis (800) 331-1212
- Budget (800) 527-0700
- Dollar (800) 800-4000
- Enterprise (800) 736-8227/ (800) RENT-A-CAR
- E-Z Rent-A-Car (888) 755-4555
- Hertz (800) 654-3131
- Hertz Gold Club Reservations (800) CAR-GOLD
- National (800) 227-7368
- Payless Car Rental (800) PAY-LESS
- Rent A Wreck (407) 823-8388
- Thrifty (800) 367-2277

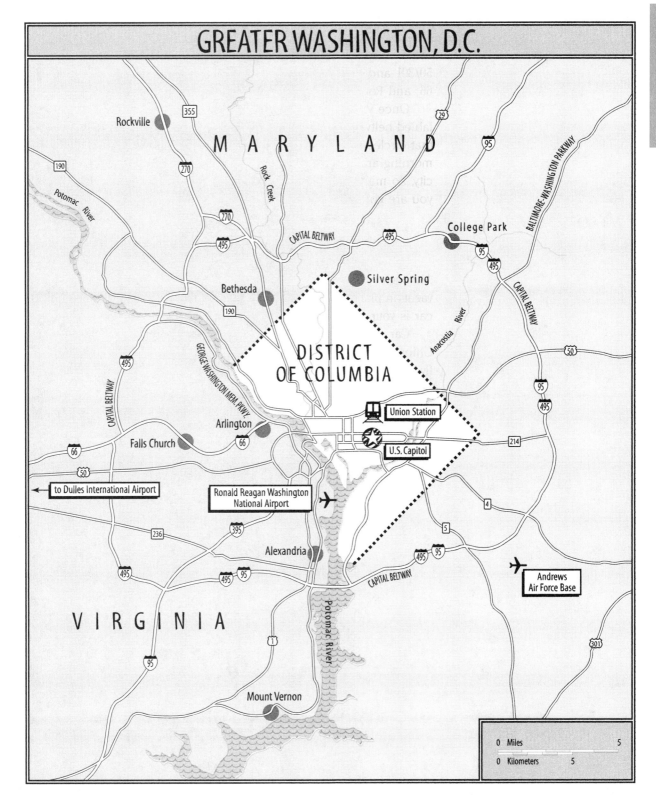

GREATER WASHINGTON, D.C.

Rockville
355
190
Potomac River
270
270
495
Rock Creek

M A R Y L A N D

29
95
BALTIMORE-WASHINGTON PARKWAY
CAPITAL BELTWAY
495
College Park
95
495
CAPITAL BELTWAY

Bethesda
190
Silver Spring
495

DISTRICT OF COLUMBIA
Anacostia River
50
95
495

GEORGE WASHINGTON MEM. PKWY.
CAPITAL BELTWAY
Arlington
Falls Church
66
66
Union Station
U.S. Capitol
214

to Dulles International Airport
50
Ronald Reagan Washington National Airport
4
5

236
395
495
95
Alexandria
495
95
CAPITAL BELTWAY
Andrews Air Force Base

V I R G I N I A
1
Potomac River
301

95
Mount Vernon

| 0 | Miles | 5 |
| 0 | Kilometers | 5 |

Chapter Three

Getting to
Know the City

Washington, D.C. is a planned city that was designed by George Washington and Charles L'Enfant (who designed Paris). It was chosen at the end of the eighteenth century for its central location between the existing states, as well as its location on a beautiful river, the Potomac. The city also includes Georgetown, which was an old independent town that to this day is so separate that it has no Metro access.

Washington, D.C. was carved out of Maryland and Virginia and is quite marvelously designed so that east-west streets use the letters of the alphabet and north-south streets are numbered (When the alphabet is used up, the east-west streets continue alphabetically with two-syllable names—Adams, Belmont, etc.—and then move on to three syllable ones.) Diagonal avenues named after various states intersect the grid and form several traffic circles. The city is divided into four quadrants—NW, NE, SW, SE—with the Capitol as the more or less center. These quadrant locators are important when writing to someone in the city or when you give cab drivers addresses.

While this design is quite wonderful, it is meaningless when you are trying to find a movie theater in the Adams Morgan neighborhood using only a subway map, which has no street names, just Metro station names and routes in bright colors. Therefore, one of the first things you need to do when you get to your hotel room (or on your way to the city) is orient yourself with the dozen or so neighborhoods that make up the city, as well as the distance from your hotel to your destination. This will help you in planning Metro trips, as well as judging how expensive a cab ride will be.

The Neighborhoods of Washington, D.C.

Following is an introduction to D.C.'s neighborhoods. It begins with the three most frequented areas (Downtown, the National Mall, and Capitol Hill) and then describes the other neighborhoods in alphabetical order.

Most of Washington, D.C.'s hotels, both upscale and budget, are located in what is referred to as the downtown area, so this will most likely be your first stop from the airport. Downtown is also the location of many of the city's finest tourist sites, outside of the Mall

Downtown

This is a fifteen-block area, between 7th and 22nd Streets along Pennsylvania Ave., that has undergone a major renovation in the past four years. Almost every block in the area has or will be undergoing construction.

Many of the city's tourist attractions are located in this neighborhood and include:

- National Aquarium
- Ford's Theatre
- Peterson House
- MCI Center
- Old Post Office Pavilion
- National Museum of Women in the Arts
- National Museum of American Art
- National Portrait Gallery
- Washington, D.C. Convention Center
- The White House
- FBI building
- National Archives

These are only the stand-outs in a very concentrated area of things to see. If you have comfortable walking shoes, you can walk throughout the downtown area, but you don't have to because there are frequent Metro stops along the way. Most of them are not named after the nearest site (they include Federal Triangle, Metro Center, National Archives-Navy Memorial and the far exit of the Gallery Place-Chinatown station). This means you have to carry two maps with you at all times—a street map and a Metro map.

The downtown neighborhood has plenty to do. There are many fabulous restaurants for every budget and occasion. A strip

Close-Up: Chinatown

When you exit the Metro station at the Gallery Place/Chinatown on 7th and H Streets, you will see a gilded arch of gold and red that marks the beginning of Washington's small Chinatown (about two blocks). The arch was given to D.C. by its sister city, Beijing, in 1984, and is referred to as The Chinese Friendship archway. During the Chinese New Year celebration in February, the twenty-meter archway (the world's widest Chinese arch) is lit up and topped by 300 painted dragons.

on 7th Street, lined with art galleries, has become one of the best places to view local art. There's plenty of nightlife in the downtown area too.

The National Mall

Everyone who comes to D.C. heads to the Mall at some point during their stay. The Smithsonian museums are here, as are most of the monuments and memorials. It is easy to find on most street maps, as it is defined by a two and a half miles of parkland between Constitution and Independence Avenues from the Capitol to the Lincoln Memorial.

Popular sites in this area include:

- Smithsonian Castle
- National Air and Space Museum
- National Museum of Natural History
- National Museum of American History
- Hirshhorn Museum and Sculpture Garden
- National Gallery of Art
- Freer Gallery of Art & the Arthur M. Sackler Gallery
- National Museum of African Art
- Arts and Industries Building
- Washington Monument
- U.S. Holocaust Museum
- Korean War Veterans Memorial
- Vietnam Veterans Memorial
- Lincoln Memorial

There are few restaurants in this area other than those in the museums. The Smithsonian Metro stop will leave you in the middle of the Mall.

Capitol Hill

Even though the Capitol and a number of heavily visited sites are in this neighborhood, Capitol Hill is mainly residential, with many apartment buildings and neighborhood restaurants.

Consequently, the food is good and less expensive than in other parts of the city. It is also the location of the city's famed Eastern Market (7th and C St., SE), which has been a site of free-for-all commerce since the Victorian days, with vendors selling everything from crafts to produce on a daily basis. It's especially bustling on weekends.

Sites in the Capitol Hill area include:

- Capitol Building
- Library of Congress
- Folger Shakespeare Library
- National Postal Museum
- Union Station
- United States Botanic Garden
- Supreme Court Building

Metro stops in this area are Eastern Market, Capital South, Judiciary Square, and Union Station.

Adams Morgan

This is a slightly off-the-beaten track neighborhood that features a wealth of ethnic restaurants, cafes, nightclubs, bookstores, and the National Zoo. It is centered around 18th St. and Columbia Rd. NW. The Kalorama district, ("Kalorama" is a Greek word for "beautiful view") runs from Adams Morgan to North Dupont Circle and showcases a number of beautiful homes and apartment buildings.

The Metro stop is Woodley Park Zoo, or you can walk up from Dupont Circle.

Dupont Circle

You just might find yourself returning to Dupont Circle over and over again, though it is a relatively small part of the city. It has wonderful restaurants of all varieties, bookstores, art galleries, movie theaters, and a thriving nightlife. Tourist sites in this area include the Heurich and Woodrow Wilson Houses, the Textile Museum, and the Phillips Collection. The Metro stop is Dupont Circle.

Close-Up: Dupont Circle

Dupont Circle is named after Samuel F. Dupont, of New Jersey, a commander of the navy during the Civil War, who captured the confederate site of Port Royal, S. C. A statue of Dupont stands in the center of the circle.

In the 1870s the circle was surrounded by a wooden fence, which was later replaced by iron posts and chains, and then again replaced around the turn of the century with stone coping.

Today it is the center of D.C.'s gay nightlife, with several gay bars within walking distance of one another.

Foggy Bottom

This neighborhood was the industrial area of the city in the late eighteenth and early nineteenth centuries. It became infested with mosquitoes in the summer, which is where it got its name. Before that nickname it had been named after Jacob Funk, the owner of a particularly nasty local factory, and was known as Funkstown. Of course, it has been drained and spiffed up now and it lies just southwest of the downtown tourist district and northwest of Georgetown.

Tourist sites in this neighborhood include the U.S. Department of State, The John F. Kennedy Center for the Performing Arts, and the luxurious (and notorious) Watergate complex. The Metro stops are Foggy Bottom and Farragut North, which you walk up from.

Georgetown

Georgetown is one of the oldest colonial townships in the country and has some of the oldest homes in the city. One of its prime tourist sites is the Old Stone House, which was built before the Revolutionary War. It was an independent town when Washington was planned, and while it is now part of the city, it does keep its distance from the heart of downtown by being nearly inaccessible without a car and having some of the highest-priced homes in the region.

However, it is also a charming part of the city and wonderful to walk through to see its historic homes (Dumbarton Oaks is only one). It is packed with interesting, youth-oriented shops (Georgetown University is located here), as well as many restaurants and pubs and a co-op of art galleries. Georgetown is one of the city's nightlife centers, especially on weekends. You can walk from the Foggy Bottom Metro stop, but it's a long walk. A cab ride from downtown is one fare zone (about $4) and Georgetown is always full of cabs.

Close-Up: Foggy Bottom

Foggy Bottom was the industrial center of the city even before the American revolution. In 1765, Jacob Funk, a German immigrant, bought 130 acres of land where he placed his factories, and the area became known as "funkstown," both for the owner and the smell. The first brewery is said to have opened in 1796.

The neighborhood also became the home to two universities by the early 1800s—a theological seminary and Columbian College, which later became George Washington University.

During the Civil War, most of the Foggy Bottom neighborhood became a military camp, known as Camp Fry. After the war, numerous churches and hospitals were built, as well as the Catholic University.

Glover Park

This is the residential neighborhood bordering the Washington National Cathedral. There are a number of good restaurants in this area, as well as movie theaters. The former mansions and now embassies that make up Embassy Row (a must-see walk or drive) are located between Glover Park and Woodley Park. The nearest Metro station is Tenleytown, but it's a ten-minute walk to the National Cathedral, so take a bus transfer when you exit the train station and you can hop on any bus for twenty-five cents.

Woodley Park

This is a beautiful residential neighborhood that grew up around Martin Van Buren and Grover Cleveland's summer homes. It borders the Adams Morgan neighborhood and starts at the National Zoo. There are a number of good restaurants in the area. Its largest landmark is the Washington Marriot Wardman Park, and it is also home to the Omni Shorehawk, another large hotel. Cleveland Park and Woodley Park-Zoo are the closest Metro stops.

U Street Corridor

This stretch of the city between 12th and 16th streets on U Street NW was once the center of African-American nightlife in the city (known as "Black Broadway") where such luminaries as Duke Ellington and Cab Calloway performed when they were in town. It still retains its reputation for nightlife, with a number of jazz and rock nightclubs, and now features the recently restored Lincoln Theater where the annual D.C. movie festival is held. Metro stops include U Street-Cardozo and Shaw-Howard University.

Tysons Corner, VA

Though not technically a D.C. neighborhood, Tysons Corner is a shopping hotspot and a bargain-shopping mecca for tourists and residents alike. It is one of the largest retail centers outside of New York City.

Close-Up: Embassy Row

Washington's Embassy Row is an entire neighborhood devoted to the city's diplomatic community. It houses more than 160 different embassies and the homes of ambassadors along Massachusetts Ave., many of whom have restored some of the city's grand mansions (General Patton's home is now the home of the Australian Ambassador). Others have commissioned fabulous (and quirky) buildings and homes. There's an idyllic park across from the British Embassy featuring a statue of Kahlil Gibran.

In the midst of Embassy Row lies the Naval Observatory, where the nation's master clocks are set. Next door is the vice president's mansion, which is so far off the road that it can hardly be seen from the street. You never read about demonstrations outside its gates.

The name comes from two of the malls—Tysons Corner Center and Tysons Galleria—which together feature a total of eight major department stores, including Bloomingdale's and Nordstroms, as well as more than 400 stores and restaurants. By car, take Route 7.

Getting Around Town

Once you know where you are and where you want to go, Washington, D.C. is a very easy city to navigate. The Metro system is safe, convenient, affordable, and fairly extensive throughout downtown. If the Metro doesn't go somewhere, the Metrobus system probably does, but it takes much longer and does not run as frequently. Taxis are abundant and usually quite affordable.

By Metro

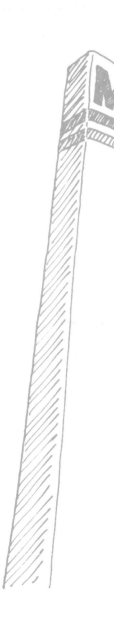

The Metro system now includes 78 stops over 107 miles of track. The final five-stop expansion is due to be completed in March 2000, bringing the system to a total of 83 stops and 103 miles of track.

The system runs efficiently throughout the downtown area (where most of the tourist sites are located) and to specific destinations in suburban Maryland and northern Virginia. If the Metro system can get you where you need to go, it is the best way to travel in the nation's capital.

Kids love the Metro system; it's often an attraction in itself for them. Many of the stations (such as Dupont Circle) are deep below the ground, with long escalators and high, domed ceilings. The deepest station is at Forest Glen on the red line, which is 196 feet below ground (twenty-one stories). The longest escalator is at Wheaton Station (also on the red line), which at 230 feet is the longest escalator in the western hemisphere.

My seven-year-old son says the gray, vaulted, honey-combed ceilings of the Metro system remind him of the Space Mountain ride at Disneyland, and it is a popular urban myth that the system was designed by Disney architects. When I called the Metro's media department, they said they had never heard of this, but I've heard this story from many different people ever since the Metro was operational in 1976, so you be the judge.

Stations are marked by a brown obelisk with the capital letter M at the top. Once you enter a station, you have to buy a ticket at an automated machine. A chart shows you how much the fare is from your starting station to your destination. The Metro Area Transit Authority has pledged that fares will not rise in the next two years. Currently, most rides are $1.10 except during rush hour when fares are $1.35 (the system is very crowded during these times). The machines take bills up to $20 and change, but they will only give you up to five dollars in change. You can buy a roundtrip or a $5 one-day fare. If you plan your trips around a central location and use a combination of the Metro system, the bus system, and walking, it's unlikely that you'll spend $5 on the Metro in one day. A roundtrip ticket is probably all you'll need.

Once you have walked through the entrance turnstile, your ticket will pop back out at you. You *must* retain it and put it in the exit turnstile at your destination station. If you lose your ticket, you can buy another one inside the station to exit. You can buy $20 worth of trips and receive a 10 percent discount on your rides. Children six and older must have a ticket, and there is no discount for children. Senior citizens pay half price with I.D.

All stations have a station manager in a kiosk on the premises and you can usually ask them questions and directions. There are pocket Metro maps available in six languages outside most of these kiosks.

There are five lines in the D.C. Metro system: red, orange, green, yellow, and blue. The Metro Center Station (in downtown Washington) connects three of them (red, blue, and orange) and the next stop, Gallery Place-Chinatown, links the other two (yellow and green), so it is very easy to change trains.

If you know you are going to take a bus later on in the day (or you think you may get tired walking from one tourist site to another), look for the bus ticket machine on the inside of the station (before you exit) and take a transfer ticket. This will enable you to take a Metro bus for a quarter (otherwise you will have to pay $1.10). There is no transfer from the bus to the train.

Metro History

It took four decades of planning to create Washington, D.C.'s mass transit system, which today consists of 78 stations and 107 miles of track. Congress authorized the creation of a planning commission to study mass transit in 1952, but the first Metro station didn't open until 1976, just in time for the masses who descended upon the city for the bicentennial.

On the first day of service in March 1976, there were 19,913 passengers. In August of 1988, Metro-rail carried its one-billionth rider.

The Metro system is open from 5:30 A.M. to midnight during weekdays (every train station lists the time of the last train for the evening) and is open from 8:00 A.M. to midnight on weekends. Eating and drinking on the Metro system is strictly prohibited.

For more information on the Metro system call (202) 637-7000 or visit their Web site at www.WMATA.com. There is a search engine on the Web site that will plot your route for you if you type in your start and destination.

A complete Metro map has been reproduced in the inside covers of this book.

By Bus

The city's surface transit system is also extensive (over 15,000 stops) and works great in conjunction with the Metro system or for short rides when your feet just give out on you. You can usually catch a bus in five to ten minutes of waiting, and there is usually a bus shelter for you to wait in.

You will need exact change for the bus, as the driver cannot give change, but the bus does take dollar bills. Rides are $1.10, and transfers are free. If you have a transfer from the Metro, you only pay a quarter.

By Taxi

Washington, D.C.'s taxis run on a zone system, instead of a meter system, which is posted in every cab. Most rides in the downtown area, or from downtown to Georgetown, are one

fare zone, which should be $4 for one person and $1.50 extra for each additional person. There is a dollar surcharge for night trips and/or rush hour traffic. Of course, you have to tip the driver, usually a dollar or two, depending on how expensive the ride was.

If you ask a cab to take you outside of the city, you will be charged by the mile, which is how the airport fares are calculated. This fare system starts at $2 for the first half mile and adds $.70 for each half mile after that.

The *Washington Post* Web site has a taxi fare calculator, which you can use to get a specific idea of how much your trip should cost. You can also call (202) 331-1671 to find out the fare between a location in D.C. and a destination in Maryland or Virginia. For fares within the city, call (202) 645-6018.

You can also call a cab, but there is a $1.50 surcharge for this service. Taxi cab companies available for radio service include Capital Cab, (202) 546-2400, and Yellow Cab, (202) 544-1212. All cab drivers will give you a receipt when asked.

Make sure you notice the driver's license number and the cab number when you get in the taxi. If you have a complaint about a driver, you can call (202) 645-6005.

Guided Tours

Washington, D.C. offers a number of options to touring the city, from faux trolley cars to buses to boat and helicopter tours. These tours are good orientations to the city, if you have the time, and they're a great way to tour the monuments at night after a full day of hoofing it.

Walking Tours

Washington, D.C. has a large variety of walking tours that you can take, some of which last an entire day, and others which are just a few hours. There so much to choose from here, from the off-beat (such as the scandal tours) to more traditional historic tours.

City Tours—Washington author and tour guide Anthony S. Pitch offers five different anecdotal history tours of Washington, D.C. on such topics as Georgetown, the Adams Morgan neighborhood, homes of the presidents, around the White House, and the White House to the Capitol. Tours are given on Sundays from 11:00 a.m.–1:00 p.m. for $10 per person. Call (301) 295-9514.

Celebrity Tours—Of course, many rich and famous people live in Washington, D.C., or at least have residences here, such as Arnold Schwartzenegger and Elizabeth Taylor, who have homes in Georgetown. If you are one of those who love to see how the

Close-Up: George Washington University

Some of the notable personalities who have received honorary degrees and doctorates from George Washington University include:

- President Harry S. Truman, whose daughter Margaret received her B.A. from the University on the same day

- President John F. Kennedy

- Bill Cosby

other half lives, you can join author Jan Pottker, author of *Celebrity Washington*, on a guided tour of the city's famous past and present residences, watering holes, and movie locations. Tours are $15 and last about two hours. Call (301) 762-3049.

Historic Downtown Tours—D.C. Heritage Tours feature costumed tour guides offering a 90-minute walking tour of historic downtown D.C. with stops along the way that include the site of Lincoln's inaugural ball and the house where his assassination was plotted. Tickets are $7.50 for adults and $5 for seniors and children. Call (202) 639-0908. The tour departs from the Discovery Store on 7th and F St, where you can catch an eighteen-minute film on the history of the city for $2.50 for adults and $1.50 for children.

African-American Heritage Tour: Visit the Frederick Douglass national Historic Site, Lincoln Park, the Supreme Court, the From Field to Factory exhibit in the Smithsonian's National Museum of American history, and more. Tickets are $15 for adults and $8 for children ages 3–11. Call (202) 636-9203.

Duke Ellington's D.C. neighborhood Tour—See Duke Ellington's D.C., by bus and by foot, which shows you the Shaw neighborhood where Ellington grew up, as well as the Lincoln Theater, the Mary McLeod Bethune House, Whitelaw Hotel, and more. The tour includes lunch with a theater performance. Tickets are $39.95 for adults and $29.95 for children. Call 636-9203.

Scandal Tours—Costumed members of the Washington comedy group Gross National Product impersonate political figures and offer a humor-filled tour of the city's most notorious history, from the Watergate to the Tidal Basin to Gary Hart's townhouse and the White House itself. Tickets are $30. Call (202) 783-7212.

Old Town Trolley

This is a narrated two-hour tour on an orange and green open-air trolley. Its eighteen stops include most of the downtown sites, as well as Arlington National Cemetery, Georgetown, Embassy Row, and the National Cathedral. You can get off and on throughout the day by showing the bus driver your ticket stub or a sticker they give you to wear (trolleys come every thirty minutes). They also have printed flyers of walking tours of Georgetown and the Mall. There's a map of tour stops, which also features a number of discounts on food and shopping if you show the establishment your ticket.

Tours start at 9:00 A.M. and end at 4:00 P.M. You may be able to buy a ticket at your hotel (and therefore charge it to your room) or you can pay on the trolley or buy a ticket at the counter in Union Station (which is the first stop). Tickets are $24 for adults, $12 for children.

Old Town Trolley also offers a Washington After Hours tour. This two-and-a-half-hour, narrated night tour features ghost stories and views of the city's monuments. Tickets are $25 for adults and $13 for children. These tours are often sold out before noon during the busy season, so call early for reservations (202) 832-9800.

Tourmobile

The blue-and-white tourmobile travels to many of the same locations as Old Town Trolley, but it does not go to Georgetown or the National Cathedral. It is also the only vehicle allowed to tour inside Arlington National Cemetery (it is authorized to do so by the National Park Service). Instead of trudging up the green hills on foot, you can sit as the trolley takes you by the Kennedy graves, the Tomb of the Unknown Soldier, Arlington House, and the Women in Service Memorial on the cemetery grounds. This is a definite consideration if you have young children or visitors who have a hard time walking long distances. You can also buy a Tourmobile ticket to tour just the cemetery, which costs $4.75 for adults and $2.25 for children and can be purchased at the cemetery's visitor's center. Tourmobile, by the way, offers the only guided tour of the cemetery—vehicle-driven or otherwise.

You can board the Tourmobile at any of its twenty-five stops and pay the driver when you get on. As with Old Town Trolley, you can get on and off the tourmobile at any stop and reboard later (with ticket). Tourmobiles come every twenty minutes.

The cost of the tourmobile is $14 for adults and $7 for children. The tourmobile operates from 9:00 A.M. to 6:30 P.M. from Memorial Day through Labor Day, and until 4:30 P.M. during the winter and

Embassy Tours

The embassies and mansions of Embassy Row house some incredible art and culture from the various countries represented, but you can't just go up to a door and go in to view it. However, two times a year (fall and spring), there is an all-day Embassy Row guided tour, so check the *Washington Post* calendar listings for this event. Proceeds usually go to charity.

spring months. It is available all year long, except Christmas Day, when most national and government sites are also closed.

Tourmobile also offers narrated tours to Mount Vernon, George Washington's Virginia estate from April through October. These tours leave from the Arlington National Cemetery Visitor's Center at 10:00 A.M., noon, and 2:00 P.M., and run $22 for adults and $12 for children. Prices include admission to Mount Vernon.

Tourmobile also offers a narrated tour to Cedar Hill, Frederick Douglass's last address. This is a good deal: The residence is beautiful and a unique piece of Washington's history, and it's very difficult to get to by public transportation. This tour also leaves from Arlington National Cemetery's Visitor's Center at noon. The cost is $7 for adults and $3.50 for children and includes the price of the National Park ranger's guided tour.

There is also a Washington by Night tour, which is a four-hour narrated tour of the Jefferson, FDR, and Lincoln Memorials (which you can visit), with stops outside the White House and the Capitol building. It departs from Union Station and is $14 for adults and $7 for children.

There are combination two-day packages for various tours such as Arlington Cemetery, Washington, D.C., Mount Vernon and/or Cedar Hill. Call or visit the Tourmobile (www.Tourmobile.com) Web site for prices and more information.

Reservations are suggested for the Mount Vernon, Cedar Hill, or Washington by Night tours, which you can call for at (202) 554-5100 or obtain at the Web site. There's a quiz on the Web site where you can attempt to win free tour tickets by answering Washington, D.C. trivia. You can also purchase tickets at Ticketmaster by calling (800) 832-9800, but there is a small fee for this service.

By Motorcoach

Gold Line/Gray Line offers full (nine hours) and half-day (four hours) narrated tours of the city that leave from Union Station or pick you up and drop you off at your hotel (you can pay by credit card). If you would like to hear a tour of the city in a language other than English, they offer tours in Spanish, French, Italian, German, and Japanese, but you must call for information and reservations at (202) 289-1995.

There is also a Twilight Tour of five memorials (Jefferson, Lincoln, FDR, Vietnam, and Korean War), as well as the Statue of Iwo Jima at Arlington National Cemetery and the John F. Kennedy Center that leaves Union Station at 7:30 P.M. and drops you off at your hotel about four hours later. If the other night tours are booked, you can usually get a seat on one of these. The cost is $25 for adults and $12 for children (you can pay by credit card).

Another bus tour operator is All About Town, which offers guided all-day tours and half-day tours in the city's only glass-topped sightseeing coaches, as well as evening tours on buses to major sites throughout the city, as well as Mount Vernon, with pickup and drop-off at your hotel. Call (301) 856-5566 for prices and information.

Atlantic Canoe & Kayak

This aquatic tour leads you through Georgetown's C&O Canal and focuses on the city's architecture and history. Guides paddle alongside tourists in small groups of boats. No children under ten years old can take this tour, but the tour operators state that no experience is necessary. Tickets are $39 and $49. Call (703) 838-9072 for schedules.

Capital River Cruises

This fifty-minute, narrated tour on the Potomac on a sixty-five-foot riverboat departs from the Georgetown waterfront and circles the city, offering views of the Kennedy Center, the various monuments, and the Capitol building. Tours leave daily from noon until 7:00 P.M. Tickets are $10 for adults, $5 for children. Call (301) 460-7447 for more information.

DC Ducks

This famous tour uses white amphibious vehicles (boats on wheels), which were built for the U.S. Army during WWII to transport

JFK Center for the Performing Arts

The Center for the Performing Arts is situated on eighteen and a half acres of Foggy Bottom real estate that once featured a brewery, a restaurant, and a riding stable. Our national performing arts center, the complex is also a memorial to John F. Kennedy.

troops, to provide tourists a one-hour tour of the city on the ground followed by a half-hour tour ride on the Potomac. Tours leave from Union Station beginning at 10:00 A.M. from April through October (perhaps longer, depending upon the weather). Tickets are $23 for adults and $12 for children. Call (202) 832-9800 for more information.

Potomac Spirit

This climate-controlled riverboat tours the Potomac River and allows a tour of Mount Vernon. The boat departs Pier 4, at 6th and Water Street SW, at 9:00 A.M. and returns at 2:30 P.M., Tuesday through Sunday. You can purchase breakfast and lunch on board. Round trip fares include the admission to Mount Vernon and are $26.50 for adults and $17 for children. Reservations are recommended. Call (202) 554-8000.

Shore Shot Cruises

This narrated tour of the Potomac departs from Georgetown Harbor, 31st and K St. NW. The cost is $10 for adults, $5 for children. Call (202) 554-6500 for information.

Washington Water Bus

Water buses make a number of regular stops along the Potomac stopping at such locations as the Jefferson, FDR, and Lincoln Memorials. One fare allows you to hop on and off all day. Call (800) 288-7925.

Bike the Sites

For the athletic, this tour group offers a three-hour guided bicycle tour on eight miles of paths and trails that pass fifty-five landmarks and monuments. The tour is recommended for ages nine and up and includes bicycle rental, as well as gear and a licensed guide. Tickets are $35 per person.

There is a longer tour for the truly athletic that takes you from Old Town to Mount Vernon on a nine-mile bike path along the Potomac River. Tickets are $55 per person, which includes lunch and admission fees. There are also evening tours ending in Georgetown. Call (202) 966-8662 for more information.

Capital Helicopters

This narrated tour of the city concentrates on the monuments and major buildings. Free transportation to and from Ronald Reagan national Airport is included in the $95-per-person fee. Call (703) 417-2150 for information and reservations.

C&O Canal Barge Rides

This tour offers mule-drawn canal rides along the C&O Canal with commentary. It departs from Georgetown and operates from April through October. Call (301) 739-4200 for prices and information.

University Helicopters

Up to four passengers can tour the city in a Bell 206 JetRanger on this fifteen-minute narrated tour that flies over the Capital's major sights. Daily flights begin at 10:00 A.M. and cost $84 per person. Van service is available for pickup and drop-off if prearranged. Helicopter departs from the South Capital St. Heliport. Credit cards accepted. Call (202) 484-8484 for more information and schedule.

Washington's Cherry Blossoms

When the cherry trees along the Tidal Basin near the Jefferson Memorial are in bloom in the early spring, Washington, D.C. is at its finest in a sea of pink. For this two-week period in late March or early April, there are constant festivities, marked by a parade at the end of the Cherry Blossom season.

The 3,700 cherry trees were a gift to the U.S. from Japan in 1912. The first two trees were planted by First Lady Mrs. William Howard Taft and Viscountess Chinda of Japan, the Japanese Ambassador's wife. Those two trees are still standing today near the statue of John Paul Jones on 17th St.

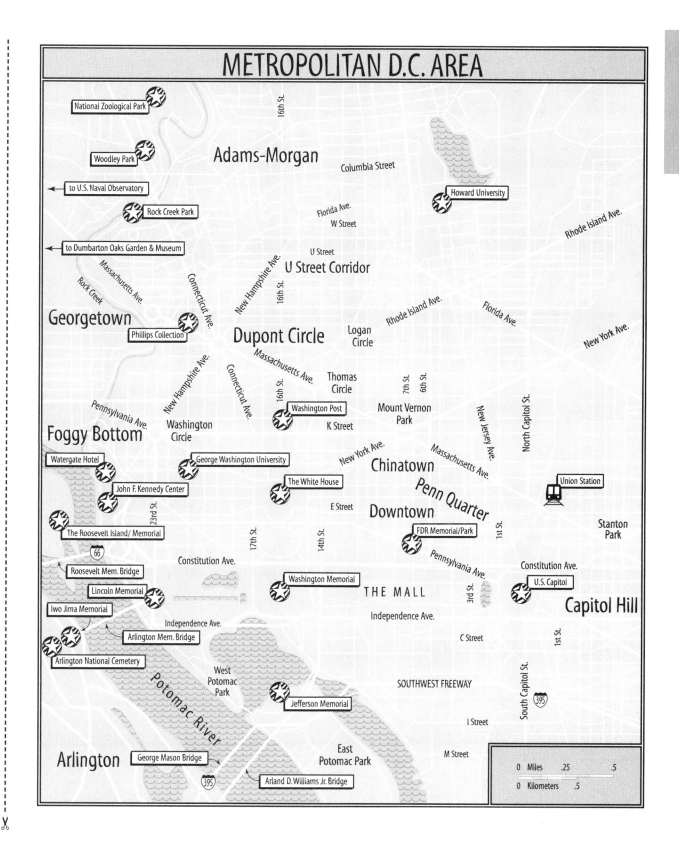

METROPOLITAN D.C. AREA

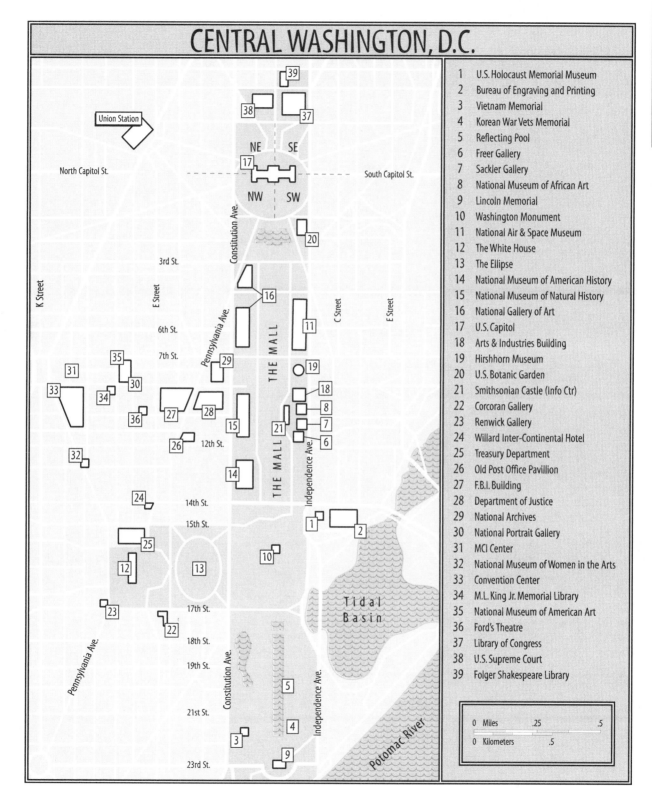

CENTRAL WASHINGTON, D.C.

Union Station

NE SE

NW SW

North Capitol St.

South Capitol St.

Constitution Ave.

3rd St.

E Street

K Street

6th St.

Pennsylvania Ave.

7th St.

THE MALL

C Street

E Street

Independence Ave.

THE MALL

12th St.

14th St.

15th St.

Pennsylvania Ave.

17th St.

18th St.

Constitution Ave.

19th St.

Independence Ave.

21st St.

23rd St.

Pennsylvania Ave.

Tidal Basin

Potomac River

1	U.S. Holocaust Memorial Museum
2	Bureau of Engraving and Printing
3	Vietnam Memorial
4	Korean War Vets Memorial
5	Reflecting Pool
6	Freer Gallery
7	Sackler Gallery
8	National Museum of African Art
9	Lincoln Memorial
10	Washington Monument
11	National Air & Space Museum
12	The White House
13	The Ellipse
14	National Museum of American History
15	National Museum of Natural History
16	National Gallery of Art
17	U.S. Capitol
18	Arts & Industries Building
19	Hirshhorn Museum
20	U.S. Botanic Garden
21	Smithsonian Castle (Info Ctr)
22	Corcoran Gallery
23	Renwick Gallery
24	Willard Inter-Continental Hotel
25	Treasury Department
26	Old Post Office Pavillion
27	F.B.I. Building
28	Department of Justice
29	National Archives
30	National Portrait Gallery
31	MCI Center
32	National Museum of Women in the Arts
33	Convention Center
34	M.L. King Jr. Memorial Library
35	National Museum of American Art
36	Ford's Theatre
37	Library of Congress
38	U.S. Supreme Court
39	Folger Shakespeare Library

0 Miles .25 .5
0 Kilometers .5

Chapter Four

Where to Stay

Washington D.C.
MAP

There are hundreds of hotels in Washington, D.C., from those that cater to the family to some of the most luxurious suites in the nation to those for people on a very tight budget.

Because Washington, D.C. is the nation's capital and so many business travelers come to the city to try to work with the government agencies around town, hotel rooms are usually more expensive during the week than during the weekend. Rates are also lower during the summer when Congress isn't in session.

The average hotel room runs about $137.50 for double occupancy, according to 1997 figures compiled by the Washington, D.C. Convention and Visitor's Association. Hotel taxes are another $15 a night, and parking charges can be as high as $20 a night.

There are many ways to cut the cost of your hotel stay, from using Automobile Association of America (AAA) and the American Association of Retired Persons (AARP) discounts, which are usually around 10 percent, to looking for a room that gives you free breakfast or even has a kitchenette. There are often discounts for business travelers, as well as summer and weekend specials and family rates, so ask for the lowest rate when you call for reservations.

You can also try a number of Internet search engines that offer hotel rooms (some offer discounts too) such as:

- *www.washington.org/planning/stay* is a searchable hotel listing prepared by the D.C. Convention and Visitor's Association that is based on price and location, offering listings from hotels to bed & breakfasts to hostels and even campgrounds. It has a special weekend rate search engine too.
- *www.fodors.com* offers a similar hotel index that you can use to search by name or category, as well as its own list of best hotels.
- *www.priceline.com* will book you a discounted hotel room in D.C., but you can't see where it is until you try their service. They say that all their hotels are members of major chains, and you can probably get a very good rate this way

(you set the price and see what comes in), but just be aware that there are parts of downtown Washington that you have to take a cab to once the sun sets.

- *www.washingtonpost.com* also has a search engine that will list hotels by neighborhood and price.
- *www.preferredhotels.com* is a site put up by Travelweb, which is a reservation system for the hotel industry.
- *www.holidayinn.com* and *www.radisson.com*, the hotel chains also have Internet sites, and sometimes they offer packages and last-minute deals.

The two most important elements to choosing your accommodations in D.C. should be location and price. Of course, if you are traveling as a family or visiting the city on business, there might be additional amenities that you will want (such as a pool or a fax machine). If you are not coming by car or don't plan on renting one, try to find a hotel near a Metro station.

The following hotel reviews are organized by location first, beginning with the downtown and Capitol Hill hotels, and then by price categories. All listings include nearby Metro stops.

The monetary rating system I've employed follows these basic price categories:

- Luxury—Over $200
- Expensive—$150-$200
- Average—$150-$100
- Budget—Under $100

Remember that even the most luxurious hotels have special rates during the summer, so you may be able to stay at a first-class hotel for half price if you ask for a summer rate.

Downtown Washington, D.C.

Luxury

Grand Hyatt Washington, 1000 H St. NW, (800) 233-1234. This is a luxurious mega-hotel with 900 rooms. The lobby

Best Buys for Hotel Rooms

During the summer months, when Washington empties its hotel rooms of lobbyists because the House and Senate are on vacation, some of the best hotels in the city offer incredibly reduced rates. These include:

- Hotel Washington, one of the most centrally located hotels in the city, right across from the White House.
- Hotel Lombardy, a quaint hotel in a charming, refurbished apartment building.
- Henley Park, a fine hotel with gargoyles on its facade and large rooms.
- Governor's House, in a restored home of a former governor.
- Morrison-Clark, a restored Victorian mansion.

Great Hotel Restaurants

Some of the best restaurants in the city can be found in Washington's hotels:

- Lespinasse at the Sheraton-Carlton is considered by many Washingtonians, and local food critics, to be the best restaurant in Washington serving elegant, and expensive, French food.
- Citronelle at the Latham Hotel has been a Washington haute cuisine hot spot since it reopened in 1998 with a $2 million dollar renovation.
- Gabriel in the Radisson Barcelo Hotel has long been considered the best Spanish restaurant in Washington, and everyone who is anyone goes there for tapas and the Sunday brunch.

alone is stupendous, with a glass-enclosed atrium that is twelve stories high and features fountains and a waterfall; a baby grand piano floating on its own island in a "lagoon" surrounded by a bar; and two floors of shops and restaurants. The hotel is across the street from the Convention Center and near the MCI Center. Rooms are large but relatively standard with hair dryers, cable TV, and a basket of toiletries. The health club is two stories, with a lap pool and sauna. For an additional $15 you can get the business plan, which includes a large desk, fax machine, and coffeemaker. Room rates are $290 double weekdays, $119–$139 weekends. There are a number of special packages available (such as the winter holiday package), so ask for specials when you make your reservations. Parking is an additional $12. Major credit cards accepted. Metro Center (red, orange, and blue lines).

Hay-Adams Hotel, 16th & H Sts. NW, (800) 678-8946. This hotel was built on the former land of John Hay and Henry Adams, two prominent Washington social and political big-wigs whose homes faced Lafayette Square and were across the street from the White House. When the hotel opened in 1927, such luminaries as Charles Lindbergh and Amelia Earhart stayed here. *W* magazine said of the recent restoration, "this is as close as one gets to staying at the White House, short of being invited by the President." It was the first member of the Historic Hotels of America. The hotel's restaurant, The Lafayette, overlooking the White House and Lafayette Square, offers contemporary American cuisine as well as afternoon tea. Rooms on the fifth through eighth floors on the H St. side have spectacular views of the White House with the Washington Monument behind it. Some rooms have fireplaces. Off the Record, a wine and champagne bar, serves cocktails and light fare. Hotel amenities include bathrobes, nightly turndown service, daily newspaper and health club privileges. Rumor has it that the ghost of Hay's wife haunts the hotel's fourth floor. Room rates are $265–$450 for a single/double. Major credit cards accepted. Metro Station (red, orange and blue lines).

Hotel Reservation Considerations

Before making any hotel reservation, consider the following:

- What type of accommodations do you need? How many beds? Does the hotel charge per night for extra cots?

- Since most room rates are based on double occupancy, is there an extra charge per person for children staying in your room?

- What type of amenities do you need?

- What type of hotel services are you looking for? Should the hotel have a swimming pool (indoor or outdoor), a hot tub, an exercise room/fitness center, tennis courts, or an on-property restaurant? Should the hotel offer room service? Will you be needing self-serve laundry facilities?

- Is a complimentary shuttle bus offered to and from the airport?

- How close is the hotel to The National Mall and other attractions you plan on visiting?

- Does the hotel offer complimentary parking? If not, how much will parking fees increase your overall hotel bill?

- Does the hotel charge for local phone calls or for calling toll-free numbers? If so, how much? Is the hotel equipped with phone jacks that allow you to connect a laptop computer so you can access the Internet, check your e-mail, or access one of the major online services?

- Is an in-room safe provided so you can store your valuables?

- Will the hotel be able to guarantee you a nonsmoking room (if you request one when you make your reservation)?

- What is your nightly budget for a hotel room?

Romantic Hotel

The Jefferson has long been considered one of the most romantic hotels in the city. The view is spectacular, it's centrally located, and the restaurant is one of Washington's best and most romantic.

Hotel Washington, 515 15th St. N.W., (800)424-9540. This elegant hotel is right across the street from the White House. Its lobby features green velvet chairs that you can sit in and look out over the White House and the Treasury Building. Its 350 rooms are mostly small but furnished in Colonial-style antiques (some rooms feature four-poster beds). The rooftop deck offers dinner and drinks and a stupendous view of the city, which you can always take in even if you are not staying here. Rooms run $174–$240 single, $189–$240 double. However, in the summer when Congress is not in session, the hotel runs a super family sale for $106 per night (ask for the *New York Times* rate or the Family Plan). All major credit cards accepted. Parking is an additional $20 per day in their on-site garage. Metro Center (red, orange, and blue lines).

The Jefferson, 16th & M Sts. NW, (800) 678-8946. This former luxury apartment building was built in 1923 and was a hotel for military personnel during WWII. In 1986, it was restored and transformed into a 100-room hotel, which is now a popular hotel for dignitaries and celebrities but is best known as the location for Dick Morris's private (and now public) moments with his paid paramour. Both the lobby and some rooms feature some genuine Jefferson artifacts (on loan from Monticello), such as signed documents and letters, as well as a bust of Jefferson in the lobby and Jefferson prints in the restaurant. Some rooms have fireplaces and four-poster beds. Hotel amenities include fax machines, nightly turndown service with Godiva chocolate, morning newspaper, VCRs, CD players, bathrobes, and a health club with a pool across the street. The Restaurant at the Jefferson features American cuisine, as well as an afternoon tea. It is located four blocks from the White House. Published hotel rates are $230/$310 for a single/double room. Major credit cards accepted. Metro Center (red, orange, and blue lines).

Loew's L'Enfant Plaza Hotel, 480 L'Enfant Plaza SW, (800) 235-6397. This posh hotel is located a hop, skip, and a jump from the Mall, and has a reputation for catering to visitors traveling with pets (who can take their dogs for a run on the

Mall). It's also quite child-friendly, offering free meals in the hotel restaurant for children under five and a welcoming gift to all children under the age of twelve. The hotel has a year-round rooftop pool and a fitness center and offers a complimentary continental breakfast. Room rates are $189–$229, but there are occasional specials. Parking is an additional $16 a night. Major credit cards accepted. L'Enfant Plaza Metro station (orange and blue lines) leads you right into the hotel.

Renaissance Mayflower Hotel, 1127 Connecticut Ave. NW, (800) 678-8946. The Mayflower is one of the most historic and luxurious hotels in the city and offers 660 deluxe guest rooms. It was where Calvin Coolidge held his 1925 inauguration for 1,000 people, which was also the hotel's grand opening. It was designed by Warren & Wetmore, the same architectural firm that designed New York's Grand Central Station, and it is almost as big, taking up most of the block. FDR lived at the Mayflower between his election and inauguration; JFK used to stay here when he was a Congressman; and Jean Harlow was so fascinated by the switchboard that she played operator for a day when she visited. When it opened its doors, it boasted more gold leaf than any other building in the city except the Library of Congress and was one of the capital's first air-conditioned buildings. Forty-six thousand square feet of Italian marble was used to create the hotel's bathrooms. A recent renovation in the '80s uncovered a sixty-foot skylight that had been blacked out during WW II, as well as murals painted by Edward Lanning. Hotel amenities include bathrobes, morning newspaper and your own pot of coffee with wake-up call, a small TV in the bathroom, and a fitness center. The hotel is so historic that there's a coffee table book about it on sale at the gift shop. Published room rates are $270–$300 for a single, $300–$330 for a double. In the summer, the rates drop to as low as $129, with free breakfast (ask for their leisure rate). Major credit cards accepted. Located four blocks south of the White House. Metro Center (red, orange, and blue lines).

The Sheraton Carlton, 923 16th St. NW, (800) 562-5661.
This ornate hotel is a favorite of celebrities of all sorts, from Queen
Elizabeth to the Rolling Stones. Designed to look like an Italian
palazzo, the Carlton's lobby features chandeliers and Empire furniture. Rooms are on the smallish side, but elegantly furnished with
desks set aside in alcoves and marble bathrooms stocked with
everything from cottonballs to mouthwash. There's also an umbrella
tucked away inside the closet. Other amenities include bathrobes,
hair dryers, personal safes, coffee with wake-up call, nightly turndown, and fitness club. The hotel's restaurant, Lespinasse, is considered one of the best in Washington. The hotel bar, the Library
Lounge, is book-lined and features a working fireplace. Room rates
are $225 single or double. Major credit cards accepted. Parking is
an additional $22 per day. Within walking distance to the White
House. Farragut West and McPherson Sq. are the closest Metro
stops (orange and blue lines).

**Willard Inter-Continental, 1401 Pennsylvania Ave. NW,
(800) 327-0200.** This is one of the best hotels in D.C. because of
its location near the White House, its fabulous restaurant, its luxurious rooms, and its historical importance. Most U.S. Presidents
have stayed or dined here, from Lincoln to Clinton. Julia Ward
Howe wrote "The Battle Hymn of the Republic" at the Willard in
the same room that Martin Luther King, Jr. later penned his "I
Have a Dream" speech. Grant was known to smoke cigars and sip
brandy in the lobby and was constantly sought out here by those
wanting something from him, which is how the word "lobbyist"
came into being.

The Willard was designed by the same architect who built the
Plaza Hotel in New York. The lobby features seals of the forty-
eight states on the ceiling, as well as chandeliers, marble
columns, and gilt trim. Rooms are large and decorated in Empire
or Federal style and feature an in-room safe, mini-bar, hair dryer,
scale, and TV speaker in the marble bathrooms. Other amenities
include twice-daily maid service, nightly turndown service, and a
choice of newspaper delivery. The Willard Room is a beautiful
restaurant that features exquisite cuisine and fabulous desserts. The
Round Robin Bar has been a popular drinking place for two cen-

turies, with such noted guests as Mark Twain, Walt Whitman, and Nathaniel Hawthorne. There is also the cafe Espresso, which offers coffees and pastries, and the Nest Lounge, which plays live jazz on weekends. Room rates are $400–$440 double weekdays, $199 double weekends, but the hotel does offer a 50 percent discount to people over sixty-five. Parking is $20 additional per night. Major credit cards accepted. Metro Center station (red, orange, and blue lines).

Expensive

Capitol Hill Hilton, 16th & K St. NW, (202) 393-1000. This is a mega hotel (549 rooms) that is popular because of its location two blocks from the White House. It underwent a major renovation in the early '90s, and most rooms feature three phones and a small TV in the bathroom. The tower floors (ten through fourteen) offer extra amenities such as complimentary breakfast, afternoon tea, and hors d'oeuvres (cocktails are extra). There are three restaurants on the premises: Fran O'Brian's, which used to be Trader Vic's and is now named after a former Redskin, offers steak and seafood; Twigg's Grill, a more elegant eatery; and just Twigg's, which is less expensive. Room rates are $127–$275 double, add $30 for Tower units. Major credit cards accepted. Parking is $22 additional per day. Farragut West or Farragut North, or McPherson Sq. Metro stations (orange and blue lines).

Holiday Inn Capital at the Smithsonian, 550 C St. NW, (202) 479-4000. Location, location, location. This 529-room hotel is a block away from the Smithsonian's National Air and Space Museum, the most popular museum in the Smithsonian Institution, as well as the other Smithsonian museums and the National Archives. Rooms are designed in traditional hotel-chain style, with hair dryers and irons. There's a rooftop pool and a health club. On-site dining includes Smithson's Restaurant, the Shuttle Express Deli, and a Lobby Bar for cocktails. Rooms are $169 per night. Parking is an additional $10 per night. All major credit cards accepted. L'Enfant Plaza Metro station (green, yellow, orange, and blue lines).

Willard Hotel History

The Willard Hotel was founded by two brothers, Henry and Edwin Willard (who were distant relatives of early American clock makers, whose clocks can be seen in the Capitol Statuary Hall and the Supreme Court). They bought the "City Hotel" from Benjamin Tayloe (owner of the Octagon House) and turned it into a much larger and more sumptuous hotel. Charles Dickens was one of the hotel's first guests.

Its nickname, "the hotel of Presidents," was given to it by Franklin Pierce who stayed there while waiting for his inauguration in 1853. Every American president since Zachary Taylor has stayed in the hotel.

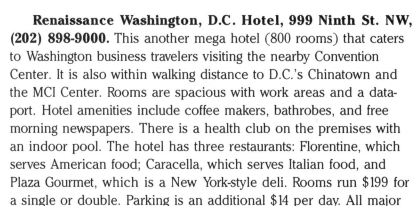

D. C. Hotel Fun Facts

The classic movie, *Mr. Smith Goes to Washington*, was filmed at the Hotel Washington.

Albert Einstein once lived at the St. Regis Hotel (now the Sheraton-Carlton).

Renaissance Washington, D.C. Hotel, 999 Ninth St. NW, (202) 898-9000. This another mega hotel (800 rooms) that caters to Washington business travelers visiting the nearby Convention Center. It is also within walking distance to D.C.'s Chinatown and the MCI Center. Rooms are spacious with work areas and a dataport. Hotel amenities include coffee makers, bathrobes, and free morning newspapers. There is a health club on the premises with an indoor pool. The hotel has three restaurants: Florentine, which serves American food; Caracella, which serves Italian food, and Plaza Gourmet, which is a New York-style deli. Rooms run $199 for a single or double. Parking is an additional $14 per day. All major credit cards accepted. Metro Center (red, orange, and blue lines).

Average

Days Inn Premier, 1201 K St. NW, (800) 562-3350. Near the Convention Center and family-friendly, this eight-story hotel has a rooftop pool, which is always popular with kids. Rooms are fairly standard, with hair dryers, satellite TV and pay-per-view movies, and coffeemakers. There is a fitness center on the premises. Room rates run $99–$125 weekdays, $79–$99 weekends, but there are a number of supersaver packages, so ask for the best price when you call. Parking is an additional $14. Major credit cards accepted. McPherson Sq. or Metro Center stations (red, orange, and blue lines).

Governor's House Hotel, 17th St. and Massachusetts Ave. NW, (800) 821-4367. A 146-room hotel built in the refurbished home of a former Governor of Pennsylvania, this elegant hotel is within walking distance to many of the city's popular attractions. The on-site restaurant, The 17th Street Bar & Grill, features traditional American fare. The hotel has a fitness center and a pool. There are also deluxe accommodations in the top two floors that include a coffee maker, wine, and flowers in each room. Rates are $145 and up, but in the summer the hotel has a $74 special rate (ask for the *New York Times* rate). Parking is an additional $7 a night. Farragut North Metro station (orange and blue lines).

Henley Park, 926 Massachusetts Ave. NW, (800) 678-8946. Once an elegant apartment building, the Henley Park is now a 96-room hotel with 118 gargoyles on its facade (including the faces of the architect and his wife). The rooms are large and nicely decorated, with a fax machine in most rooms, as well as a bathrobe, coffeemaker, hair dryer, and iron. Other hotel amenities include free newspaper, nightly turndown service with chocolates, and a free limousine service in the morning. The hotel restaurant, Coeur de Lion, is one of the best hotel restaurants in the city, and nightly hors d'oeuvres are served in the jazz club, Marley's Lounge, with dancing on weekends. There is also a fireside afternoon tea in the hotel's lobby, which has stained glass windows and original Mercer tiled floors. The hotel is within walking distance to the National Gallery, Ford's Theatre, the National Museum of Women in the Arts, and Chinatown. Published rates are $165 for a single, $225 for a double, but there is an $89 summer rate (mention the *New York Times* rate). Major credit cards accepted. Closest Metro station is Metro enter (about five blocks).

Howard Johnson Hotel & Suites of Washington, D.C. (a Taj Hotel), 1430 Rhode Island Ave. NW, (202) 462-7777. This is a hotel and suite, so some rooms have kitchen facilities, which is great for families. There is a restaurant on the premises, as well as a fitness center and a rooftop pool. Room rates are $129–$189 single, $10 more for double, and even more for suites. Parking is an additional $10 per night. All major credit cards accepted. McPherson Sq. Metro station (orange and blue lines).

Holiday Inn Downtown, 1155 14th St. NW, (800) HOL-IDAY. Five blocks from the White House, this fourteen-story hotel is very family friendly, with a kids-eat-free promo that is part of the chain's many extra perks. The hotel features a roof top pool and sun deck, a fitness center next door, as well as washers and dryers. The restaurant offers breakfast and dinner buffets. Room rates are $130–$170 weekdays, $100–$170 weekends. Inquire about summer rates. Valet parking is $10 per night. McPherson Sq. Metro station (orange and blue lines).

Lincoln Suites Downtown, 1823 L St. NW, (800) 424-2970. This is an all-suite, ten-story hotel with ninety-nine suites. Many guests stay for weeks or longer when doing business in the city because it is only five blocks from the White House and central to most of the capital's attractions. About one-third of the suites feature full kitchens; others have microwaves and refrigerators. Other amenities include a wet bar, hair dryer, complimentary milk and cookies in the evening, and continental breakfast in the morning. There are two restaurants on site: Samantha's features traditional American food and Beatrice is an Italian restaurant. Suites are $99–$159. Major credit cards accepted. Parking is an additional $9 per day in the adjoining garage. Farragut North or Farragut West Metro stations (orange and blue lines).

J.W. Marriott, 1331 Pennsylvania Ave. NW at E St., (800) 228-9290. This hotel's location is central to lots of downtown activity, such as the Convention Center and National Theater, and is two blocks from the White House. There are three restaurants on the premises, but the hotel connects to a mall with eighty shops and restaurants. The hotel has a fitness center, indoor pool, and game room. Rooms are comfortable and feature a desk area, hair dryer, iron, and toiletries. Other amenities include twice-daily maid service, nightly turndown, and morning paper. Rates are $234 double weekdays, $109–$234 weekends. The hotel does run a number of specials, such as their $89-per-night holiday package before Christmas, so ask for special rates. Parking is an additional $20. Major credit cards accepted. Metro Center station (red, orange, and blue lines).

Morrison-Clark Inn, 1015 L St. NW, (800) 678-8946. This hotel was once two separate townhouses, which have been joined to create this unique inn, the only city inn to be listed in the National Register of Historic Places. From 1923 until the 1980s, the site was the Soldiers, Sailors, Marines and Airmen's Club. Some rooms are small but elegantly detailed and furnished with wonderful antiques. There are transformed carriage houses on the first floor, which offer spacious accommodations, and some rooms feature fireplaces and pier mirrors and wrought iron ceiling medallions. Hotel amenities include a lovely continental breakfast in the hotel's dining area with scones, pastries, and cereal, nightly turn down service with chocolates, free morning newspaper, complimentary fitness center (open twenty-four hours with your room key), and a mini-bar in every room. The hotel restaurant is nationally acclaimed and offers fabulous southern and American cuisine, including great desserts. Walking distance to the National Gallery, Ford's Theatre, MCI Center, and the Convention Center. Published room rates are $150 for single, $210 for double, but there is an $89 summer rate (ask for the *New York Times* rate). Major credit cards accepted. Closest Metro stop is Metro Center (red, orange, and blue lines).

Washington Plaza, 10 Thomas Circle NW. at 14th St., (800) 424-1140. A little off the beaten track, but trying to be family friendly, the Washington Plaza offers many family-oriented activities in the summer, such as Friday night poolside barbecues. Recently renovated, this large hotel (339 rooms) brings back the International style of the '60s in its lobby furnished with Mies van der Rohe chairs. Rooms are large with in-room coffee makers. Other amenities include twice-daily maid service, twenty-four-hour room service, and a morning paper. There is nightly jazz in the plaza lounge, free American breakfast buffet, and a fitness center. Published rates are $125–$175 for single, $145–$175 for a double, but the hotel offers an $89 summer rate (ask for the *New York Times* rate). Major credit cards accepted. Parking is an additional $10 a night. McPherson Metro station (orange and blue lines).

Budget

Braxton Hotel, 1440 Rhode Island Ave. NW at 14th St., (202) 232-7800. This sixty-two-room hotel is decorated with a hodgepodge of themed antiques, which certainly has its own unique

Historic Hotels

The Mayflower Renaissance Hotel, built in 1925 has so much Washington, D.C. history that a book has been written about it, which you can buy in the hotel lobby gift store. It has been the site of many inaugural balls, and the makeshift home of most of our presidents while they waited to occupy the White House. Here, Franklin Delano Roosevelt wrote his famous words, "The only thing we have to fear is fear itself."

charm. A free continental breakfast is offered in the dining room, with twenty-four-hour coffee and tea. Room rates are $39–$79 for single, $45–$89 for double. Parking is an additional $5 per night. Most major credit cards accepted, excluding American Express. McPherson Sq. Metro station (orange and blue lines).

Red Roof Inn, 500 H St. NW, (800) THE-ROOF (843-7663). A ten-story hotel in the heart of the capital's Chinatown, right across the street from one of the best Chinese restaurants (Full Kee), the Red Roof is also within walking distance to many of the city's major attractions such as the MCI Center, Ford's Theatre, and the Convention Center. Rooms are spacious and decorated in contemporary hotel decor, with pay-per-view movie service, as well as Nintendo for children. The hotel's restaurant serves an inexpensive breakfast and lunch, and there is a washer/dryer on the premises, as well as a health club and sauna. Weekdays rates are $97.99–$102 double, weekend rates are $70–$102. Outdoor parking is $8.50 per day. Major credit cards accepted. Gallery Place Metro station (green line).

Swiss Inn, 1204 Massachusetts Ave. NW, (202) 371-1816. This is an affordable hotel in a former brownstone within walking distance to almost everything you'll need, but it's a small hotel, so book in advance. Rooms are simple but nicely decorated with a kitchenette in each room. Pets are allowed. Room rates are $79 for a single, $89 for a double. Most major credit cards accepted. Parking is free on weekends, $6 during the week. Metro Center (orange, red, and blue lines).

Travelodge City Center Hotel, 1201 13th St. NW at M St., (202) 682-5300. This is fairly standard hotel accommodations at a central, if somewhat urban, location. There is a free continental breakfast and a coffeemaker in each room. Room rates are $79 for single, $89 for double. Parking is an additional $11–$21 depending on the size of the vehicle. Major credit cards accepted. McPherson Sq. Metro station (orange and blue lines).

Capitol Hill

Luxury

Hyatt Regency Washington on Capital Hill, 400 New Jersey Ave. NW (between First and D Sts.), (202) 737-1234. This mega hotel (834 rooms) is the perfect location for travelers who need to be within walking distance of the Capitol, the Supreme Court, or the House or Senate, which is one of the reasons why the rooms are so pricey. The hotel offers a business plan, which offers free membership to its health club that includes a heated pool, free local phone calls, morning newspaper, and a continental breakfast at the Park Promenade restaurant. There are two other restaurants in the hotel: The Capital View Club, which features a stellar rooftop view of the city, and the Spy's Eye Lounge, which has a big TV screen and a nightly happy hour. Rooms are $225 for single, $250 for double. Parking is an additional $22 per day. All major credit cards accepted. Union Station (red line).

Expensive

Holiday Inn on the Hill, 415 New Jersey Ave. NW, (202) 638-1616. This hotel is down the street from the Capitol, near the Library of Congress and the Folger Shakespeare Library. Rooms are large with work areas, hair dryers, mini-bars, and coffee makers. There is a rooftop pool, a fitness club, and sauna. The Senators All-American Sports Grille features memorabilia from the now defunct D.C. baseball team. Room rates are $184 per night. Parking is an additional $11 per night. All major credit cards accepted. Union Station (red line).

Hotel George, 15 E St. NW, (800) 576-8331. This is an old building that has been rehabbed and presents itself as the hip hotel for those doing business on the Hill. Posters throughout the hotel depict images of George Washington in contemporary gear, without the wig. Rooms are spacious, with desks, hair dryers, coffeemakers, irons, and a TV speaker in the bathroom. The hotel restaurant, Bis, serves French bistro food. The hotel has a fitness club and steam rooms, as well as a billiard room. Other amenities

Recently Renovated Hotels

Two of Washington's largest hotels in the Woodley Park area (right near the zoo) have recently undergone major renovations, making them more business and family friendly.

The Marriott Wardman Park Hotel, which is the largest hotel in the city with over 1,000 rooms, has just undergone a head-to-toe renovation, which includes its two pools and restaurants.

The neighboring Omni Shoreham, with a mere 860 rooms, has also undergone a major rehab, with a recently added children's pool and poolside snackbar, and a totally redone fitness center. The Omni is also one of the two "haunted" hotels in the city.

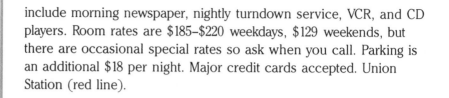

include morning newspaper, nightly turndown service, VCR, and CD players. Room rates are $185–$220 weekdays, $129 weekends, but there are occasional special rates so ask when you call. Parking is an additional $18 per night. Major credit cards accepted. Union Station (red line).

Phoenix Park Hotel, 520 N. Capitol St. NW, (800) 824-5419. This hotel is a block away from Union Station and two blocks from the Capitol and was once known as the Commodore Hotel. The hotel has an Irish pub, the Dubliner, on the premises and in keeping with that theme has tried to make things Irish throughout, with Irish toiletries and linens in the bathrooms and much green in the decor. The 150 rooms are comfortable and feature hair dryers and coffeemakers. Room rates are $189–$219 for a double on weekdays, $89 and up on weekends. Parking is an additional $15. Union Station (red line).

Average

Capitol Hill Suites, 200 C St. NW, (800) 424-9165. Its location on the House of Representatives side of the Capitol makes this a regular haunt of congresspeople, whose recent photos adorn the lobby walls. This is an all-suite hotel with 152 rooms, most of which have kitchens and dining rooms, so it is also a good family place to stay. There is no on-site restaurant, but there is a food court and many restaurants nearby, which the hotel staff will gladly inform you about. Amenities include a continental breakfast, washer and dryer on premises, and use of a nearby health club. Suite rates are $89–$199, with a $20 surcharge for extra adults. Parking is an additional $15 per night. Major credit cards accepted. Capitol South Metro stop (orange and blue lines).

Adams Morgan/Woodley Park

Expensive

Marriott Wardman Park, 2660 Woodley Rd. NW at Connecticut Ave., (202) 328-2000. The former site of the

Sheraton Washington, this is the largest hotel in the city, sitting on a sixteen-acre plot of land a hop, skip, and a jump away from the National Zoo. Its more than 1,000 rooms have just undergone a major renovation. Because of its size, the hotel tends to cater to conventiongoers, but it's also a good place for families because of its two pools and proximity to the zoo (there are reduced rates in the summer and when the hotel is not at capacity). The hotel is composed of two parts. The oldest, Wardman Park, is a former apartment building for the rich and famous (Gore Vidal and Douglas Fairbanks, Jr. once lived here), and the 200-odd rooms in this section retain a bit of its earlier charm with high ceilings and intricate moldings. In-room amenities include hair dryers, complimentary Starbucks coffee and tea, irons, and morning newspaper delivery. The hotel has two outdoor pools (one of which is heated with a sundeck), a fitness center, a number of shops and services, and its own post office. On-site dining is available at Americus, while breakfast and lunch are served in the Courtyard Cafe. L'Espresso serves sandwiches and pastries. Room rates are $189–235 weekdays double, $89–$149 weekends double, but there are specials all year round. Self parking is $14 additional per night. Major credit cards accepted. Woodley Park Metro station (red line).

Omni Shoreham, 2500 Calvert St. NW at Connecticut Ave., (800) 843-6664. Recently renovated from top to bottom, this is another mega hotel (860 rooms) on an eleven-acre plot of land overlooking Rock Creek Park that serves the convention crowd, within walking distance to the National Zoo. It was built in the 1930s and has been the site of many an inaugural ball. A suite on the eighth floor is said to be haunted and bears a plaque marked "Ghost Suite" (see sidebar on Haunted Hotel Rooms). Rooms are very spacious (some have marvelous views of Rock Creek) and nicely decorated. The hotel has a brand new swimming pool with poolside snackbar and a children's pool, fitness center, steam room and whirlpool, completely new spa facilities, and nearby jogging and bicycling paths. The upscale restaurant serves elegant meals and overlooks the park. There is a bar on the premises, as well as a lounge. The grounds have been completely relandscaped, with an elliptical lawn (like the

Historic Hotels

The Watergate, next door to the notorious apartment and office complex, where the fateful burglary took place in the '70s, has long been a favorite of celebrities, politicians, and performing artists. (The John F. Kennedy Center for the Performing Arts is nearby.)

one in front of the White House but smaller) and a new formal garden with fountains, which is a popular location for weddings and parties. Room rates are $109–$290 for double. Parking is an additional $14. Major credit cards accepted. Woodley Park Metro station (red line).

Average

Windsor Park Hotel, 2116 Kalorama Rd. NW at Connecticut Ave., (202) 483-0770. This charming forty-three-room hotel is furnished with antiques and dried flowers, giving it a Victorian feel. Hotel amenities include a mini-bar, free newspaper delivery, and a continental breakfast buffet in the Tea Room. Room rates are $98 single, $108 double. Parking is available on the street. Major credit cards accepted. Woodley Park Metro station (red line).

Budget

Adams Inn, 1744 Lanier Place NW (between Calvert St. and Ontario Rd.), (800) 578-6807. This hotel is composed of three turn-of-the-century townhouses that have been combined to make a total of twenty-five rooms, some of which do not have bathrooms of their own. This is a charming old-world inn furnished in a faux Victorian style, and in keeping with that decor the rooms do not have TVs or phones, but there is a pay phone in the lobby and the hotel will take messages for you. There is also a communal TV room and a refrigerator and microwave for guest use. There is a washer/dryer for guest use, and a free continental breakfast is offered in the morning. Room rates are $55 for a double without a bathroom, $70–$95 with bathroom. Weekly rates are available. Major credit cards accepted. Parking is an additional $7 per night. Woodley Park Metro station (red line), but it's a hike.

Kalorama Guest House, 1854 Mintwood Place NW (between 19th and Columbia Rd.), (202) 667-6369 and 2700 Cathedral Ave. NW at 27th St. The Mintwood Place location is composed of four townhouses and the Cathedral Ave. location is housed in two townhouses. Though small by hotel standards, these charming inns both offer a great location for a great price, if you don't mind sharing a bathroom (this is actually great for families or friends traveling together) and not having a TV or phone in your room. There is a communal TV room for those who just can't live without and a phone in the lobby where you can make free local calls (the inn will take messages for you). There is a free continental breakfast in the morning and a snack and drinks on Friday and Saturday afternoons. Room rates are $45-$80 for a double with a shared bathroom, $55–$105 for a double with bathroom. Parking is an additional $7. Major credit cards accepted. Woodley Park Metro station (red line).

Dupont Circle

Luxury

Canterbury Hotel, 1733 N St. NW, (202) 393-3000. This is a historic and luxurious hotel that once served as "The Little White House" when it was Teddy Roosevelt's private residence. Built in 1901, it now has ninety rooms, most of which are decorated with prints from Chaucer's Canterbury Tales. A continental breakfast of muffins and pastries is included in the price of your hotel room. There is also the Brighton Restaurant on the premises, which offers an English menu, as well as pub food and dart games. Rooms range from $195 single, $215 double. Parking is an additional $14 per night. All major credit cards accepted. Dupont Circle (red line).

Washington Hilton & Towers, 1919 Connecticut Ave. NW at T St., (202) 483-3000. This is the hotel where John Hinkley, Jr. tried to assassinate President Reagan. It has been a major stop for presidential events and continues to be one with a new bullet proof side entrance added after the shooting. It has the largest ballroom on the East Coast, and therefore has a steady stream of important shindigs from inaugural balls to society events. The more than 1,100 rooms are designed in a contemporary

Hotel Lounges

Although there is plenty of nightlife in Washington, most of the better hotels have highly recommended lounges, where you can hear piano and/or jazz, and some even have dancing.

Among those that stand out are:

- Dancing at the Hilton Tower
- Grand Hyatt's piano bar on its own island in a "lagoon"
- Marley's Lounge in the Henley Park, a jazz club that offers dancing on the weekends
- The Fairfax Club in the Westin Fairfax has a popular piano bar
- A pianist performs at the West End cafe at One Washington Circle Hotel
- On Friday and Saturday night a quartet performs at the Washington Plaza Hotel

decor with the work of local artists on the walls. Above the fifth floor there is a panoramic city view from most hotel windows. The hotel offers five on-site dining alternatives from the more upscale 1919 Grill to poolside dining. In-room amenities include newspaper delivery of your choice. The hotel features a heated outdoor pool and a children's pool, tennis courts, and a health club. Room rates are $230–$270 weekdays, $119–$129 weekends, tower rooms are slightly more expensive. Parking is an additional $12 per night. Major credit cards accepted. Dupont Circle Metro station (red line).

Westin Fairfax, 2100 Massachusetts Ave. NW at 21st St., (800) 325-3589. Vice President Al Gore just about grew up in the Westin, which has been one of *the* places to stay in Washington for the rich, famous, and powerful since it opened in 1927 (it was once the Ritz Hotel). It was renovated in the '90s, and rooms are elegantly decorated, many featuring armchairs and ottomans and marble tubs. Some rooms have a view of Embassy Row. Views from upper floors include the Washington Monument and Georgetown. Amenities include robes, three phones, hair dryers, and a toiletry basket, as well as morning newspaper delivery, nightly turndown service with chocolates, twice-daily maid service, and a mini-bar. The hotel has a fitness club with sauna. The Jockey Club restaurant has been a Washington hangout since the Kennedy days, and still has the red leather booths. The Fairfax Club, which serves cocktails, has a working fireplace and a piano bar. Room rates are $235 single/double. Parking is an additional $13–$23 a night. Major credit cards accepted. Dupont Circle Metro station (red line).

Expensive

Hotel Sofitel, 1914 Connecticut Ave. NW, (800) 424-2464. This hotel is part of a French hotel chain, and they try very hard to add those extra touches that will constantly remind you of this fact, such as French toiletries and Evian water as part of your in-room amenities. This 144-unit hotel is in a historic building and because it is prewar, the rooms are spacious, with a work alcove. Those on the upper floors have a nice city view. The hotel provides nightly turndown, twice-daily maid service, and a fitness center. There is a free limo service on weekdays in the morning and late afternoon. The on-site restaurant, Tracedero, serves French food and there is a piano lounge. Room rates are $199–$259 weekdays, $139–$159 weekends. Valet parking is an additional $15. Major credit cards accepted. Dupont Circle Metro station (red line).

Average

Hampshire Hotel, 1310 New Hampshire Ave. NW at 20th St., (202) 296-7600. A good location off of Dupont Circle, near Embassy Row, the hotel's rooms are spacious, with desk work areas and a nice decor. Some rooms have balconies; others have kitchenettes. There is an outdoor cafe on site. Amenities include newspaper delivery and minibar in room. Room rates are $109 for suites, but there are even lower summer rates. Parking is $13.44 extra a night. Major credit cards accepted. Dupont Circle Metro station (red line).

H.H. Leonard's Mansion on O St., 2020 O St. NW, (202) 496-2000. This very small inn, with its six suites and five-bedroom guest house, offers one-of-a-kind lodging. It is housed in a five-story brownstone that has a number of other tenants, such as an art gallery and antiques store. Rooms are decorated in one-of-a-kind themes; some have fireplaces, some have whirlpools and/or kitchens, but all have interesting touches. There is an outdoor pool and exercise room. Free breakfast comes with your stay and you can order whatever you want. Room rates are $150 to $1,000. Parking is an additional $15. Only Mastercard and Visa accepted. Dupont Circle Metro station (red line).

Hotel Tabard Inn, 1739 N St. NW, (202) 785-1227. This small hotel (forty units) is made up of three Victorian townhouses. It retains much of the charm of its original architecture, such as bay windows in several rooms, and a beamed ceiling and working

Bed & Breakfasts

In addition to hotels, Washington has many wonderful small inns and bed-and-breakfasts. You can receive a list of 65 bed-and-breakfasts by calling the Bed & Breakfast League/Sweet Dreams and Toast (202) 363-7767. Bed & Breakfast Accommodations Ltd. (202) 332-3885, www.bnbaccom.com also offers a listing of B&Bs in the city. The *Washington Post's* Web site *(www.washingtonpost.com)* also has a database of places to stay in the city that includes bed-and-breakfasts.

fireplace in the lounge. The on-site restaurant is known for its Sunday brunch, but is also popular with Washingtonians. Rooms are quirky but nice, although some do not have bathrooms of their own. A free continental breakfast is available to guests. Room rates are $90–$100 with shared bathroom, $114–$165 with bathroom, but there are summer specials. Major credit cards accepted. Valet parking is $14; self-parking is an additional $10 per night. Dupont Circle Metro station (red line).

Normandy Inn, 2118 Wyoming Ave NW at Connecticut Ave., (800) 424-3729. This is a lovely small hotel (seventy-five rooms) in the midst of Embassy Row, so many of your fellow travelers are here on foreign affairs business. The hotel has a European air (it's run by an Irish company) and serves coffee and tea all day long in the appropriately named Tea Room, as well as afternoon cookies. This is also where the complimentary continental breakfast is served every morning. In-room amenities include a small refrigerator and a coffeemaker, and the hotel shares facilities with the nearby Washington Courtyard Marriott (which is owned by the same company), so you can use their fitness center and pool. Room rates are $79–$155 double. Parking is an additional $10. Major credit cards accepted. Dupont Circle Metro station (red line).

Radisson Barcelo Hotel, 2121 P St. NW., (800) 333-3333. This Spanish-owned, 301-room hotel occupies a former apartment building and is said to have the largest hotel rooms in Washington. All rooms have desks, armchairs, and couches, and marble bathrooms with shaving mirrors. You can choose between 200 movies on their pay-per-view system. Other amenities include hair dryers, coffeemaker, nightly turndown service, morning newspaper, and three phones. The hotel also has a tree-lined outdoor pool and a fitness center. The on-site restaurant, Gabriel, features Spanish food as well as tapas. Room rates are $135–$169 single, $155–$189 double; there are weekend and summer specials, so ask when you make reservations. Parking is $15 per night. Major credit cards accepted. Dupont Circle Metro station (red line).

Swann House, 1808 New Hampshire Ave. NW, (202) 265-7677. This eleven-unit inn is housed in a mansion built in 1883, and each room is uniquely and handsomely decorated. Most have working fireplaces. The main floor features high ceilings, original woodwork, and a sunroom where a continental breakfast of home-made pastries is served daily. The hotel has an outdoor swimming pool set in a garden. Room rates are $110–235. Mastercard and Visa only. Dupont Circle Metro station (red line).

Washington Courtyard by Marriott, 1900 Connecticut Ave. NW, (800) 842-4211. This 147-unit hotel is operated by the same Irish company as the Normandy Inn and has brought many of the same European amenities to the hotel, such as coffee and tea served all day in the lobby and cookies in the afternoon. In-room amenities include coffeemakers and hair dryers, and the hotel has an outdoor pool and a fitness center. The on-site restaurant, Claret's, serves American food, and there is a lounge, Bailey's, on the premises as well. Room rates are $89–$190 double. Parking is an additional $15 per night. Major credit cards accepted. Dupont Circle Metro station (red line).

Budget

Embassy Inn, 1627 16th St. NW, between Q and R Sts., (800) 423-9111. This thirty-eight-room hotel in a four-story townhouse is on a nice block with other turn-of-century townhouses. Much of its interior architecture is original, which is why the sinks are in the bedroom and some interior rooms have no windows. Amenities include a free continental breakfast, evening sherry, and snacks. Room rates are $79–$110 weekdays, weekends $59. Street parking only. Major credit cards accepted. Dupont Circle Metro station (red line).

Windsor Inn, 1842 16th St. NW, at T St., (800) 423-9111. This hotel is operated by the same management as the Embassy Inn and offers some of the same amenities, such as free continental breakfast and afternoon snack and sherry. The forty-seven-room hotel is composed of two buildings, with two separate

Hotel Bars with Something Special

- The Hotel Washington has a rooftop deck where you can get a drink or a bite to eat and see a spectacular view of the city.

- The Round Robin Bar in the Willard Hotel has quite a drinking history. It has been a popular drinking place for two centuries, serving such luminaries as Mark Twain, Walt Whitman, and Nathaniel Hawthorne. It is said that Washington Irving brought Charles Dickens here for a drink.

- Aquarelle in the Watergate offers breath-taking views of the Potomac and themed happy hours.

entrances, that sit side by side. Hotel rooms are nicely laid out and a handful have fireplaces. Most rooms have tubs and showers, but six rooms have showers only, so ask when you make your reservations. Room rates are $79–$125 double on weekdays, $59 on weekends. Parking is on the street. Major credit cards accepted. Dupont Circle Metro station (red line).

Foggy Bottom/West End

Luxury

Washington Monarch, 2401 M St. NW, (202) 429-2400. This 415-room hotel, formerly the ANA Hotel, has become a mecca for celebrities because of its state-of-the-art fitness center, which is an additional $10 per person, although the pool, sauna, steam room, and whirlpool are free to guests. The hotel was refurbished in 1999 and has a beautiful garden courtyard, which about one-third of the rooms overlook. In-room amenities include bathrobes, three phones, high-end toiletries, and in-room safes. There is twice-daily maid service and nightly turndown service. Room rates are $280 weekday for double, $139 weekends for a double. Valet parking is an additional $19. Major credit cards accepted. Foggy Bottom Metro station (orange and blue lines).

Park Hyatt Hotel, 1201 24th St. NW at M St., (800) 922-PARK. Designed as a luxury hotel by the famed New York architectural firm of Skidmore, Owings & Merrill, this 224-room hotel has a wrought iron fountain on its side and a pair of large Chinese Y'ang horses in the lobby. Rooms are dotted with modern art, much of it copies of works hanging in the National Gallery. In-room amenities include marble bathrooms with oversize tubs, twice-daily maid service, weekday newspaper delivery, nightly turndown service, and an afternoon snack. The health club is excellent, with a pool and a separate kid's pool. The Melrose Restaurant is topnotch with many seafood entrees. Afternoon tea is served on the weekends. Room rates are $280 single, $308 double. Parking is an additional $20 per night. Major credit cards accepted. Foggy Bottom Metro station (orange and blue lines).

Watergate Hotel (Swisshotel Washington), 2650 Virginia Ave. NW, (800) 424-2736. This has always been one of the best hotels in Washington, legendary long before the Watergate break-in the nearby apartment complex and the press hordes that waited for Monica Lewinsky to emerge from her mother's apartment. Its location is one of its many drawing cards, as well as the view of the Potomac. Many of the performers playing at the Kennedy Center right next door have stayed here; other notable guests Ingrid Bergman, Muhammad Ali, and Gloria Estefan. Rooms are spacious, and the suites are reported to be some of the largest in the city. Many rooms have balconies. The hotel has an excellent health club and a heated indoor lap pool. In-room amenities include a robe, minibar, hair dryer, toiletries, nightly turndown service, and daily newspaper delivery. There is a complimentary weekday limo service and free coffee in the morning in the Potomac Lounge, which also serves afternoon tea. The hotel restaurant, Aquarelle, is considered one of the best hotel restaurants and often offers themed happy hours, such as Japanese sushi. Rooms rates are $270–$960 single/double, but there are some specials. Major credit cards accepted. Valet parking is an additional $20. Foggy Bottom-GWU Metro station (orange and blue lines.)

Expensive

Doubletree Guest Suites, 801 New Hampshire Ave. NW (at H St.), (202) 785-2000. This 101-room chain offers larger rooms to business travelers (and touring families in the summer months) with a fully stocked kitchen (with free coffee and tea) and an in-season rooftop pool. There is no restaurant on the premises, although there are many nearby. Rooms rates are $129–$200 for a single, $20 more for a double. Parking is an additional $15 per day. All major credit cards accepted. Foggy Bottom Metro station (orange and blue lines).

Great Hotels for Families

- Red Roof Inn in Chinatown has in-room pay-per-service Nintendo game systems.

- Days Inn has a rooftop pool, as does the Holiday Inn Capital.

- Loew's L'Enfant Plaza offers free meals and a welcoming gift to every child under 12.

- Kitchenettes can be found at the Howard Johnson Hotel & Suites, The Lincoln Suites Downtown, Hampshire Hotel, Doubletree Guest Suites, The River Inn, the Georgetown Dutch Inn and Georgetown Suites.

- Washington Plaza has a pool and family oriented activities all summer long.

- Marriott Wardman Park and the Omni Shoreham both have fabulous pools for kids, are located near the zoo, and have extensive grounds featuring a host of outdoor activities.

Doubletree Guest Suites, 2500 Pennsylvania Ave. NW (at 25th St.), (202) 333-8060. This two-room suite hotel is a great location for families traveling to the city. It's within walking distance to Georgetown, so the rooms are furnished in a more faux Colonial decor, but there's a TV in every room and a fully stocked kitchen (with free coffee and tea). On weekends there is a complimentary breakfast. Room rates are $119–$229. Parking is an additional $15 per day. All major credit cards accepted. Foggy Bottom-GWU Metro station (orange and blue lines).

Hotel Lombardy, 2019 Pennsylvania Ave. NW (at 21st St.), (800) 424-5486. This was once an elegant apartment building and has been recently refurbished into an elegant ten-story hotel (with a handful of apartment like suites for rental). The hotel still has an elevator operated by a human being. The rooms are individually decorated and have retained some of the apartment building flavor, such as crystal doorknobs and breakfast nooks. Hotel amenities include a coffee maker, hair dryer, and complimentary newspaper. There's a very good restaurant on the premises, Cafe Lombardy, as well as The Venetian Room, which is a more elegant dining area. The location of the hotel makes it within walking distance to both the White House in one direction and Georgetown in the other. Room rates vary wildly. In the summer you can get a room for $79 a night (ask for the *New York Times* rate), but the list price is $120–$155 for a single, $140–$175 for a double. All major credit cards accepted. Parking is an additional $16 per night. Foggy Bottom Metro station (orange and blue lines).

Hotel St. James, 950 24th St. NW (at K St.), (800) 852-8512. This 195-room suite hotel was once a Catholic all-girls school. Each suite has two TVs, a dual-line phone, and a fully stocked kitchen. There is no restaurant on the premises, but you can order from room service. A continental breakfast is served in the morning. There is a small pool on site, as well as a health club. The hotel is within walking distance to Georgetown. Quoted rates are $185 single, $205 double, but the hotel offers a $79 rate in the summer (ask for the *New York Times* rate). Parking is an additional $16 per night. All major credit cards accepted. Foggy Bottom Metro station (orange and blue lines).

State Plaza Hotel, 2117 E St. NW, (800) 424-2859. This all-suite hotel is located about five blocks from the White House and the Mall. From one of its two towers (they are connected through the garage) you can see the mall and the Washington Monument. From the North tower you can see downtown Washington. The restaurant is in the North tower, which serves three meals a day, and there are complimentary hors d'oeuvres during happy hour. The hotel has a fitness center and offers free coffee, local phone calls, and morning newspaper. All rooms have kitchens; one-bedrooms have a dining area. Room rates are $125–$150 for an efficiency, $175–$225 for a one bedroom. In the summer, the hotel offers a $79 rate (ask for the *New York Times* rate). Parking is an additional $12 per night. All major credit cards accepted. Foggy Bottom Metro station (orange and blue lines).

Moderate

The George Washington University Inn, 824 New Hampshire Ave. NW, (800) 426-4455. This former apartment building was turned into a hotel in the '60s and was purchased by George Washington University in the late '90s and updated. Because it was once an apartment building, the rooms have a certain charm that makes the hotel unique, such as dressing chambers. In-room features include a small refrigerator, microwave, and coffeemaker, and the hotel also gives guests free newspaper delivery. There is a laundromat on the premises. The on-site restaurant serves mostly Japanese food. Room rates are $120–$150 weekdays, $99–$135 weekends. Even though the hotel only has ninety-four units, there are often vacancies, so ask about special rates. In the summer the hotel runs a $74 rate (ask for the *New York Times* rate). Limited parking is an additional $14. Major credit cars accepted. Foggy Bottom Metro station (orange and blue lines).

Hotels with Pools

Washington gets frightfully hot in the summer, so many of the city's hotels have outdoor, or even rooftop pools. Most of the chains have pools (Marriotts, Howard Johnsons, Holiday Inn, Hyatt, Hilton, Days Inn, etc.) as do most of the more luxurious hotels (Willard, Latham, Watergate, Loews L'Enfant Plaza, etc.). and some of the smaller hotels will allow you to share a neighboring hotel's facilities.

Below is a partial list of some of the smaller hotels with pools:

- Governor's House
- Radisson Barcelo
- St. James Hotel
- Hampshire Inn
- Westin

Sheraton City Center Hotel, 1143 New Hampshire Ave. NW at M St., (202) 775-0800. This hotel is the site of a former private hospital, and its 353 rooms are spacious and have some interesting decorative features (there are hand-carved green marble vanities in the bathrooms). Rooms feature a coffeemaker. There is a fitness club on the premises and a good restaurant, The Washington Grill. Room rates are $89–$179 for a single to double. Parking is an additional $16 per night. Major credit cards accepted. Foggy Bottom Metro station (orange and blue lines).

One Washington Circle Hotel, 1 Washington Circle NW, (800) 424-9671. (As of this writing, the hotel was planning to call itself the W Hotel beginning in January 2000.) This is an all-suite hotel with a variety of suite sizes and is said to be where President Nixon stayed when hiding out in town after the Watergate scandal. All suites include a kitchen, dining area, and a terrace. The on-site restaurant, West End Cafe, serves American food. Suite rates are $135–165 weekdays for smaller suites, $59–$99 on weekends; larger suites are more expensive. Valet parking $8–$15 per night. Foggy Bottom Metro station (orange and blue lines).

Westin Hotel, 2350 M St. NW (at 24th St.), (202) 429-0100. This 263-room hotel has a number of unique features, such as working fireplaces in some rooms and French doors that open up on terraces overlooking the street. It is within walking distance to Georgetown and the Kennedy Center. There is a heated outdoor pool and a good on-site restaurant, as well as a bistro that features a mahogany bar, etched-glass windows, and wallpaper designed by William Morris. Room rates are $139–259 for a single, $159–$259 double, suites $259. Parking is an additional $15–$20 a night. All major credit cards accepted. Foggy Bottom Metro station (orange and blue lines).

Budget

Allen Lee Hotel, 2224 F St. NW at 23 St., (202) 331-1224. This is a real find—a nice, clean, safe, and very inexpensive

Haunted Hotels

The Hay-Adams Hotel on 16th and H Street is said to be haunted by the unhappy wife of Henry Adams, who has been haunting the property for over a hundred years.

Henry Adams, a popular novelist, historian, and minister to Britain, was the grandson of John Quincy Adams and the great-grandson of John Adams. He met his wife, Marian Hooper Adams, known as "Clover" to her friends, in London, and they set up residence in the 16th Street house, which they rented from the art collector, W.W. Corcoran. With their next-door neighbors, John Hay, Lincoln's biographer, and his wife, Clara, the two couples' home became a major center for Washington's society of the time.

However, Mrs. Adams was not happy in her marriage. One day Mr. Adams came home to find his wife dead in front of the fireplace in her room, and many suspected it was suicide caused by taking potassium cyanide, which she used in developing film.

Soon after her death, Mr. Adams moved out of the 16th St. home, which was suddenly very difficult to rent. Visitors were said to become uneasy in the home, and they could hear a woman crying at twilight. The house was said to be very cold, especially around the fireplace where Mrs. Adams died. A newspaper article published in 1890 reported that visitors heard the sound of a chair rocking and would see a ghost of a sad-eyed woman sitting in the chair. Some people who had seen the ghost would break out sobbing themselves.

This ghost is also said to haunt the Rock Creek Cemetery where Mrs. Adams is buried, and visitors to her grave who have been there at sunset report feeling that same sense of overwhelming grief.

Another haunted hotel in Washington, D.C. is the Omni Shoreham in Woodley Park. Originally built as a residence hotel in the 1930s, a suite on the eighth floor was rented by a wealthy South American businessman with political dealings who moved his whole family into the hotel. The housekeeper died in the hotel room, and shortly after so did the wife and daughter.

After their deaths, the businessman continued to pay rent on the suite but no longer lived there. Eventually the suite was abandoned, and became a large storage space for the bustling hotel. Workers would hear things moving, but no one would be there when they opened the door. People have reported that they have heard a piano playing or the TV blaring when neither was in the room. Some guests have reported seeing a little old lady in the elevator who vanished when it reached the eighth floor.

The hotel has returned the old storage space to its original use as a suite, which is now 6,000 sq. ft. They have placed a plaque on the door calling it the "ghost suite" and it can be rented for $3,000 a night. Most years a Halloween party is held in the suite.

hotel near a Metro stop. Many of the people who stay here are prospective George Washington University students or their visiting parents. The hotel is also within walking distance to the Kennedy Center. There are only eighty-five rooms so book early. Room rates are $34 for a single, $47 for a double. Street parking only, although there is parking in a nearby lot for $10. Mastercard/Visa only. Foggy Bottom Metro station (orange and blue lines)

The River Inn, 924 25th St. NW, between K and I Sts., (202) 337-7600. Within walking distance to the Kennedy Center and Georgetown (a long walk), the River Inn is a very affordable hotel offering guests fully stocked kitchens and microwave ovens. The Foggy Bottom Cafe has everything from sandwiches to romantic dinners. Hotel amenities include a free continental breakfast, health club, and newspaper delivery. Rooms rates are $99 single, $150 double. Major credit cards accepted. Parking is an additional $12–$15. Foggy Bottom Metro station (orange and blue lines).

Georgetown

Luxury

Four Seasons Hotel, 2800 Pennsylvania Ave., (800) 332-3442. This is one of Washington's premier hotels and has been the hotel of choice for celebrities for years. The rooms are well appointed with plants and art, armchairs and desks, as well as down comforters on the beds. Rooms come stocked with a minibar, CD players, bathrobes, hair dryers, and a toiletry basket. The on-site health club is considered one of the best in the hotel business with weights, equipment, a two-lane pool, and classes in everything from yoga to Tai Chi. Other hotel amenities include twice-daily maid service, complimentary car service weekdays, and morning newspaper of your choice.

Rooms rates are $360 single, $380–$445 double. Major credit cards accepted. Parking is an additional $15 per night. Foggy Bottom Metro station, but you have to walk.

Expensive

The Latham Hotel, 3000 M St. NW, (800) 528-4261. Set in the center of Georgetown, this hotel is conveniently located near all the good restaurants and nightlife, but it is quiet because it is set back from the street. There are two excellent French restaurants on the premises—Citronelle, which is one of the more talked about D.C. eateries, and La Madeleine. The rooms have a French country flair. In-room amenities include desks, fax machine, hair dryers, and robes. The hotel offers free newspaper delivery and nightly turn-down service and has an outdoor pool and a fitness center. Room rates are $160–$189 for a double on weekdays, $119–$139 for a double on weekends. Valet parking is an additional $14. Major credit cards accepted. No Metro service.

Moderate

The Georgetown Dutch Inn, 1075 Thomas Jefferson St. NW, (800) 388-2410. This small, forty-seven-unit inn offers spacious one- and two-bedroom apartment-like suites with fully stocked kitchens. In-room amenities include three phones. The hotel offers a free continental breakfast in the lobby and use of a nearby health club. Room rates are $125–$195 double weekdays, $105–$115 weekends, and more for larger suites. Major credit cards accepted. Limited free parking. No Metro service.

Georgetown Suites, 1000 29th St., NW between K and M Sts., (800) 348-7203. This seventy-eight-unit, all-suite hotel in the heart of Georgetown offers a living room, dining area, and fully stocked kitchen in all suites. In-room amenities include a hair dryer, iron, and writing area. Hotel amenities include a free continental breakfast, fitness center, washer and dryer, and an outdoor barbecue grill for guest use. Room rates are $139 double weekdays, $99 double weekends, and more for larger suites. Parking is an additional $15. No Metro service. A sister hotel with an additional 136 suites (same phone number and rates) is located at 1111 30th St. NW, between K and M Streets.

Historic Hotels

The Jefferson, opened in 1923, is one of D.C.'s finest and most exclusive hotels. It features an exquisite collection of fine art and antiques and is home to several original documents signed by Thomas Jefferson.

Chapter Five

Dining in D.C.

Washington, D.C. has an incredible number and variety of restaurants, from haute cuisine to Japanese tea houses to cafeterias. Many neighborhoods have more restaurants than stores (the main drags of Dupont Circle and Adams Morgan come to mind).

Washingtonians like to dine out, and much Washington business is done over lunch, drinks, and dinner. There are always new restaurants opening and many well-known landmarks that visitors and locals return to again and again. Washington has attracted a number of well-respected chefs from all over the country, and even some from Europe and Asia. It's a great city to eat in.

Washington, D.C. has a large number of French restaurants because of the presence of the French-influenced diplomatic corp (and I like to think it has something to do with Lafayette's legacy), as well as a lot of Vietnamese restaurants and more Ethiopian restaurants than any other American city.

Many hotel restaurants offer stellar examples of Washington cuisine, from the mega hotels to the tiny little inns. The museum restaurants can also be surprisingly good (try the Corcoran Cafe and restaurant at the National Gallery of Art or the tiny restaurant at the National Museum of Women in the Arts). Afternoon tea and Sunday brunch are also a big dining to-do in this town, and some of these are spectacular or at least unique (the National Cathedral's afternoon tea is legendary, and the drag queen brunch at Perry's is one-of-a-kind).

Of course, there are also many branches of some good chain restaurants, such as New York's Smith & Wollensky, Morton's of Chicago, Seattle's fabulous Palomino Restaurant, or even Washington's own pub chain, Clyde's. There's also a Hard Rock Cafe, a Planet Hollywood, and a Rain Forest Cafe (in Virginia) from which you can bring back souvenir Washington, D.C. T-shirts. The city also has plenty of Burger Kings and McDonald's, should the desire for such fast food arise. Most tourist attractions and malls have food courts, which offer an array of tastes where you can eat quickly and affordably. Two especially good food courts are the ones at Union Station (featuring over forty types of cuisine) and the Shops at Georgetown mall.

With so much to see and do in the city, you don't want to be walking through the streets looking for a good or affordable place to eat when the museum closes at 4:45 p.m. So it's a good idea to plan your meals in conjunction with your sightseeing, and if a place is highly recommended, make a reservation just in case (during the summer, restaurants are packed).

This list of restaurants is by no means comprehensive: D.C. eateries could fill a whole book alone. The following list offers recommendations for good, even excellent, restaurants for you to dine in during your stay, organized by location first, and then price.

The pricing guide is as follows:

Expensive—Main courses start at $20
Affordable—Main courses are $12–$20
Budget—Main courses are under $12

Special attire recommendations (such as jacket and tie, or no shorts), are noted in the review. Otherwise, you should be able to wear whatever you are sightseeing in.

Aside from hotel restaurants, most Washington restaurants do not have parking.

Downtown
Expensive

Capitol Grille, 601 Pennsylvania Ave. NW, (202) 737-6200. This is a popular bar and restaurant where locals eat and hang out. Noted for its steaks and dry-aged cuts of beef, there's an aging room on the premises with sides of beef hanging on display. They also serve lobster, large portions of fish, and generous side dishes. Some seats have a view of the Capitol Building. Entrees run $19–$27. Jacket and tie strongly suggested. Major credit cards accepted. National Archives metro station.

Les Halles, 1201 Pennsylvania Ave. NW, (202) 347-6848. A slightly expensive French restaurant with an

emphasis on beef and desserts, Les Halles is located just opposite the Federal Triangle Metro stop. The decor is authentically French, with lace curtains, a homey wooden interior, and popular French songs playing in the background. The fare is mainly beef, which is well-prepared (the filet with béarnaise sauce is divine), but there are other traditionally French items on the menu such as cassoulet and a marvelous onion soup, which is a meal in itself. They also feature rich and wonderful desserts, such as Peach Melba. A meal for one with a glass of wine will run about $40. Major credit cards accepted.

Lespinasse, 923 16th St. NW, in the Sheraton-Carlton Hotel (formerly the St. Regis), (202) 879-6900. This is where Washington goes to celebrate or show off. The interior is rich, with gold tones and fine china. The menu changes daily, but there are some constants such as the fois gras appetizer and the risotto with truffles. Aside from a wonderful array of pastries for dessert, there's also a cheese platter. Entrees run $23–$36; prix fixe $48 for four courses, $85 for 6; there's also a prix fixe lunch, which is much less expensive. Major credit cards accepted. Reservations a must. Jacket required. Complimentary valet parking with dinner. Farragut North Metro station.

Morton's of Chicago, 1050 Connecticut Ave. NW, (202) 955-5997. This is the quintessential Washington, D.C. steakhouse, even though it's part of the Chicago chain. This is where Washingtonians go for prime rib, which is thick and juicy but runs out early in the evening, so it is recommended that you get there early if this is what you want. Portions are generous. Most people, even the swells, leave with doggy bags. Meals run $20 to $65, slightly less for lunch. Business attire is essential. Most major credit cards accepted. Reservations are strongly suggested. Metro Center metro station.

Willard Room, 1401 Pennsylvania Ave. NW, in the Willard Hotel, (202) 637-7440. This is the very best that D.C. dining has to offer. It is known as the "residence of the presidents" because it has served most presidents dinner the night before their inauguration. Lincoln is said to have come here for the corned beef and blueberry pie, and Henry Clay is said to have invented the mint julep at Willard's bar. The setting is palatial, restored to its turn-of-the-century grandeur with chandeliers, wood paneling, and columns. It is considered one of the most romantic settings in town, and many marriage proposals have been made in this dining room. For such a spectacular, historical setting, the food is reasonably priced. The menu changes daily, but the seafood is especially wonderful under a new chef from Florida, as are the desserts. Main courses run $15–$30. Major credit cards accepted. Jacket and tie required. Reservations a must. Complimentary valet parking with diner. Metro Center Metro station.

Affordable

Arena Cafe, 521 G St. NW, (202) 789-2055. While the Velocity Grill in the MCI Center is closed for renovation, this nearby diner-looking (from the outside) restaurant is a real treat. It is known for its excellent salads, great crab cake sandwiches, and a full selection of beers. Entrees run $10–$18. Major credit cards accepted. Gallery Place Metro station.

Bis, 15th E St. NW, (202) 661-2700. Located in the trendy Hotel George, and a sister restaurant of the ever-popular Vidalia, this is one of the hottest new restaurants in town, so make reservations. Its food is Parisian with an American flair as evidenced by such entrees as calamari with chorizo or duck breast with olives and citrus fruit. Entrees range from $17.50–$25. Major credit cards accepted. Union Station Metro stop.

Bombay Club, 815 Connecticut Ave. NW, (202) 659-3727. A very popular upscale Indian restaurant, the presidential couple has been seen dining here many times. The setting is very British colonial, with ceiling fans and wicker chairs. The food is often very hot and spicy, but well done, and many of the seafood entrees are unique to this restaurant. Entrees run $8–$18, but there's a prethe-

Romantic Restaurants

- Coeur de Lion in the Henley Park Hotel is considered by many to be one of the most romantic hotel restaurants in town, for both its setting of fireplaces and candlesticks, as well as its superb food.
- The Willard Room is said to be one of the places where Washingtonians propose to one another, with cozy, yet elegant table settings (lots of chandeliers) and consistently fabulous food.
- Morrison-Clark Inn seats only about forty diners in its Victorian living room turned restaurant. There are white marble fireplaces, beautiful crystal chandeliers, and candles, as well as creative and delicious food.

ater prix fixe meal, as well as a Sunday brunch. Major credit cards accepted. Farragut West Metro station.

Cafe Atlantico, 405 8th St. NW, (202) 393-0892. A popular Latin three-level restaurant and nightclub, this place is usually packed, so make a reservation. The decor is colorful with artwork on the walls. The restaurant has a number of signature drinks to choose from, and your server will make guacamole at your table right in front of you. There are many great appetizers to choose from and many people make a meal out of them (there is a tastings menu). Desserts are also rich and creative. Entrees run $7–$18; lunch is less expensive and the appetizers start at about $5. Most major credit cards accepted. National Archives Metro station.

El Catalan, 1319 F St. NW, at 14th St., (202) 628-2299. A wonderful mix of Spanish and French cooking, it is named after the region in Spain where the two cuisines (and languages) meet. The interior features murals, iron work, and Spanish tiles. Of course, there's a wide selection of tapas, and the homemade soups are excellent, as are the seafood and meat dishes. Jacket and tie suggested for dinner. Entrees are $13–$36, but you can make a meal of the tapas. Most major credit cards accepted. Complimentary parking during dinner. Metro Center Metro station.

Coco Loco, 810 7th St. NW, (202) 289-2626. This is a very popular Latin restaurant, and its carnival atmosphere is enhanced by mosaic tiles and bright colors on the walls. This is a hot night spot with a packed dance floor in the evenings and weekends, so make reservations. It's also popular for the food, which is Euro/Pan-American (a little Mexican, a little Brazilian, and a little Spanish). Also featured are a bountiful array of original Mexican tapas (mushroom quesadilla) as well as a fixed price churrasquiera, which is an ample array of grilled meats, colorful salad bar, rice, and condiments. Meals run $10–$27. Major credit cards accepted. Gallery Place Metro station.

Coeur de Lion, 926 Massachusetts Ave. NW in the Henley-Park Hotel, (202) 414-0500. A local favorite because of its romantic, elegant decor and cozy atmosphere, this restaurant serves a wonderfully rich continental cuisine with an American flair. The cognac-flavored lobster bisque is a favorite, as are the crab cakes, but the menu changes seasonally and there are a lot of lighter entrees. Desserts are a specialty, so save room for the cheesecake or crème brûlée. Entrees run $15–$22. Major credit cards accepted. Jacket required. This is an intimate restaurant with candle-light tables, so reservations are recommended. Metro Center Metro station.

D.C. Coast, 1401 K St. NW, (202) 216-5988. This is the hottest new restaurant of the year, so don't even think about going without making reservations. Set in the Tower Building, the art deco interior with its two-story dining room and glass-enclosed balcony make the place airy, and the bronze mermaid at the door lets you know you're in for some fun too. Seafood is a specialty on the menu, which includes crab cakes, tuna tartar, and Chinese smoked lobster, and there are also some hearty entrees like the double-cut pork chop. Entrees run $12–$30. Major credit cards accepted. McPherson Sq. Metro station.

Equinox, 818 Connecticut Ave. NW, (202) 331-8118. Founded by Todd Gray, one of chef Roberto Donna's disciples, this is one of the hottest new restaurants in town. The food is American bistro fare with a wide variety of creative appetizers, as well as a good selection of meat, fish, and game. Everyone raves about the lamb with beans. A honey butter and a fruit butter are served with your bread basket, and homemade cookies are served after the meal, so you don't need dessert. Entrees run $12–$20, but there are a number of more elaborate tasting menus. Major credit cards accepted. Farragut West Metro station.

Hard Rock Cafe, 999 E St., (202) 737-7625. This theme restaurant is located right around the corner from Ford's Theatre and the Peterson House, and it might be a good lunch stop for children or teens who are tired of "ancient" history. It serves

Classic D. C. Eateries

- Old Ebbitt Grill has been a Washington watering hole and business lunch spot for years. It's where many visiting celebrities can be seen (Clint Eastwood and the Rolling Stones), and President Clinton has been spotted there occasionally.
- The Jockey Club in the Westin Fairfax was a Kennedy clan hang-out in the '60s.
- Clyde's in Georgetown is a popular favorite both for its location (right near the Georgetown Shops mall) and its hearty appetizers. It started out as a hangout for Georgetown University students and has become a chain.
- Kinkead's is a popular American brasserie within walking distance to the White House.
- Hogate's, a popular water-front restaurant that's big on seafood, features leg-endary rum buns.

average American fare jam-packed with rock memorabilia in a fun atmosphere. Clever items on the menu include Tupelo chicken with apricot sauce and honey mustard ($7), the Ringo Combo of rings, rolls and chicken ($9), Bruce's ribs ($16), and Lovely Rita's Pot Roast ($11), as well as burgers, chili, and pizza. The kids menu includes macaroni and cheese, pizza, Jimi Tenderstix, or a cheese sandwich for $6.99. An amusing painting depicts George Washington in a Hard Rock T-shirt. Other items of interest include displays on the Beatles, the Rolling Stones, the Jackson Five, Jimi Hendrix, and the Doors, as well as some of Elvis's gold records and the saxophone President Clinton played at his 1993 inauguration. Major credit cards accepted. Souvenir shop on premises sells a very cute D.C. T-shirt featuring the Capitol and the Washington Monument ($24). There is a coupon for a free souvenir with the purchase of an entree in various hotel hand-outs. Metro Center Metro station.

Hogate's, 800 Water St. SW, (202) 484-6300. This is a very popular waterfront seafood restaurant that has been serving Washingtonians (Newt Gingrich and Jesse Jackson have been spotted here) for more than sixty years. There are nautical tchotches throughout the lobby, but the food is great and the atmosphere is casual; sightseers often come in wearing shorts and sneakers. Everyone raves about the rum buns that are served with the meal and the creamy crab soup is a favorite. There's a New England clam bake, lots of lobster, some interesting grilled salmon, and fried fish for those who insist. It seats up to 1,000 and is often packed during the tourist season, so call for reservations. Entrees run from $11 to $35. Major credit cards accepted. L'Enfant Plaza Metro station.

Jaleo, 480 7th St. NW, (202) 628-7949. This popular tapas bar is named after a John Singer Sargent painting, *El Jaleo,* of a Spanish dancer, which is recreated on the back wall. The sangria is refreshing, and the tapas selection is wide—Spanish cheeses, sausages, gazpacho, the traditional torta omelette, etc. There is also paella for two. A meal for one (two tapas with a half carafe of sangria) should run about $20. Home-made bread, Spanish olive oil, and a dish of olives are served with your meal. Major credit cards accepted. Call for reservations as this place is popular with the locals (also right next door to the National Shakespeare theater), and you might have to wait up to an hour without a reservation in the summer months. Metro Center Metro station.

The Mark, 401 7th St. NW, (202) 783-3133. This trendy new hot spot, painted emerald green and mustard yellow with contemporary art on the walls, is located in one of the art gallery centers of Washington, D.C. Chef Alison Swope serves up American/southern/Santa Fe food that's original and creative, with a good by-the-glass wine list and fabulous desserts. Dinner entrees run $13–$20; lunch is about half that. Reservations are suggested. Major credit cards accepted. National Archives Metro station.

McCormick & Schmick's Seafood Restaurant, 1652 K St. at Connecticut Ave. NW, (202) 861-233. Although part of an Oregon chain, this is one of the better restaurants in town and it features linen tablecloths and fancy chandeliers. People come here for the oyster bar and the crab cakes, and the desserts are highly recommended. There is an all-day light fare menu where entrees run under $10, otherwise entrees are $11–$24. There's a daily happy hour where appetizers are about $2, which makes this a very popular afterwork place. Major credit cards accepted. Business attire suggested. Farragut North or West Metro stations.

Morrison-Clark Historic Inn Restaurant, 1015 L St. NW, (800) 332-7898. Award-winning creative cuisine in an historic landmark served amid Victorian decor. The goat cheese and phyllo roll is excellent, as are the many delicious desserts such as the homemade chocolate napoleon. Entrees change from season to season, but the menu offers a full array of fish, duck, rabbit, pork, and lamb on a regular basis. All the ice cream is made on the premises. Reservations are strongly suggested since the dining area only seats about forty and this restaurant is popular with the local crowd for business lunches and romantic dinners. Entrees run $15–$30. Major credit cards accepted. Metro Center station, but it's a bit of a walk.

Great Views

- Aquarelle, in the Watergate Hotel, offers spectacular views of the Potomac and is a great place to go for drinks, appetizers (often with a theme, such as Japanese sushi or Spanish tapas) or dinner when you are taking in a show at the Kennedy Center for the Performing Arts.
- Pier 7 is where locals go for waterfront and city views, as well as good seafood.
- Roof Terrace is the Kennedy Center restaurant which offers wonderful vistas of the Potomac and good food that will coincide with performance schedules. There's also a fabulous brunch every Sunday.
- Sequoia is a popular drinks-after-work spot for locals that offers a view of the Potomac along the Washington Harbor.

M & S Grill, 600 13th St. at F St. NW, (202) 347-0234. This is the surf-and-turf sister restaurant of McCormick & Schmick's and it's right near the MCI Center. A little more relaxed and much heavier on the meat (ribs and steaks abound), there's a regular happy hour special of $2 appetizers and plenty of sandwiches under $10. Meals run $7 to $22. Major credit cards accepted. Metro Center or Gallery Place Metro station.

Mykonos, 1835 K St. NW, (202) 331-0370. The interior has whitewashed walls and tiled floors to make you think of the Greek Islands. There's always a daily special, but the standards of moussaka and lamb dishes, as well as the two choices of mezethes plates with fifteen dishes, are favorites. Entrees run $7–$20. Major credit cards accepted. Complimentary valet parking with dinner. Farragut West Metro station.

Old Ebbitt Grill, 675 15th St., (202) 437-4801. Now part of the Clyde's chain, this very old Washington watering hole is still a popular place for the power lunch and wellknown for its Sunday brunches. Famous patrons include most presidents (including Clinton) as well as the Rolling Stones and Clint Eastwood. It was opened as a saloon in 1856, and its etched glass partitions and paneled, wooden booths are surrounded by political memorabilia such as Teddy Roosevelt's animal trophies and Alexander Hamilton's wooden bears. While a restaurant this old has standards that regulars return for—the burgers, the New England clam chowder, and the Maryland crab cakes—the menu does vary seasonally, and it is said that this is the only place in Washington where you can get fresh Alaskan halibut when it's in season. Entrees run $10–$16; lunch is a little less expensive. This is one of the few restaurants downtown that serves breakfast ($4–$7), and if you wake up early to get White House tickets, this is a good place to kill time and eat a big meal while waiting for your tour. Sunday brunch is $6–$16. Major credit cards accepted. McPherson Sq. or Metro Center stations.

Oval Room, 800 Connecticut Ave. NW, (202) 463-8700. Within walking distance to the White House, there are some charming murals of Washington, D.C.'s past and present (presidents and Hollywood stars) on the walls and oval ceiling and an oval table. The restaurant's soups are highly recommended, as are the tuna tartare and crab cake appetizers, but there's also a wide selection of meat and seafood entrees. Entrees run $6 to $25. Major credit cards accepted. Jacket and tie required. Complimentary valet parking with dinner. Farragut West Metro station.

Palomino, 1399 Pennsylvania Ave. NW, (202) 842-8900. This new Euro-bistro next door to the Ronald Reagan Trade Building is surprisingly good. The interior is alive with red walls and giant copies of Fernand Léger paintings. There are outside tables for dining in warm weather, a large wooden bar, and tables around the bar, and a nonsmoking area downstairs. The food is a little Italian, a little French, and a little Mediterranean. The chef seems to like Gorgonzola cheese and hazelnuts, so you'll find them on pasta (the penne Gorgonzola is delicious), in salads, and even on grilled salmon. There are three signature drinks; of these, the Palini, a champagne and peach nectar drink, is particularly good. Major credit cards accepted. Main courses run from $10–$22 for a seafood sampler. Federal Triangle Metro station.

Pier 7, Maine Ave. and 7th St.. Waterfront, (202) 554-2500. This is another waterfront dining experience with panoramic views of the Potomac and various monuments. The restaurant is known for its seafood, such as the crab cakes and bouillabaisse, but there is also a wide selection of pastas and meat dishes on the menu, as well as a pretheater prix fixe menu. Entrees run $15–$30. Major credit cards accepted. L'Enfant Plaza Metro station.

Planet Hollywood, 1101 Pennsylvania Ave. NW, (202) 783-7827. The food is pretty standard (burgers, salads, pizzas) and moderately priced, with a good children's menu. Kids love this popular food attraction when visiting the White House or Mall because there is some unique Hollywood memorabilia to see. Two video screens play nonstop Hollywood snippets. Don't miss Darth Vader's helmet, Arnold Schwarzenegger's *Terminator* costume, Freddy Krueger's *Nightmare on Elm Street* glove, Jack Nicholson's ax from

Planet Hollywood Hidden Treasures

Aside from the *Titantic* and Washington, D.C. movie memorabilia, other "treasures" at the D.C. location of Planet Hollywood include:

- *Beverly Hills 90210*'s Luke Perry's high school yearbook
- The futuristic skateboard from *Back to the Future II*
- *Star Trek* memorabilia

The Shining, and the props from *Titanic.* Specific to the Washington, D.C. locale are the computer set from *Wargames,* which is in the back of the restaurant toward the ceiling (it's used as a frame for the second video screen), the desk from *Mr. Smith Goes to Washington,* and the gun Wesley Snipes used in *Murder at 1600.* Major credit cards accepted. There is a coupon in the Old Town Trolley map and various hotel handouts that give you a free magnet with your meal of over $15. Federal Triangle Metro station.

Prime Rib, 2020 K St. NW, (202) 466-8811. This is considered one of Washington's best places for roast beef, and it has a real men's club feel with lots of wood and leather. Steaks are thick and juicy, and the prime rib served with fresh horseradish is excellent. There's plenty of fish on the menu too. Meals run $18–$30, less for lunch. Jacket and tie required. Most major credit cards accepted. There's a pianist in the evenings. Farragut West Metro station.

Red Sage, 605 14th St. NW, (202) 638-4444. Ask anyone who's been here and they'll refer to this restaurant as "a Wild West fantasy." Think of it as an upscale theme restaurant, with unique western touches such as buffalo chandeliers. The menu offers many creative southwestern opportunities, such as barbecued ostrich and catfish tacos, but it's best when you stick to traditional western food, like chili or burritos, or their fabulous signature homemade sausage. Reservations are recommended for the main dining area (it's a very popular tourist draw in the summer), but the Cafe and Chili Bar don't accept them. Meals run $12–$31.50, but the Cafe and Chili Bar are less expensive, as is lunch. Major credit cards accepted. Metro Center Metro station.

Budget

Fado Irish Pub, 808 7th St. NW, (202) 789-0066. Right near the great Chinese arch, close to the MCI Center, is this interesting Irish pub. Its interior is broken up into separate rooms that have their own themes, such as the library room or the interior of an Irish cottage. All the decorative pieces were imported from

Ireland. The menu features such Irish staples as corned beef and cabbage, and there are some interesting deviations such as oysters and mussels and salmon, plus a wide selection of Irish beer and whiskey. Entrees are very reasonably priced, most under $10. Major credit cards accepted. Gallery Place Metro station.

Havana Breeze, 1401 K St. at 14th St. NW, (202) 789-1470. This is a two-tier, down-home Cuban restaurant with both table and cafeteria-like counter service. The lower level is geared toward the fast lunch for the working crowd and offers such Latin staples as Ropa Vieja (old clothes), a sort of Cuban beef stew, as well as the classic Cuban sandwich of ham, pork, cheese, and pickles, with the side dishes that make Latin food so satisfying—rice and beans, plantains, yucca. Upstairs is more of a bar, but you can order food there as well. Entrees run $6–$11. Major credit cards accepted. Farragut North Metro station.

Tony Cheng's, 619 H St., NW (202) 842-8669. This well-known two-story restaurant offers lunch and dinner specials for as little as $5 and a "Mongolian grill" (all-you-can-eat BBQ) for $14.95 in the downstairs dining area. Also featured are dim sum and exotic seafood specialties. Chef and owner Tony Cheng is usually on the premises, and you can see pictures of him with presidents of the past thirty years, from Carter to Clinton. American Express, Mastercard, and Visa accepted. Gallery Place Metro station.

Full Kee, 509 H St. NW, (202) 371-2233. This is one of the best little Chinese restaurants in town, with a daily menu of specialties (featuring a lot of fish and shellfish in the summer) that includes such unique fare as Hong Kong wonton soup (eight wontons stuffed with shrimp in a spicy broth) and wonderful casseroles of pork and tofu or oysters. Most entrees are $5–$12. Cash only. Gallery Place Metro station.

Go-Lo's, 604 H St., (202) 437-4656. After viewing Ford's Theater and Peterson House, you might want to eat here and dine in a bit of history. Conspirators met here in Mary Surratt's boarding house to plan the kidnapping of President Lincoln. There is a land-

Rock and Roll Artifacts

Among the rock memorabilia on view at Washington, D.C.'s Hard Rock Cafe are:

- A green leisure suit worn by James Brown
- Freddy Mercury's red leather pants from 1982
- 8 Beatles gold records, as well as the piccolo trumpet used in "Penny Lane"
- Led Zepplin's Jimmy Page's guitar
- Rolling Stones' Brian Jones' nehru jacket
- Jimi Hendrix's brown leather shoulder bag in which he kept his lyrics

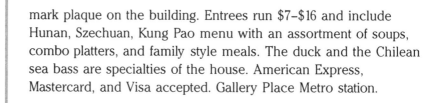

mark plaque on the building. Entrees run $7–$16 and include Hunan, Szechuan, Kung Pao menu with an assortment of soups, combo platters, and family style meals. The duck and the Chilean sea bass are specialties of the house. American Express, Mastercard, and Visa accepted. Gallery Place Metro station.

National Museum of Natural History, 10th St. and Constitution Ave. There's a new cafeteria at the museum, which has many child-pleasing meals (hamburgers, pizza), as well as homemade soups, hot food, and personally prepared sandwiches, desserts, coffee, and tea. Meals run $5–$10. Major credit cards accepted. Smithsonian Metro station.

National Museum of American History, Constitution Ave. between 12th and 14th Sts. There's a wonderful old-fashioned ice cream parlor and three other restaurants in the museum, so you don't have to leave the premises for lunch or dinner. Meals are under $10. Major credit cards accepted. Smithsonian Metro station.

TGI Friday's, 1201 Pennsylvania Ave. NW at 12th St., (202) 628-8443. Across the street from the Federal Triangle Metro stop, this often very crowded restaurant offers very basic lunch and dinner fare of the Tex-Mex variety—hamburgers, chicken fingers, etc. It is kid friendly with a good and inexpensive kids menu. Entrees run $7–$15, less for lunch and appetizers, from which you can make a meal. Most major credit cards accepted.

Sholl's Colonial Cafeteria, 1990 K St. NW in the Esplanade mall, (202) 296-3065. This family-owned cafeteria has been a Washington landmark for over seventy years. It has all that 1950s meat-and-potatoes charm, and everything is homemade. Regulars come for the meatloaf, chopped steak and potatoes, liver and onions, crab cakes, and the desserts—rice pudding and fruit pies—and everything is extremely cheap. Entrees run $1.85 to $5.50. Cash only. Breakfast, lunch, and dinner served, but it is closed by 8:00 p.m., Sundays 8:00 a.m. to 3:00 p.m. Farragut West Metro station.

Eat Like a Washingtonian

Most Washington office workers and political aides don't have the time to go to the fancier restaurants for heavy, leisurely lunches because they need to rush back to their desks should the big kahuna need them at a moment's notice, so they eat in cafeterias hidden in office buildings throughout the downtown area and Capitol Hill. Many of these offer wonderful meals right in or nearby major sightseeing locations, and you get to feel what it's like to be a Washington drone.

Below is a list of the inside cafeterias and lunch spots of working Washington:

- Dirkson Senate Office Building, 1st and C Sts. NW, (202) 224-4410. There's a lunch buffet here that includes a carving station and a number of hot and cold entrees for about $10 for an adult and $7 for children. The meal includes a beverage and dessert too!

- Library of Congress Cafeteria, (202) 707-8300. This is a pretty standard office workers' cafeteria, but there's a buffet lunch for $8.50 in the neighboring Montpelier Room.

- Longworth Building Cafeteria, Independence Ave. and South Capitol St. NE, (202) 225-4410. This is an indoor food court, with a wide array of quick-meal choices.

- House of Representatives Restaurant, U.S. Capitol Building, (202) 225-6300. This is a fancier dining room, with chandeliers, also known as the "Members Dining Room" or "Room H118," where you might actually spot a congressperson or two. It serves breakfast as well as lunch. It's crowded for lunch, so get there a few minutes before noon if you'd really like to eat here.

- Supreme Court Cafeteria, (202) 479-3246. Like the House of Representatives Restaurant, this is a real working cafeteria for the court, so you might just see a justice or two during lunch. There are plenty of hot and cold daily specials at a reasonable price.

Capitol Hill
Affordable

America, 50 Massachusetts Ave. NE, inside Union Station, (202) 682-9555. This is a great location for a leisurely meal after getting off the train. If you sit in the dining area in Union Station, you can people-watch as busy travelers head to and fro. The fourth floor offers a view of the Capitol building. The food is supposed to be traditional American and offers fare from all fifty states, with selections like roast turkey and stuffing, macaroni and cheese, and spaghetti and meatballs. Meals run $12–$17 for dinner, less for lunch. Major credit cards accepted. Union Station Metro station.

B. Smith's, 50 Massachusetts Ave. in Union Station, (202) 289-6188. This is the most expensive restaurant in Union Station and is a branch of a New York restaurant founded by model Barbara Smith (the Oil of Olay beauty). It is built in a beautiful Beaux Art building and former presidential waiting area where presidents once greeted visiting dignitaries. The food is creative southern/Creole/soul food, which means wonderful corn bread, red beans and rice, catfish, jambalaya, and pecan pie. Meals run $11- $22. Major credit cards accepted. Union Station Metro station.

Thunder Grill, 50 Massachusetts Ave. in Union Station, (202) 898-0051. This is high concept southwestern food, with a beautiful wooden interior and portraits of Native Americans on the walls. Entrees include traditional southwestern fare such as fajitas and quesadillas, as well as hot and spicy shrimp, salads, and sandwiches. There's a selection of thirty-one tequilas on the menu and happy hour features a different frozen margarita every day.

Most entrees are under $15. Major credit cards accepted. Union Station Metro station.

Brunch in Washington

Washingtonians love Sunday brunch, so you'll find it offered at most hotel restaurants and most of the chain restaurants. Of course, not all brunches are equal. Some are opulent food extravaganzas that offer everything but the kitchen sink and unlimited champagne; others are so quirky they seem like something out of Alice in Wonderland.

Below is a list of the stand-outs in town:

- Bistro Francais in Georgetown offers a moderately priced brunch with a selection of eggs or French fare and all the champagne you can drink for $15.95.

- Bombay Club offers a sumptuous buffet that includes an array of Indian dishes, as well as a carving station, for $16.50.

- Corcoran Gospel brunch in the Corcoran Gallery's Cafe des Artistes features gospel music as you dine in the museum's atrium drinking mimosas. The $18.95 brunch includes your entry fee.

- Clyde's of Georgetown is a popular brunch spot ($7–$11) with a nice selection of omelettes, steak and eggs, etc. Its sister restaurant, the Old Ebbitt Grill, downtown has a much fancier brunch menu ($6–$13).

- Gabriel in the Hotel Radisson Barcelo is packed on Sundays with locals and tourists who come for the extravagant array of food. Everything from salads to quesadillas, with a carving station offering beef, lamb, and suckling pig, plus a fabulous selection of desserts can be had for $17.95.

- Kramers & Afterwords offers Sunday brunch all day in a very affordable price range, so it is a popular Sunday destination in the Dupont Circle area.

- Roof Top Terrace at the Kennedy Center is one of the best brunch deals in town with a lavish buffet of pasta, smoked meats, omelettes made to order, and desserts, as well as your choice of a drink for $25.95

- The Morrison-Clark Hotel offers an exquisite upscale brunch, with unlimited champagne, for $29.95.

- Perry's, in the Adams Morgan area, is the most creative Sunday brunch in town. Take in the funky, funny drag show while you eat from a buffet of pasta, breakfast meats, bagels, dessert, and coffee for $15.95. Alcoholic drinks are additional. The crowd is mixed, and you'll even see some couples with baby carriages.

- Castle Common at the Smithsonian. Here's your chance to eat in this wonderful old building and then rush out and see the sights on the Mall. Sunday brunch offers a "noble feast" of carved meats, omelettes, and the famous spiced shrimp buffet for $18.95 for adults, $8.95 for children. Reservations are recommended because this is such a popular brunch spot (202) 357-2957.

Budget

Union Station food court, lower level of Union Station. This is an entire floor of fast food establishments that offer everything from sushi to quiche and sauerbraten. Most meals are $5. Union Station Metro station.

Adams Morgan/Woodley Park
Affordable

Lebanese Taverna, 2641 Connecticut Ave. NW, (202) 667-5350. A mainstay of the Woodley Park dining zone since it opened more than twenty years ago, this is a very popular Lebanese restaurant, and it is usually packed on the weekends (reservations are only accepted until 6:30 p.m.). The interior is decorated with prints of Old Lebanon, and prayer rugs hang on the wall while Lebanese music plays in the background. The big hit on the menu is the demi mezze, where you are given a sampling of a dozen appetizers, such as humus, baba ganush, spinach pies, etc., as well as homemade pita cooked in the wood-burning oven on site. There's also a wonderful selection of main courses, such as kabobs, falafel, fish, and vegetarian dishes. Meals run from $10–$16. Free parking at a nearby garage. Most major credit cards accepted. Woodley Park Metro station.

Merskerem, 2434 18th St. NW, (202) 462-4100. Some say that this is the best Ethiopian restaurant in the city. Its spicy fare of lamb, chicken, beef, and vegetables is served with the traditional Ethiopian bread, injera, by a staff dressed in Ethiopian clothing. Ethiopian wine and beer is served and live Ethiopian music is performed after 11:30 p.m. on Friday and Saturday nights. Meals run $8–$15. Major credit cards accepted.

New Heights, 2317 Calvert St. NW, at Connecticut Ave., (202) 234-4110. This two-story restaurant with large windows is popular because you can order any selection in appetizer or meal sizes, and the menu is creative but dependable. People come back for the butter-fried oysters and the crab cakes. Full

entrees run from $16–$25, but appetizer portions are about half that. Major credit cards accepted. Free valet parking. Woodley Park Metro station.

Peyote Cafe/Roxanne, 2319 18th St. NW, (202) 462-8330. Housed in an Adams Morgan brownstone, Peyote cafe is a small, fun Santa Fe-style Mexican restaurant with brightly colored walls and a good menu of tacos and white cheese pizza (a real kid pleaser), and more exotic fare, such as chili-grilled shrimp, from Roxanne, the up-scale restaurant upstairs. Entrees are $10–$16. Most major credit cards accepted.

Perry's, 1811 Columbia Rd., (202) 234-6218. Known for its legendary drag queen brunch on Sundays, Perry's—a disco in a former life—is a hip, fun restaurant with cozy sofas around tables and a funky, bizarre, alien-like chandelier. It serves Asian fusion food in the evenings, and there's a rooftop dining area open in the spring and summer where you can eat sushi or sesame-crusted tuna with mango salad. Most meals run between $10–$17, but you can make a meal out of sushi and an appetizer. Major credit cards accepted.

Georgetown
Expensive

1789, 1226 36th St. NW, (202) 965-1789. This upscale restaurant, named for the year that Georgetown was founded, is located in an old townhouse with working fireplaces and old maps of Washington, D.C. on the walls. The food is based on traditional American cooking, with an updated twist by Chef Ris Lacoste who varies the menu according to what's available seasonally, and emphasizes seafood. The oyster stew is creamy and the desserts are rich. Entrees run from $18–$39, but there is a pre-theater prix fixe that offers three courses for $25. Jacket required. Free valet parking. Major credit cards accepted.

Michel Richard Citronelle, 3000 M St. NW in the Latham Hotel, (202) 625-2150. This is the place to dine in Washington, where everyone who is anyone goes for both the food and to be seen. (Reservations are a must!) The award-winning chef and owner, Michel Richard, left his Citrus Restaurant in L.A. to set up this signature contemporary French restaurant, and everyone in Washington seems to have appreciated his move. There is a wall in the restaurant that changes colors (sort of a mood wall) and a see-through glass-enclosed wine "library" of thousands of bottles surrounds the dining area. The menu is exotic and comprehensive; you can get everything from sweetbreads to lamb to duck, all of it creatively displayed and prepared, most with wonderful sauces. Meals run $16 to $32. Jacket and tie required at dinner, business attire for lunch.

Morton's of Chicago, 3251 Prospect St. NW, (202) 342-6258. (See downtown listing.)

Affordable

Bistro Francais, 3124-28 N St., (202) 338-3830. This charming French bistro offers terrific prix fixe meals of $13.95 that include wine, salad or soup, a selection of main courses, as well as four choices of fruit tart for dessert. Weekend brunches include all you can drink champagne with a choice of an omelette, steak and eggs, eggs benedict, and so on. There are also post- and pretheater dinner specials. The restaurant is open until 3:00 A.M. on weekdays and 4:00 A.M. on weekends, so it is a popular late-night dining spot. Major credit cards accepted.

Bistrot Lepic, 1736 Wisconsin Ave. NW, (202) 333-0111. A Georgetown favorite for both the authentic French bistro food and the quirkiness of the tiny restaurant, Bistrot Lepic is often crowded, even for lunch. The food is the kind of bistro fare you might actually find in a Parisian restaurant—plenty of kidney, liver, even pig's feet, as well as salmon, tuna, and lamb. The desserts are quite good too. Meals run from $14–$17, lunch is less expensive. Major credit cards accepted.

Kid Food Hot Spots

It's not as if there's nothing for your kids to eat in Washington, but sometimes, in order to get them to sit quietly at a place like Les Halles, you have to promise to take them somewhere that's more child-oriented in return. Below is a list of places that promise to be kid pleasers and where kids are made to feel truly welcome:

- Hard Rock Cafe. Right near Ford's Theatre and the Peterson House, it's chock full of rock-'n'roll memorabilia that older kids find fascinating, and it has a good, varied children's menu, as well as some great frozen drinks for both kids and adults. The souvenir shop is a hit with kids too.

- Full Kee. This hole-in-the-wall Chinese restaurant is so authentic it fascinates children (there are smoked ducks hanging in the window). There are wonderful egg rolls and wonton soups for the kids to enjoy, and the staff is very child friendly.

- Museum of Natural History Cafe. When I asked my son what his favorite dining experience in the city was, he answered with the cafeteria in this museum. He said he loved the soup and watching the staff put together his sandwich, but he also loved not having to leave the museum to get something to eat.

- Soda Fountain at the Museum of American History. Designed to recall the old-fashioned soda shoppe in main street U.S.A. in 1950s America, the Soda Fountain is a nice retreat. Kids love it because they can get a milkshake or a sundae in the middle of the day, and it's a great place for their parents to take a break from all that museum sightseeing.

- Planet Hollywood. Not too far from the White House and the aquarium, this is a kid's delight, with great movie paraphernalia for kids and a generally fun atmosphere. The kid's menu is good and inexpensive, and the staff knows that kids are the reason that many adults are there, so they treat them right.

- Sholl's Cafeteria. Unless you have something like this back home (and for most urban kids the answer is a resounding no), Sholl's is a rare treat. Kids are fascinated by the array of food and by the opportunity to pick just about anything they want without their parents saying no. They also love the mashed potatoes with gravy and all those desserts.

- TGI Friday's, near the White House and the aquarium, is another kid pleaser. They like the children's menu, which is varied (and cheap—most meals are under $5) and the decor, which looks like Huck Finn's attic.

- Union Station food court. There are more than forty food stalls for your hungry child to choose from here (mine wanted sushi), while you also get to eat what you want (quiche Lorraine) without spending a bundle.

Café Deluxe, Wisconsin Ave. NW, (202) 686-2233. Ask any Washingtonian what their favorite restaurants are, and after they try to impress you with the fact that they've been to the latest hotspot, they will all mention Café Deluxe. It's always packed and full of lively energy. The food is consistent and never expensive. The interior is fairly plain, with white tablecloths and simple white plates—a step up from a diner—but the burgers are excellent (both beef and tuna), and so is the meatloaf. The desserts are home-made, as are the soups. Meals run $7–$16. Most major credit cards accepted.

Clyde's of Georgetown, 3236 M St. NW, (202) 333-9180. Founded in 1963 as a faux-Victorian pub for Georgetown University students, this has become a popular chain of local restaurants (that include the venerated Old Ebbitt Grill and several other Clyde's locations) where you can always get good American saloon food. The standard selection includes a juicy burger, buffalo wings, crab cake sandwich, hearty soups, and a surprisingly excellent cheese platter that pairs blackberries with your four cheese selections. Most people order from the appetizer menu, which is varied and creative. Of course, there's a wide selection of beers on tap and a good wine list. Weekend brunches have become a tradition (especially since this restaurant is located in the Georgetown Shops mall). Meals run from $10–$17, lunch is less. Validated parking is available in the nearby mall. Major credit cards accepted.

Sea Catch, 1054 31st St. NW, (202) 337-8855. Conveniently located in a courtyard of art galleries in the Georgetown mall, Sea Catch overlooks the C&O Canal and features a fireplace and tables on a deck. The raw bar features oysters, clams, shrimp, and lobster. Entrees run the gamut from shellfish to tuna nicoise or sesame-crusted scallops. Most entrees run from $13–$20. Major credit cards accepted. Free parking.

Sequoia, 3000 K St. NW at 30th St. (at Washington Harbour), (202) 944-4200. This is one of the spectacular view-with-a-meal dining experiences in D.C. Most people come for the view of the Potomac (especially for drinks after work), but the food is decent too—crab cakes, calamari, pizza, catfish, salads. There's a pre- and post-theater special prix fixe Monday through Thursday that offers house wine, soup or salad, choice of entree, and dessert for $19.95. Meals run $8 to $29. If you want a window table with a view, it's a good idea to make a reservation. Major credit cards accepted.

Budget

Georgetown Shops food court, off of M St. There are a dozen or so fast food establishments offering pizza, philly cheese steaks, pretzels, ice cream, gyros, etc., all reasonably priced.

Myth.com, 3243 M St. NW, (202) 625-6984. At this cyber-cafe and restaurant, you can partake of a wide selection of coffees, teas, and fruit drinks, as well as a killer hamburger, while you check your e-mail. Internet usage is free to students and faculty with I.D. cards ($2.50/15 minutes, $10 hour otherwise). Major credit cards accepted.

Zed's, 1201 28th St., (202) 333-4710. Now in a new two-story location, this very popular Ethiopian restaurant is where Chelsea and Hillary bring their personal friends for a fun meal (photos line the wall). Meals of lamb, beef, chicken, seafood, and vegetables are very spicy and are served with an Ethiopian injera bread and no silverware. Most meals are under $10. Ethiopian beer available. Major credit cards accepted.

Dupont Circle
Expensive

The Jockey Club, 2100 Massachusetts Ave. NW in the Westin Fairfax Hotel, (202) 293-2100. A Washington, D.C. standby since the Kennedy days, and a still popular place for a power lunch, the Jockey Club is the same as it ever

was (in spite of a number of renovations and changes in hotel management)—red leather banquettes, red and white tablecloths, horsey do-dads. The menu changes from chef to chef and food trend to food trend, but the standards are still there—French onion soup, Caesar salad and crab cakes, as well as the pommes souffles side dish of puffy French fries. There's a dessert cart for those who care to indulge. Reservations are a must. Jacket and tie required for dinner, but strongly suggested for lunch. Complimentary valet parking with dinner. Entrees run $24–$34, less for breakfast and lunch. Most major credit cards accepted. Dupont Circle Metro station.

Nora, 2132 Florida Ave. NW at R St., (202) 462-5143.
This is one of the best restaurants in Washington, D.C., in spite of the fact (or because of it, depending upon your culinary tastes) that all the food is organically grown. The setting is lovely, in a private townhouse with a skylight and restored stable as the main dining room with quilts and local art on the walls. This is not your tofu and bean sprout burger restaurant, but haute cuisine for the culinarily correct. There's an emphasis on seafood, but there's also free-range chicken and even kidney on the menu. Desserts are wonderful, especially the pies and homemade ice cream, and there's a varied wine list. Of course, a restaurant like this varies the menu depending upon seasonal produce, so there is always something new and different to try. Entrees range from $20–$25. Reservations strongly recommended. Mastercard, Visa, and Discover only. Dupont Circle Metro station.

Smith & Wollensky, 1112 19th St. NW (between L and M streets), (202) 466-1100. Since Washington, D.C. is a town that loves its red meat, this is just the restaurant that the city needs. This branch of the famed New York steakhouse, with its famous green and white exterior, serves lots of steak (even a double sirloin for close to $60), as well as lamb chops and lobster. There's a smaller, sister restaurant next door, Wollensky's Grill, that is open until 2:00 A.M. Entrees run $15–$60. Major credit cards accepted. Business attire suggested. Farragut West Metro station.

High Tea in Washington

Don't ask me why, but afternoon tea is a big deal in this town. You'll find it offered at most of the better hotel restaurants. There are a handful of truly stellar afternoon tea experiences in the city, and if you like a late light lunch or a little something before dinner, you should really try to fit them into your schedule.

- Tea at the National Cathedral (Massachusetts and Wisconsin Avenues, 202-537-8993) is grand, but you really should make a reservation because it's also very popular with tourists and regulars. It is served on Tuesday and Wednesdays only at 1:30 p.m. and costs a flat $15, for which you are offered a selection of tea sandwiches, pastries, scones, a selection of delicious desserts, and tea. A tour of the cathedral comes with the tea.
- Coeur de Lion, in the elegant Henley-Park Hotel in the downtown area serves a wonderful afternoon tea in their dining room from 4:00 p.m. to 6:00 p.m., with a wide selection of pastries and scones.

Other hotel restaurants that feature afternoon tea include Lespinasse at the Sheraton-Carlton during the winter months only, the Lafayette in the Hay-Adams Hotel, Melrose in the Park Hyatt, and Seasons in the Four Seasons Hotel.

Vidalia, 1990 M St. NW, (202) 659-1990. Considered one of the most creative southern restaurants in D.C., Vidalia has been a popular favorite for a long time. The dining room is down a flight of stairs and has no windows, but no one seems to mind as they slap apple butter on the delicious corn bread and try the new ways that the chef has come up with to flavor grits (such as goat cheese and mushrooms!). There are many interesting seafood entrees on the menu. Desserts are superb too. Try the pecan pie. Entrees run $13–$27. Most major credit cards accepted. Dupont Circle Metro station.

Affordable

Athens Taverna, 1732 Connecticut Ave. NW, (202) 667-9211. This moderately priced Greek restaurant features a good selection of food and seafood, including a three-entree combo plate of stuffed grape leaves with a lemon sauce, moussaka, and pastito, as well as an excellent retsina wine. Galatobutiko (literally "milk and butter," a rich Greek dessert made of sugared farina wrapped in filo dough) is on the dessert menu. Entrees run $9–$20. Major credit cards accepted. Dupont Circle Metro station.

Buca di Beppo, 1825 Connecticut Ave. NW, (202) 232-8466. Family-style, large portions of southern Italian cuisine are this new restaurant's claim to fame, designed as a '50s-style supper club. Platters of pasta, oversized pizza, and standards such as chicken cacciatore are featured on the menu. Entrees run $16–$20 but are meant to be shared. Most major credit cards accepted. Three blocks north of the Dupont Circle Metro station.

Gabriel, 2121 P St. NW in the Radisson Barcelo Hotel, (202) 956-6690. Upscale Spanish food is featured with an emphasis on European, as opposed to Latin American, influences. There's a wonderful selection of tapas and some delicious Spanish dishes, such as roast pig, and exquisite desserts. However, Gabriel's is known for its sumptuous Sunday brunch, so make a reservation for this. As in all tapas restaurants, you can get away with making a meal out of two tapas selections. Dinner can run you as little as

$12, but entrees are $15–$22. Major credit cards accepted. Complimentary valet parking. Dupont Circle Metro station.

Levante's, 1320 19th St. NW, (202) 293-3244. This upscale Mediterranean restaurant (Turkish cuisine via Europe) has an outdoor patio and features a terrific appetizer plate of fried cheese and salad, cigars, dolmathes, as well as a terrific spinach pie. Entrees run $6–$16.50. Most major credit cards accepted. Dupont Circle Metro station.

Budget

Kramerbooks & Afterwords, 1517 Connecticut Ave. NW at Q St., (202) 387-1400. This is a good restaurant, and it's located in one of the late-night bookstores and cybercafes in town (free fifteen-minute e-mail check). The menu is pages long, featuring a variety of dishes from vegetable chili to lamb chops to quesadilla, with a wide selection of beers. Sunday brunch (served all day) is very popular here. Entrees run $7 to $11. Major credit cards accepted. Dupont Circle Metro station.

Teaism, 800 Connecticut Ave. (202) 835-2233, Dupont Circle Metro station, and 2009 R St., (202) 667-3827. This wonderful Asian restaurant serves a wide selection of personal potted teas, ice creams (green tea and ginger are first rate) and meals, including Japanese bento boxes, kebobs, curries, salads, and even an ostrich burger. Most meals are under $5, except for the ostrich burger. Most credit cards accepted.

Zorba's Cafe, 1612 20th St. NW at Connecticut Ave., (202) 387-8555. This inexpensive Greek restaurant is located in a rowhouse on Dupont Circle's main drag. It features a wonderful selection of fast Greek food from dips to fried cheese to a souvlaki plate and baklava for dessert. Entrees start at around $5. Some credit cards accepted. Dupont Circle Metro station.

Foggy Bottom/West End

Expensive

Aquarelle, 2650 Virginia Ave. NW (in the Watergate Hotel), (202) 298-4455. Here's your chance to get inside the infamous Watergate and see how the other half lives, or eats. If you're going to the Kennedy Center, this is actually a good place to go for an exquisite pretheater meal (prix fixe $38, which is a bargain at this upscale restaurant) and some fabulous views of the Potomac. (Call ahead for a reservation if you want a good table with a view.) The menu includes such upper crust entrees as quail, rack of lamb, squab, and sweetbreads, all wonderfully prepared. Entrees run $18.50 to $38. Free valet parking. Jacket required with dinner. Major credit cards accepted. Foggy Bottom Metro station.

Galileo, 1110 21st St. NW, (202) 293-7191. This was one of the most talked about restaurants in the late '80s, as it was the first restaurant in chef Roberto Donna's Italian eatery empire (others include the Il Radicchio chain and Pesce). It's so popular you cannot get in for dinner without a reservation, and some book weeks in advance. The food is rich (Italian with French and Swiss influences), and hazelnuts and porcini mushrooms seem to be a chef's favorite as they appear on everything from fish to game. Entrees are on the expensive side, with pasta dishes starting at $22, but it's worth it. There's even a cookbook you can buy. Major credit cards accepted.

Affordable

Goldoni, 1120 20th St. NW, (202) 293-1511. This highly praised restaurant with Venetian Italian cuisine has just moved to a new location. The food is a little more complicated than southern Italian—lots of light sauces and intricate food layering. The rack of lamb is a favorite, as is the salmon wrapped in prosciutto. The desserts are supreme. Entrees run $12–$18. Major credit cards accepted. Parking in validated lot. Foggy Bottom Metro station.

Kinkead's, 2000 Pennsylvania Ave. NW, (202) 296-7700. This is a popular American brasserie just a few blocks west of the White House. It is known for its seafood entrees, such as the grilled squid and polenta appetizer and the signature dish of a pepitia-crusted salmon with shellfish and chili ragout, but there is always at least one meat and poultry entree on the menu. During evenings and Sunday brunch, the restaurant features a jazz group or a pianist. Dinner entrees run $18–$25; lunch is less expensive. Major credit cards accepted. Foggy Bottom Metro station.

Melrose, 1201 24th St. NW at M St., in the Park Hyatt Hotel, (202) 955-3899. A very popular seafood restaurant in an upscale hotel, reservations are strongly recommended for the weekends when there's dancing, and for lunch when the business crowd comes here. There's a sunken terrace outdoors with a garden and fountain for warm-weather dining, and the glass-enclosed dining area overlooks this. Everyone loves the shrimp-filled ravioli and the house crab cakes. Meals run $14–$34, slightly less for lunch. Major credit cards accepted. Free valet parking. Foggy Bottom Metro station.

Roof Terrace Restaurant/Hors D'oeuvrerie, New Hampshire Ave. at Rock Creek Parkway in the Kennedy Center, (202) 416-8555. Needless to say that an excellent restaurant with fabulous Potomac views in Washington's premier entertainment showcase requires a reservation (but the lighter fare Hors D'oeuvrerie doesn't accept them). On some evenings you can choose from selections on either menu. The beef is recommended, as is the fish; the appetizers are always good and there's always a daily special. There's a spectacular Sunday brunch that attracts a crowd. Hours of operation are really geared around performances, so call to make sure that the restaurant is open. Entrees run $12–$29, less for appetizers and lunch. Major credit cards accepted. There is garage parking, but you have to pay for it. Foggy Bottom Metro station.

Budget

Moby Dick's House of Kabob, 1070 31st St. NW, (202) 333-4400. A very popular restaurant with the locals, this is the

Washington's Trendy Restaurants

Bis, a Parisian bistro with an American flair, features a James Beard-award-winning chef.

Coco Loco, both a nightclub and a restaurant, is always packed because of its carnival atmosphere and fun Euro/Pan-American cuisine.

D.C. Coast, the hot new restaurant of the moment, features a statue of a bronze mermaid at the door.

Galileo an '80s hotspot started by celebrity chef Roberto Donna, is still considered one of the best restaurants in town. Italian/French food.

Jaleo, a tapas restaurant in downtown Washington, is always packed.

Nora features "healthy" food in a townhouse with quaint decor.

third branch of a chain that started in the suburbs. It features Persian food, mainly kabobs and grilled meat, laced with a secret house seasoning. There's hardly any seating, but it's always crowded. Cash only.

Cleveland Park

Affordable

Matisse Cafe, 4934 Wisconsin Ave. NW, (202) 244-5222. This is a French/Middle-Eastern restaurant, with Matisse-inspired grill work and lots of whitewashed walls and blue accents. Specialties include calamari with mint, grilled sausage, seafood couscous, and great onion soup. Entrees run $15–$23.50, but there is a good selection of appetizers from which you can make a meal. Major credit cards accepted. Cleveland Park Metro station.

Yanyu, 3433 Connecticut Ave. NW, (202) 686-6968. A new pan-Asian restaurant (featuring entrees from China, Japan, Thailand, and Vietnam) has just opened in what is becoming a dining thoroughfare in Cleveland Park near the Uptown theater. Some of the featured entrees include lily bulb dumplings, white fish sashimi, and many other cleverly seasoned seafood dishes. The green tea creme brûlée is a one-of-a-kind dessert. Entrees run $8–$16. Major credit cards accepted. Valet parking on weekends. Cleveland Park Metro station.

Budget

Nam Viet, 3419 Connecticut Ave. NW at Macomb St., (202) 237-1015. One of the older and best Vietnamese restaurants in town, everyone recommends the pho and the fresh crispy fish, as well as the spring rolls and the shrimp toast. Entrees run $7–$14. Most major credit cars accepted. Cleveland Park Metro station.

Chapter Six

The Complete Smithsonian

You can't visit Washington, D.C. without seeing some of the Smithsonian Institution's fourteen museums and galleries in the city. They are the jewels of the crown in this town.

If you are only in town for a long weekend, the three must-see Smithsonian attractions are the National Air and Space Museum (the only one of its kind in the world), the National Museum of Natural History, and the National Museum of American History, each of which will take you a minimum of four hours to fully explore.

However, if you have the luxury of being able to explore all the Smithsonian branches in Washington, D.C., you will see a breadth of art, history, science, and culture unparalleled anywhere in the world. And it's all free (visiting a similar number of museums in any other city would run at least $100 per person) and open every day of the year except Christmas.

The story of the Smithsonian Institution is fascinating (see the sidebar on its founder, James Smithson). It was founded by an Act of Congress in 1836, after a wealthy English bachelor-scientist donated his fortune to the United States (which he had never seen but was enamored of because of its scientific and democratic principles) to create a center dedicated to the study of science and culture.

In the century and a half since the Smithsonian was founded, it has grown from a one-building science center to a sixteen-building Institution (two museums are currently housed in New York) that contains more than 141 million objects. And it is still growing today. In 1999, the Smithsonian received two major donations—one by the noted Asian art collector Dr. Paul Singer, which will complement the existing collection in the Arthur M. Sackler Gallery, and a second by billionaire Steven Udvar-Hazy, who donated $60 million to create a new wing of the Air and Space Museum at Dulles Airport that will display 180 airplanes and spacecrafts including the Space Shuttle Enterprise. By the year 2002 there will be a new museum and a new building for the National Museum of the American Indian on the Mall; and the Anacostia Museum, which features the art, history, and culture of D.C.-area African-Americans, will be housed in a larger building closer to public transportation by the year 2001.

Overview of the Smithsonian's Galleries and Museums

Below is a brief overview of the fourteen museums and galleries of the Smithsonian currently located in the nation's capital (see the map on page 45 for the locations of the nine Smithsonian museums and galleries on the Mall). Detailed descriptions follow in the later pages of this chapter.

The Anacostia Museum. This museum of African-American social and cultural history focuses on Washington, D.C., Maryland, Virginia, North Carolina, South Carolina, and Georgia. Established in 1967, the Anacostia was the first federally funded neighborhood museum. Exhibitions have highlighted the work of local southern artists, as well as the African-American culture and heritage in all walks of life, including music, religion, and more. This museum is scheduled for a relocation to another building in the near future.

Arts and Industries Building. This was the building where the Smithsonian collection was first shown, and it is a beautiful example of Victorian architecture. The museum houses collections of American Victoriana, as well as crafts and special sociological exhibits of various peoples in America (Japanese-Americans in Hawaii, for instance).

Freer Gallery of Art. This museum brilliantly pairs nineteenth- and twentieth-century European and American artists influenced by Asian art with authentic Asian works from ancient times to present. The epitome of the Freer Gallery's vision is the restored Peacock Room designed and painted by James Whistler.

Hirshhorn Museum and Sculpture Garden. A stellar museum of modern art of this century, this museum has a perma-

A Haunting at the Smithsonian?

Smithson's bones were brought over to the United States at the turn of the century when an Italian marble drilling company bought the cemetery in Genoa where Smithson was buried. His crypt was set up in a former guard room in the Smithsonian Castle.

In the 1970s, guards and Castle workers started to comment on weird occurrences in the Castle, such as alarms going off without cause and the ancient elevator jamming for no reason. Books were being pulled out and abandoned in the Woodrow Wilson Library and many latenight workers complained of feeling that someone was watching them. This went on for about a decade, and during a renovation in the late 1970s, Smithson's sarcophagus was opened. Inside was a tin box where Smithson's bones were haphazardly mixed together, along with fragments from his original coffin. After the bones were realigned properly and the sarcophagus resealed, the Castle has remained quiet.

nent collection of paintings from Picasso to Warhol, as well as three floors of small sculpture and an outdoor sculpture garden that features the work of Rodin, Matisse, Moore, etc.

National Air and Space Museum. The most popular museum in the Smithsonian, this museum's permanent collection is dedicated to the history of flight. The actual aircraft and spacecraft that made aviation history are on view to the public, as are exhibits on the science and technology of aviation and space flight. There's also an IMAX theater, a planetarium, and many special exhibits.

National Museum of African Art. This is one of the country's only museums dedicated solely to African art, with more than 7,000 pieces in the collection.

The National Museum of American Art. One of the few museums in the world dedicated solely to American art, this permanent collection houses some great colonial masterpieces, as well the paintings that tell the story of our country. This museum, and its sister museum (they share the former home of the Old Patent Office Building, the site of Lincoln's second inaugural ball), the National Portrait Gallery, will be closed until 2003 for an extensive renovation, but traveling exhibits will be shown in art museums throughout the country.

National Museum of American History. A comprehensive museum on the history and culture of America, featured are permanent exhibits on the politics, science, history, and popular culture of America's past. The two most popular exhibits are the first ladies' inaugural gowns and entertainment artifacts, which include Judy Garland's ruby slippers from *The Wizard of Oz*.

The National Museum of Natural History. This four-floor museum that takes up two city blocks has everything from dinosaur skeletons to the famed Hope diamond to an insect zoo with giant cockroaches—plus an IMAX theater.

National Portrait Gallery. This incredible museum features paintings and sculptures of Americans of note, from portraits of all the presidents to paintings of this country's leading scientists, artists, writers, and historical figures. This museum and its sister museum, the National Museum of American Art, will undergo an extensive renovation beginning in January 2000 and will be closed until 2003.

National Postal Museum. This surprisingly entertaining museum is dedicated to the history of postal service and stamps in this country. The exhibits on the Pony Express and airmail are particularly interesting, especially to children.

Renwick Gallery. A branch of the National Museum of American Art highlighting American craft and design, this is a refreshingly eclectic museum in a beautiful mansion (former home of the Corcoran Gallery of Art) with some incredible nineteenth-century paintings and a trompe l'oeil ghost clock that is mind-boggling.

Arthur M. Sackler Gallery. Housed in an underground gallery, this is a stupendous collection of artwork from China, Japan, and Southeast Asia, from pre-Christian times to the present, featuring works in bronze, jade, paintings and sculpture, as well as furniture and jewelry.

The National Zoological Park. This 163-acre zoo features what seems like almost every creature known to man. Highlights include a tropical rain forest, orangutans who use a computer-based language system, and American bison.

The Smithsonian Castle

(1000 Jefferson St. SW) When you get to the Mall, one of the landmarks to look for is the red sandstone castle-like structure that houses the Smithsonian Institution's Information Center. Though not a museum itself, this is the headquarters of the Institution, where all its main offices are located.

The Norman-style castle (a combination of twelfth-century Romanesque and Gothic architectural styles) was designed in 1855

The National Museum of American Indian on the Mall

A new museum dedicated to the history, religion, art, and culture of Native Americans will soon be opening in the last available museum site on the Mall. Dedication of this new museum is scheduled for the summer solstice of 2002.

The museum will be a five-story limestone building designed by the Canadian Blackfoot architect, Douglas Cardinal, and a committee of Native Americans. It will be built between the Capitol and the Lincoln Memorial.

The Smithsonian Institution has a vast collection of Native American artifacts, arts, and religious items from the Arctic Circle to Tierra del Fuego spanning three centuries. Many of these items had previously been housed at the Museum of the American Indian in New York City and at the Smithsonian's Cultural Resources Center in Suitland, Maryland.

The new museum will include an interactive library, as well as indoor and outdoor spaces for Native Americans to use in ceremonial and ritual care of objects in the collections.

Wright Brothers Flight

The first successful powered, controlled, sustained flight by humans took place on Dec. 17, 1903 in Kitty Hawk, N.C. using a plane designed and constructed by Orville and Wilbur Wright.

The inscription at the Air & Space Museum on the 1903 Flyer reads: "The original, Wright Brothers aeroplane, the first power-driven, heavier-than-air machine in which man made free, controlled, and sustained flight, invented and built by Wilbur and Orville Wright, flown by them at Kitty Hawk, North Carolina, December 17, 1903. By scientific research the Wright Brothers discovered the principles of human flight. As inventors, builders, and flyers they further developed the aeroplane, taught man to fly, and opened the era of aviation."

by noted architect James Renwick (who designed St. Patrick's Cathedral in New York and the Renwick Gallery, which is named after him). It has become the symbol of the Smithsonian over the years; you can find it on key chains and Christmas ornaments in any of the museum's shops.

Think of the castle as your gateway to the Smithsonian theme park. There is a visitor's information desk, where you can ask questions and get directions. You can also see models of the museums on the Mall and watch interactive videos. Information on special exhibits and events are also available at the Castle.

There is a twenty-minute film on the history of the Institution, as well as an overview of the museums and galleries that runs continuously throughout the day.

The marble sarcophagus of James Smithson, the founder of the Institution, is also housed in this building in its own room behind the information desk, and to the right (in a former guard's room) you will find a piece of Smithsonite, a zinc carbonite he discovered that was named after him. Although Smithson never visited the United States when he was alive (and never even corresponded with any Americans that we know of), his bones now lie in the centerpiece structure that bears his name.

The sumptuous Sunday brunch known as "the noble feast" is also presented here in the Castle Common Room from 11:00 A.M. until 3:00 P.M., (202) 357-2959 (see restaurant listings in Chapter 6). The Smithsonian cafeteria is closed to the public during the rest of the week.

The Museums Up Close

National Air and Space Museum

Independence Ave. and 6th St. on the south side of the Mall, with entrances on Jefferson Dr. and Independence Ave. Often open earlier and later in the summer. Call for hours. Free daily guided tours at 10:00 A.M. and 1:15 P.M., as well as science demonstrations throughout the day. L'Enfant Plaza Metro station.

This is the most visited museum in the Smithsonian complex, and some say the world, with more than seven million museum-

The History of the Smithsonian Institution

The Smithsonian Institution exists because James Smithson, a wealthy English scientist, thought the principles of our nation and the scientific discoveries that were coming out of this country in the nineteenth century, were so amazing that he wanted to found "an establishment for the increase and diffusion of knowledge among men" in the United States.

Upon his death in Italy in 1829, he willed his fortune to his nephew and stipulated that should he die without heirs, the entire Smithson fortune, which was worth about half a million dollars (which was an enormous amount of money in those days and which came to the United State in bags of gold sovereigns) would be given to the United States to fund such an institution.

It took eight years of discussion in Congress before the Smithson gift was accepted and then another nine years before the Smithsonian Institution became a reality when President Andrew Polk signed an act of Congress establishing the Smithsonian Institution. The Renwick-designed Castle was built in 1855.

Since then a trust has been established to oversee the Institution, which receives private funds and donations, as well as more than $250 million in government funding a year (which is why the museums are free to visitors).

Who was this guy who made this great gift possible? He was born James Lewis Mace in France in 1765, but later learned that his father was Hugh Smithson, Duke of North Cumberland. He changed his name to Smithson while a student at Oxford, where he studied science, and later became a noted mineralogist. He discovered a zinc carbonite, Smithsonite, which was named after him, and was invited to become a fellow of the Royal Society, a British group dedicated to scientific research, at the age of twenty-two.

goers annually. It is a vast museum that chronicles the history of flight and aviation, with twenty-three galleries, each devoted to a subject or theme, as well as 300 authentic spacecraft and rockets, spacesuits, a touchable moon rock, propellers, engines, and many interactive exhibits. Put aside at least three hours (four if you have children or if you are really interested in flight) because there is no way you can rush through this incredible museum, especially in the summer months when it's quite crowded.

The most popular exhibit is the Milestones of Flight, a two-story exhibit that you can see from the street through the glass wall of the museum and is right inside the Mall entrance. Here you will find the Wright Brothers' 1903 *Flyer,* the first human-propelled flying machine; the *Spirit of Saint Louis,* in which twenty-five-year-old Charles Lindbergh made the first transatlantic flight from New York to Paris in 33$^1/_2$ hours in 1927; the Bell X-1 *Glamorous Glennis*, in which Chuck Yaeger was the first pilot to fly faster than the speed of sound in 1947; *Gemini IV*, which carried astronauts Edward White and James A. McDivitt on the first manned space walk (their spacesuits are here too); and the *Apollo 11* command module, which was the first spacecraft to land on the moon (astronaut Michael Collins's spacesuit is on display as well). In the fall of 1999, the museum added its newest addition to the Milestones Gallery—the Breitling *Orbiter 3* gondola, which was the first balloon to successfully circle the earth nonstop in 1998.

Other highlights of the first floor include the world's only touchable moon rock, which was collected by *Apollo 17* astronauts; the Viking Lander, the test vehicle for the first spacecraft to explore the surface of Mars; Goddard rockets from 1926 and 1941; and United States's Pershing II and USSR's SS-20 missiles, which are nuclear missiles banned by the INF treaty of 1987.

First Floor Galleries: Galleries on the first floor include permanent exhibits on air transportation, the black experience in aviation, and the golden age of flight, which chronicles aviation history between the two world wars and features many classic planes such as the Beechcraft Staggerwing. There is also a gallery on the history of jet aviation, which explains how the commercial jetliner came into being, as well as a film on technological developments.

The first floor also has an exhibit on the history of early flight, from gliders that inspired the Wright Brothers to the first seaplanes and a Bleroit IX, the most popular pre-WWI monoplane. In the How Things Fly exhibit there are hands-on demonstrations of the scientific principles that enable airplanes to fly. You can also crawl into the cockpit of a Cessna 150 and manipulate the controls (a very popular experience for kids of all ages).

The first floor also features a gallery on exploring the earth from above for mapping, weather, and spying purposes, and another gallery on the stars that explains how satellites are used to map and examine radiant energy from the sun and the stars, with a host of solar instruments on display, as well as a film on the history of telescopes and our current knowledge of our galaxy and those beyond.

The Space Race gallery is one of the most popular exhibits on the first floor, with various models of American spacecraft, rocketry, missiles, spacesuits, and an overview of the space race. Here you will find a full-size test model of the Hubble Space Telescope, the Apollo-Soyuz spacecraft (the first manned international space mission), a model of the space shuttle *Columbia* on its launch pad, and the Skylab orbital workshop, which visitors can walk through (another very popular exhibit).

The Samuel P. Langley IMAX Theater, which features an IMAX screen that is five stories high and seven stories wide, is also located on the first floor, and films on the history of flight and space exploration are shown daily. This is a unique experience, and children love films on this giant screen, especially the evergreen *To Fly*. Tickets sell out quickly in the summer months, so purchase them early in the day (the 10:00 A.M. shows are usually not sold out) even if you want to see a show in the afternoon. You can also purchase tickets at the box office up to two weeks in advance, so you might want to stop in the museum when you get to town

Historical Highlights of the National Portrait Gallery

Portraits of all the American presidents are on view here, including the famous painting of George Washington by Gilbert Stuart. Charles Willson Peale's portraits of George and Martha Washington are here, as is Norman Rockwell's Richard Nixon and a bust of Bill Clinton.

The National Portrait Gallery's Civil War collection includes depictions of Civil War figures including Abraham Lincoln, Harriet Beecher Stowe, Frederick Douglass, Ulysses S. Grant, Robert E. Lee, and Jefferson Davis.

Smithsonian Hours

All Smithsonian museums and galleries are open 364 days a year (they are closed Christmas Day) from 10:00 A.M. to 5:30 P.M. Some have extended hours in the summer. There are no direct phone numbers to the museums and galleries. For information, call the general Smithsonian number at (202) 357-2700.

and buy tickets for later on in the week. Tickets are $5.50 for adults and $4.50 for children and seniors.

The Museum shop is also located on the first floor, where almost every kid who ventures in walks out with the freeze-dried "astronaut" ice cream (at $1.95, a bargain as far as kid's souvenirs are concerned). The gift shop will undergo a massive renovation in the year 2000 and will re-emerge as a three-level shopping gallery. There will be alternate sites where you can buy the space ice cream during the renovation.

The Second Floor: Galleries on the second floor include exhibits on air and sea exploration from 1911 to present and display biplanes, WWI carriers, and navy fighters. There are two separate exhibit halls on aviation during WWI and WWII, which is an extremely popular hall, displaying aircraft from five countries including a Messerschmidt and a P-51D Mustang.

Another hall on this floor features an exhibit on exploring the planets, where you can see a full-scale replica of *Voyager*, the spacecraft that explored Jupiter, Saturn, Uranus and Neptune, as well as a meteorite collected in Antarctica that scientists believe may be a piece of Mars.

The Pioneers of Flight exhibit houses many record-holding airplanes. The most popular is Amelia Earhart's Lockheed Vega, which made the first transatlantic solo flight by a woman in 1932 from Newfoundland to Northern Ireland in 14 hours, 52 minutes.

Other galleries on the second floor include a look at space exploration in the future, including a realistic Martian landscape, an overview of the Apollo program with examples of moon soil and space food and suits, as well as an exhibit of art about flight and space exploration. The final gallery looks at computers and space exploration featuring the world's fastest computer, the brain of the Minuteman missile, and interactive displays for designing spacecraft.

The Albert Einstein Planetarium is located on the second floor, where there are various shows on the night sky, astronomy, and space projected onto a domed interior. Tickets for the planetarium shows can be purchased at the Langley Theater box office.

The Air and Space museum has two restaurants, the Flight Line Cafe on the first floor, which is a cafeteria serving lunch basics such as burgers, pizza, etc., and The Wright Place on the mezzanine level above the Cafe, which is a full-service restaurant featuring a menu of regional specialties such as crab balls and the Memphis Belle pork sandwich. You can make a reservation at the Wright Place by calling (202) 371-8777.

Even More Air and Space

If you have been inspired by the Air and Space Museum and/or you just can't get enough of aviation history, there is an annex to the museum in Maryland that houses the extra aircraft that the museum just couldn't cram into its two-stories.

The Paul E. Garber Preservation, Restoration, and Storage Facility is located in Suitland, MD, about six miles from Washington, D.C. and has several buildings open to the public in what the Smithsonian bills as a "no-frills" museum (meaning they are on view in three airplane hangers and there is no heating or air conditioning). On view are more than 150 aircraft, as well as engines, propellers, and other flight-related items. Guided tours provide a behind-the-scenes look at the museum's workshop where you can learn about airplane restoration. Highlights of the Garber collection include WWII fighter planes, Roscoe Turner's RT-14 *Meteor*, and planes from the Korean War.

Tours must be made by reservation two weeks in advance ((202) 357-1400) and last about three hours. Tours are available Monday through Friday at 10:00 A.M. and Saturday and Sunday at 10:00 A.M. and 1:00 P.M.

In 2003 this collection will move to the Dulles Center at Washington Dulles International Airport, where it will be housed in a new museum made possible by the $60 million donation of Steven Udvar-Hazy, the largest individual donation in the museum's history.

The National Museum of Natural History

10th St. and Constitution Ave. NW, with entrances on both Constitution Ave. and Madison Dr., (202) 357-2700. Often open later during summer months, call for hours. Guided tours are offered at

Discovery Room

On the first floor of the National Museum of Natural History there is an interactive museum for children where they can touch and examine various exhibits. The Discovery Room is due to be expanded and moved to the third floor in 2002.

Some of its kid-pleasing opportunities include:

- Peering into a crocodile's mouth
- Examining the "Discovery Boxes" which feature a variety of shells, fossils, plants, and bones
- Touching an elephant tusk and a porcupine's spikes

Highlights of the National Museum of American Art

The National Museum of American Art shares space with the National Portrait Gallery, so it too will be closed for renovation until 2002. However, among its treasures are:

- A wonderful folk art exhibit including objects such as a giraffe made out of bottle caps

- American landscape artist Frederick Church's "Aurora Borealis"

- George Catlin's gallery of American Indian portraits (the museum has more than 400 in its collection).

- Modern art by Robert Motherwell, Jasper Johns, and Robert Rauschenberg and a wonderful mural of "Achelous and Hercules" by noted WPA artist Thomas Hart Benton, who was a Washington, D.C. artist and the son of a congressman.

10:00 A.M. and 1:00 P.M. The new Discovery Room, a family-oriented, multi-sensory experience, is located on the top floor. Call for hours of operation. Federal Triangle Metro stop.

The green-domed National Museum of Natural History is the second most visited museum in the Smithsonian complex, with more than six million annual visitors (about a million each during the summer months). To do this museum justice, you should expect to spend three or four hours in it.

Highlights of the museum include the fabled Hope diamond, which always draws a huge crowd, as does the room where all the other fabulous jewels are displayed. The nearby Hall of Minerals is actually fascinating to children, with recreations of a copper mine, many touchable geodes and rocks, and a good display of meteorites. Kids also love the insect zoo, where they can see inside termites' and bees' nests, and see a display of Madagascar cockroaches. The Hall of Bones is a great learning display of how mammal skeletons have evolved, and the replica of a giant blue whale and two preserved squid carcasses (one of only three *architeuthis*—giant squids—bodies in the country) are well displayed and explained.

Ground Floor: The ground floor entrance on Constitution Ave. opens with highlights from the collection, including geodes and crystals, a 700,000-year-old hand ax, totem poles from the Pacific Northwest, a gigantic tooth from a fossilized shark, meteorites, and butterflies from South America. A collection of 300 bird specimens is also on this floor.

The totally remodeled Atrium Cafeteria is here too, offering many child-pleasing meals (hamburgers, pizza), as well as hot food and personally prepared sandwiches.

The museum's gift shop is also on this level and has two wings—one exclusively for children. Museum artifacts, such as a lead coffin, are on display throughout the shop. The museum shop is extensive and you could spend an hour in it as well. You can also buy a replica of the Hope diamond for $70—with matching earrings!

First Floor: If you enter the museum from the Mall, you will walk into the museum's rotunda where you will be greeted by a giant display of an African Bush Elephant with his trunk extended.

This mighty creature has been a constant of childhood visits to Washington, D.C. since before the baby boomers were kids.

There are eight exhibit halls on this floor, some of which have banners over their entrances from the rotunda.

Fossils: The History of Life displays the oldest known fossil of microorganisms from 3.5 billion years ago, with a film explaining the theory of evolution and various exhibits and fossils tracing the emergence of life from the ancient sea to the conquest of land. Some of the highlights of this exhibit include rare 530-year-old fossilized soft-bodied animals in shale, which were discovered by the fourth secretary of the Smithsonian in 1910, and the fossilized skeleton of an early whale.

The exhibit charts the evolution of ancient amphibians and plants and concludes with the dinosaur exhibit, where the skeletal remains of a diplodocus, an eighty-foot sauropod and the largest land-based dinosaur, is on display with a comptosaurus, stegosaurus, and an allosaurus. Informative, hands-on exhibits on dinosaur limbs, jaws, and teeth accompany this exhibit.

The next hall is dedicated to Ice Age mammals, where there are skeletons of sabre tooth tigers (one from the La Brea Tar Pits in California) and a woolly mammoth skeleton and tusk, as well as some preserved mammoth skin! Also on view is an Ice Age bison, freeze-dried by nature and recovered by Alaskan gold miners. This hall also features life-sized tableaus of Neanderthal man and Ice Age mammals.

Asian and Pacific Cultures: The next series of exhibits on this floor is on the people of Asia and the Pacific, displaying crafts, objects, clothing, and religious artifacts of the history and culture of the region. Highlights include a recreation of a Chinese opera, Confucian and Shinto shrines, and an iron Buddha from Korea. In the Pacific exhibition, highlights include two huge stone discs used as money and one of the huge stone heads from Easter Island.

African History and Cultures: The newly renovated exhibit hall on African culture features exhibits on African peoples from the Strait of Gibraltar to the Cape of Good Hope and the historical experience of the African diaspora. Highlights include a seventeenth century Nigerian cast brass head and African headdresses from the nineteenth and twentieth centuries.

Orkin Insect Zoo

One of the many highlights of the National Museum of Natural History (especially for children) is the Orkin Insect zoo, where they can see the inside of an African termite mound, watch bees in their hive, examine a tarantula, electronically match bugs that infest a home to where they like to nest (this is a very popular kid activity) and explore the interior of an ant hill (again, popular with children after the movies *ANTZ* and *A Bug's Life*). Scientists on hand allow children to "pet" giant Madagascar cockroaches and other equally adorable insect species.

Woolworth's Lunch Counter at NMAH

The legendary lunch counter from the F.W. Woolworth store in Greensboro, North Carolina, considered by many to be where the 1960s Civil Rights movement began, is on display on the main floor of the National Museum of American History. Here, on February 1, 1960, four African-American college students sat down and tried to order lunch. When asked to leave, they remained in their seats. Their nonviolent refusal to yield to the Jim Crow laws began a movement to challenge segregation practices throughout the South. The Woolworth lunch counter was desegregated on July 25, 1960. The attention given this chain of events and the feeling of empowerment and activism it created ignited the Civil Rights movement throughout the South and the country.

Eskimo and Indian Cultures: This is an exhibit on the various Indian cultures from the Eskimo to the North American and South American Indians. Highlights include displays on seal hunting, ice fishing, and igloo construction in the Arctic region; a teepee and buffalo hides in the North American section; and an impressive 1880 Sioux headdress with seventy-seven eagle feathers.

Birds of the World: Birds are displayed in re-creations of their natural habitats from the penguins in the Arctic to Passenger pigeons, the most common American bird in the eighteenth century. The Passenger pigeon became extinct by 1914, when the last bird of the species died in captivity. Other extinct species on display include the penguin like Great Auk and the Carolina parakeet. This exhibit hall also features displays on birds' feeding habits, migration, reproduction, and importance to people.

Sea Life: Exploring Marine Ecosystems: This is one of the highlights of the museum's collection. Here you can find a ninety-two-foot model of the great blue whale, which was actually modeled after a real whale carcass, and a stellar exhibit on the giant squid, where there are two preserved specimens of two different species of squid. The films accompanying this exhibit are fascinating and informative, as are the displays that explain how squids capture their prey (with clawlike hooks) and how one species stuns prey with strobelike flash organs.

Other exhibits in this area include recreations of a Maine sea coast and a Caribbean coral reef, as well as mounted specimens of walruses and sea otters.

The World of Mammals: Specimens of mounted animals in their re-created habitats are on display here, from the Bengal tiger to the Rocky Mountain goat. Displays explain mammal classification, adaptation to the environment, and the relationship between man and beast.

Second Floor: Janet Hooker Hall of Geology, Gems, and Minerals: This exhibit hall is always packed because the legendary blue Hope diamond is on display here (see accompanying sidebar for the story of the Curse of the Hope diamond), as well as Marie Antoinette's diamond earrings and Empress Josephine's emerald necklace (copies of which are all available for purchase in the museum gift shop).

This exhibit hall also has a re-creation of a copper mine, a display of meteorites (including a fascinating story about meteorites that have dropped into people's homes), a moon rock, displays of ores and geodes to touch and examine, and many interactive displays on how minerals are formed.

South America: Continent and Culture: Like the exhibits on the first floor, this hall presents the peoples and cultures of South America in life-size dioramas such as a Patagonian grassland in the nineteenth century, a re-creation of a tropical rainforest, the arid Pacific coastlands, and Andean mountain valleys. The highlights of this hall are the objects from the Inca civilization.

Origins of Western Culture: This is one of the most interesting exhibits in the museum. It tries to explain the history of Western civilization from the end of the Ice Age to A.D. 500, when the basic patterns of human existence were set.

The exhibit includes a diorama of the cave paintings of Lascaux, France, as well as excellent displays and informative short films about the ancient Egyptians and their burial and embalming processes. The Egyptian exhibits will hold even a seven-year-old spellbound! Additional exhibits on Mesopotamian, Ancient Greek, and Roman cultures are on view here.

The Hall of Bones: Wow. Floor-to-ceiling displays of hundreds of animal skeletons, grouped by order and species, dramatically show the theory of evolution. Informative displays illustrate how bone structure adapted to the environment.

The Hall of Reptiles: This is an exhibit of alligators, frogs, turtles and snakes in natural setting dioramas. Informative displays explain feeding habits, movement, and their influence on humans.

The Orkin Insect Zoo: A relatively small but very entertaining exhibit on the world of insects, here you can see a live bee hive (put your hand on the glass and you can feel their heat), an African termite mound, and three-times-a-day tarantula feedings (10:30, 11:30, and 1:30 on weekdays). There are re-creations of rain forests and caves and swamps, all full of live bugs. The more docile members of the insect world can be held or touched by children (under supervision), including the ever popular Madagascar cockroach. There's also an insect lab where kids can see butterflies cocooning.

See a Civil War Horse at NMAH

In the hall of Armed Forces, you can find George Washington's tent, the 1776 Revolutionary War gunboat *Philadelphia*, and weapons used throughout our country's wars and battles. One of the most interesting artifacts however, is the stuffed and preserved horse ridden by general Philip Sheridan in the closing months of the Civil War. Displayed intact inside a glass case, the horse is decked in all its Union regalia. The horse was originally named Rienzi, but was rechristened Winchester, in honor of the Virginia town where a potential defeat for the Union forces turned into a victory.

Butterfly Garden: In the warmer months there's an outdoor butterfly garden on the 9th St. side of the museum building where visitors can see the interaction between butterflies and plants. This is a nice follow-up to the insect zoo.

Discovery Room: This is a hands-on, interactive room for children (and their parents) to touch and explore the many natural objects in the museum's collection. Kids can handle fossils, shells, bones, feathers, etc.

Samuel Johnson Theater: The museum has a brand new IMAX theater where visitors can see *Africa's Elephant Kingdom* and the Smithsonian's own *Galapagos* on a six-story screen in 3D. Theater admission is $5.50 for adults and $4.50 for children and seniors.

The National Museum of American History

Between 12th and 14th Sts. on Constitution and Madison Aves. Often open later during the summer. There are daily tours of the museum, which vary seasonally. There are also demonstrations throughout the day. Federal Triangle or Smithsonian Metro stations.

This is another four-floor museum where you can expect to spend at least three hours (and perhaps an hour in the exhaustive gift shop). The exhibit on the first ladies is very popular, especially the section where you can see their inaugural gowns, and Foucault's Pendulum never fails to fascinate. The pop culture touchstones on view include Archie Bunker's chair, Mr. Spock's phaser and Dorothy's red ruby slippers. There are also a number of exhibits on the scientific innovations and technological advances that have made the United States a world leader, such as Thomas Edison's lightbulb and Ford's Model T. There are also halls on the historical events and sociological experiences that define our country.

First Floor: If you enter from Constitution Avenue, you will arrive on the first floor where exhibits highlight the history and impact of science and technology with over fifteen exhibit halls. The first hall you will see displays an actual country store and post office that was transported whole from Headsville, West Virginia (to the left of the entrance), which still operates as a post office today (you can get your postcards stamped

"Smithsonian Station"). The purpose of the Material World exhibit is to explain how things are made and how those elements have changed since the beginning of our country. There's a central section on new materials and re-using existing products (such as plywood and plastic) in new ways.

The next section of the first floor highlights technological innovations from farm machines (harvesters and tractors) to ships (more than 100 models, including one of the Mayflower) and the engine room of a coast guard ship from the 1920s. There are also displays on a sailor's life (kids find the re-creation of a 1940s tattoo parlor fascinating), luxury liners, whaling and disasters at sea (very popular since *Titanic*).

This exhibit wing also includes a hall on the development of the automobile with more than forty antique cars on display (including the 1913 Model T), as well as its predecessors, horse drawn carriages, and alternate wheeled transportation such as bicycles and motorcycles. A hall on railroad innovations includes the Pacific-type steam locomotive 1401 used between 1926 and 1941, a stage coach from 1836, and a Seattle cable car from 1888. There are additional exhibit rooms on bridge technology and engine design for power machinery.

The exhibit hall on electricity starts with the work of Benjamin Franklin and traces the development of electrical power through the nineteenth century, ending with the work of Thomas Edison and his lightbulb. Other technological innovations highlighted on this floor include the development of the typewriter, the phonograph (one of Edison's first phonographs from 1877 is on display), clocks, and locks.

The exhibit on the American Industrial Revolution is vast, tying together industrial innovations and their effect on the population. It begins with a re-creation of the Crystal Palace, the site of the 1851 World's Fair in London where American technological innovations were first heralded by Europe, and goes on to examine the impact of machinery and the factory system. On display is the world's oldest operable locomotive, the *John Bull*, as well as the Colt revolver and another 250 objects.

Science in American Life chronicles scientific innovations over the past 125 years such as nylon, the atomic bomb, and emerging

Man of a Thousand Patents

When most people think of Thomas Edison, they think of only the light bulb, but Edison registered more than 1,000 patents for inventions in his lifetime. In addition to the light bulb, Edison's printing telegraph of 1873 (where would Wall Street be without this invention?) and his phonograph are on display at the NMAH.

Other Edison inventions and improvements include:

- Vote recorder
- Electric motor
- Talking doll
- Storage battery

technologies of bioscience. The hands-on science center is an incredible fascination for children interested in science. Kids can put the four proteins of DNA together in varying patterns to create different musical sounds and use a Geiger counter to test for radioactivity, among other experiments.

The final exhibit hall on the first floor is on the Information Age, which begins with Morse telegraph and continues through the developments of the phone, early computers, radio, and television. This exhibit is designed to be very interactive with opportunities to have fingerprints taken, decipher a German WWI code, and even produce an evening news program.

Second Floor: The emphasis of this floor is the political and social history of our country. It begins with an exhibit on the restoration of the flag Francis Scott Key saw was "still there" by "the dawn's early light" flying over Ft. McKinley after a battle of the War of 1812. (After that sight, of course, he wrote the poem that became the national anthem.) The huge (9-by-10-foot) historic star-spangled banner is displayed under a protective cover.

Foucault's pendulum, a copy of the nineteenth-century experiment that proved that the earth rotates, dominates a second floor gallery where the hollow brass bob swings back and forth periodically knocking down red markers set in a circle. It is somewhat mesmerizing and always surrounded by visitors.

After the Revolution looks at life in the United States in the 1780s and 1790s through the eyes of Native Americans, Europeans, and African-Americans, both slaves and freedmen, re-creating living spaces and the tools used during those times. It also re-creates the harrowing experience of coming to America on a slave ship.

As a hint that you are approaching the ever-popular exhibit on the first ladies, the next gallery features a reproduction of the Ceremonial Court of the Cross Hall of the White House at the turn of the century, with original furnishings from Teddy Roosevelt's tenure in the White House. Adjoining galleries display presidential memorabilia such as Thomas Jefferson's portable writing desk and the toys from the children who grew up in the White House.

The Peacock Room

The highlight of the Freer Gallery is the perfectly restored *Harmony in Blue and Gold: Peacock Room,* which is spectacular to behold more than 100 years after it was painted. When the museum is open late on summer evenings, or in the early morning hours, you may be able to sit for a while alone in this room and take in the all-encompassing splendor of it.

The Peacock Room was once the dining room of one of Whistler's London patrons, who had an interior architect design a room to hold his Chinese porcelain collection and his prized Whistler painting, *The Princess from the Land of Porcelain*, which was displayed above the fireplace. The architect consulted Whistler on the color of the room, and while the patron was away on a business trip Whistler took over the design of the room, having the ceiling covered in gold leaf over which he painted a pattern of peacock feathers. He echoed that pattern in four painted wooden panels of peacocks on wooden shutters.

Whistler had done all this interior design without his patron's permission, and when the patron was presented with the bill, he was not amused and refused to pay the full price. Whistler got back at him by painting a confrontational scene of two peacocks fighting, which he titled *Art and Money; or The Story of the Room.*

The room was purchased by Freer in 1904 and dismantled and brought to his home. It was willed to the gallery in 1919. The Peacock Room has been restored twice since it was installed in the Freer, the most recent installation having revealed the blue, green, and gold peacock feather pattern on the ceiling and the gold paint on the wainscoting of the room. It is indeed an inspired home for *The Princess from the Land of Porcelain*.

First Ladies Gowns

This is by far one of the most popular exhibits at the NMAH, and features the inaugural gowns worn by the past eight first ladies. Jackie Kennedy wore white; Lady Bird Johnson, Pat Nixon, and Betty Ford all chose yellow gowns, Rosalyn Carter chose a lavender gown; Nancy Reagan wore an off-the-shoulder dress; Barbara Bush went for blue velvet, and Hillary Clinton wore purple.

The First Ladies Exhibit centers on the presidential wives of the twentieth century and gives a brief biographical and political background on each one. But it's the inaugural gowns that people really come to look at, especially those of Jackie Kennedy and Hillary Clinton. A nearby exhibit focuses on the role of women in politics 1890–1925, from the middle class home to the tenement, and also includes some important memorabilia of the suffragette movement, such as Susan B. Anthony's desk.

This floor also has two exhibits examining the effect of migration on Americans. The first looks at African-American migration from the south to the north in the early part of this century, and the second hall, titled American Encounters, looks at the effect migration had on the western Native American populations.

The second of two hands-on exhibits is also located here, and visitors can operate and examine machines featured on the floor, from sending a message by telegraph to turning the handle of a cotton gin.

Third Floor: This floor features exhibits on the objects and innovations that have impacted the country, from coins to firearms. The section on armed forces history features George Washington's field headquarters tent and a Revolutionary War vessel—the gunboat *Philadelphia*—from 1776, as well as many models of war ships from the Revolution to WWI.

There is also a hall on the internment of Japanese Americans during WWII that includes the executive order signed by FDR, a barracks room from the internment camp, and audio interviews with people who were kept in the camps.

Other galleries present collections of musical instruments, ceramics, textiles (wonderful quilts are on display), money, and medals. There's a permanent exhibit on the life and music of Ella Fitzgerald, with wonderful clips. The third floor also features a doll house from the turn of the century that has more than twenty rooms and is infinitely fascinating in both detail and content.

In addition to the previously mentioned pop culture icons, cases filled to the brim with television memorabilia are on view around the escalators of both the second and third floor and include Jim Henson's muppets Elmo and Oscar the Grouch, Fonzie's jacket from *Happy Days,* and the Howdy Doody ventriloquist puppet.

Ground Floor: The three restaurants and the gift shop are located on the ground floor (there's a first floor gift shop entrance as well). The gift shop hosts a ton of fabulous knickknacks and Americana from earrings made out of pennies ($2.50) to bags of old fashioned candy to replicas of some of the White House china.

There is an old-fashioned ice cream parlor facing the Constitution Ave. entrance that offers a full lunch menu, as well as wonderful ice cream desserts. The Palm Court Coffee Bar re-creates a turn-of-the-century restaurant with wooden screens and ceiling fans and features coffee and snacks such as brownies and scones. The Main Street Cafe is a large cafeteria with a full array of breakfast and lunch items. All the restaurants are closed by 4:30, even in the summer when the museum is open later.

Freer Gallery of Art

Jefferson Dr. at 12th St. SW on the Mall. Open late on some summer evenings. Guided tours are given daily. Smithsonian Metro station.

This is a small museum in comparison to the ones previously described, but it's a real find. The Italian Renaissance-style building was designed to hold the National Museum of Fine Arts and now houses one of the world's most extensive collections of Asian art. There is an impressive collection of works by James McNeill Whistler, who was profoundly influenced by Asian art, culminating in his Peacock Room, which is a one-of-a-kind visual experience. Don't miss it.

The gallery is named after its donor, Charles Lang Freer, a Chicago industrialist who collected both Asian and nineteenth-and twentieth century American art that he believed complemented his collection. He donated 7,500 pieces of art to the gallery, as well as the money to build the gallery, and another 20,000 pieces have been donated or acquired since 1923.

Since the collection is so extensive, pieces are shown on a rotating schedule, but there are some permanent features on view. These include the largest collection of Whistler's paintings, a wing on Japanese art that features some incredible painted wooden

Dr. Singer's Gift

In the summer of 1999, the Smithsonian received an impressive gift of the 5,000 piece collection of Dr. Paul Singer, a fellow psychiatrist, Asian art collector, and friend of Dr. Sackler, which now makes the Sackler Gallery the largest museum of Chinese artifacts in America.

Dr. Singer's collection was once housed in his two-bedroom apartment in New Jersey. He specialized in collecting small items from the Chinese provinces, which curators say is a perfect complement to the existing Freer and Sackler collections that focus on Chinese art from more metropolitan cultures.

Eighteen of Dr. Singer's pieces are already on view at the Sackler Gallery including a small bronze bell (one of the earliest known in the west), a small bear sculpture, and a jade, amber, and gold necklace from the third century B.C., which shows that there was commerce between China, Africa, and the Baltic region thousands of years ago.

screens, Korean ceramics, Chinese paintings and ancient art, Buddhist art, South Asian art, Islamic art (Freer was especially found of Persian painting from the sixteenth century), Egyptian glass, which Freer collected himself on three trips to Egypt, and Luxury Arts of the Silk Route Empires exhibit. The Silk Route exhibit is on view in the underground corridor connecting the Freer Gallery with the Sackler Gallery, and it mixes holdings of both museums.

The museum shop has many beautiful Japanese tea items, as well as books about Asian art that are unique to this gift shop.

The Arthur M. Sackler Gallery

1050 Independence Ave. SW, on the Mall. Often open late on some summer evenings. Guided tours are given daily. Smithsonian Metro station.

This gallery is dedicated to the history of the artistic development of Asian and Near Eastern art from ancient times to the present. Shows of contemporary Asian artists are often on view here, as well as traveling exhibits from major museums. Some exhibits offer the visitor the chance to touch objects to feel their weight and texture. In the Japanese porcelain exhibit there are shards of porcelain for viewers to handle.

Like the Freer Gallery, the Sackler has an extensive collection shown on a rotating schedule. Permanent galleries include Art of China (from Dr. Sackler's own collection), Contemporary Japanese Porcelain, Metalwork and Ceramics from Ancient Iran, Puja: Expressions of Hindu Devotion, and Sculpture of Southeast Asia.

The museum gift shops mirrors the collection with a wide variety of prints, books, and porcelain available for purchase.

The Hirshhorn Museum and Sculpture Garden

Independence Ave. at 7th St. SW on the Mall. Often open later in the summer; sculpture garden 7:30 A.M. till dusk. Guided tours at 10:30 A.M., noon, and 1:30 P.M., and 2:30 P.M. on Sundays. L'Enfant Plaza Metro station.

Tax Free Souvenirs

Because the Smithsonian Institution is run by the government, everything you buy in the Smithsonian gift shops is tax free.

The Hirshhorn is one of the leading museums of contemporary art in America, right up there with New York's Museum of Modern Art and the Guggenheim, and something no visitor interested in modern art should miss. It has an extensive collection of twentieth-century art, from a room full of Picassos to the latest controversial works by the likes of Britain's bad boy artist Damian Hirst (the only one of his works on permanent display in the United States). The sunken outdoor sculpture garden reveals a marvelous collection of important modern sculpture, from pivotal works by Rodin to unusual three-dimensional work by de Kooning.

Latvian-born art collector Joseph Hirshhorn gave the Smithsonian more than 12,000 pieces of modern art, which is the nucleus of this museum's collection that opened in the '70s.

The museum itself is a work of art, echoing the spiraling interior design of New York's Guggenheim so that each floor is a self-contained circle around a courtyard with floor-to-ceiling windows that make wonderful use of natural light. Some have commented that the museum, designed by Gordon Bunshaft, looks like a giant donut or drum.

On the first floor there is a continuously shown twenty-minute film on the art on display in the museum, as well an overview of modern art and suggestions on how to experience the works. The first floor also houses special exhibitions and the museum's gift store, which has a quirky collection of art knickknacks, from

Picasso plates to a Red Grooms clock, as well as a good selection of books and posters.

The works on display are arranged chronologically from the turn of the century to the present, moving from the third floor to the ground floor where the new acquisitions are located. Major movements in twentieth-century art are represented here from Picasso's early Cubist painting and sculpture (the Picasso Room chronicles his entire career) to the surrealism of Magritte and Miró, as well as a sizable collection of American realists such as Edward Hopper, George Bellows, Thomas Hart Benton, and various members of the Ashcan school.

The second floor focuses on modern art of the second half of the century, with an impressive display of abstract expressionist works by Jackson Pollock, Barnett Newman's *Stations of the Cross*, and '60s pop icons such as Claes Oldenburg's *7-Up*, and Warhol's Marilyn Monroe lips.

On the lower level there is a hall that displays recent acquisitions and contemporary works where you can find the Hirst, a Cindy Sherman print, as well as a work by Sam Gilliam, a noted abstract colorist whose studio is located in D.C.

Sculpture of the century are located on the interior galleries of the first three floors, overlooking the courtyard, and these galleries chronicle the spatial developments of the last century with works by Degas, Picasso, Giacometti, Matisse, a rare wooden sculpture by Gauguin, as well as a clever Man Ray, all of which culminates in the powerful Robert Arneson giant bust of General Nuke.

Circling the museum are a number of recent sculpture acquisitions where you can sit in a tree-lined area while eating self-service from the Full Circle Cafe, which is open from May until September.

The Sculpture Garden across the street features a number of major works, including Rodin's *Burghers of Calais* and a Calder ground-based mobile, as well as works by Henry Moore, David Smith and more than thirty others.

National Museum of African Art

950 Independence Ave. SW, on the Mall. Often open later on some summer evenings. Smithsonian Metro station.

This underground museum exhibits traditional arts from Africa from ancient times to the present. The museum has special exhibits on the ground floor where you enter, and its permanent collection includes a marvelous show on the art of the personal object, with more than 100 objects on view, such as baskets, bowls, cups, etc. Another permanent exhibit on African ceramics has more than 140 bowls and figures. Also on permanent view are exhibits entitled Images of a Power and Identity, which feature a selection of masks and figures, as well as an exhibit on the African city of Benin from 1300 to the end of British colonial rule, and an exhibit on the Ancient Nubian city of Kerma, an Egyptian city, 2500–1500 B.C.

The gift shop is on the first level and offers a selection of African crafts and jewelry, as well as books and posters.

National Postal Museum

2 Massachusetts Ave. at First St. NE, in the Washington City Post Office Building next to Union Station. Guided tours are at 11:00 A.M. and 1:00 P.M. every day, with an extra tour at 2:00 P.M. on weekdays.

What a surprisingly engaging museum this is! The National Postal Museum began with a donation of a sheet of ten-cent Confederate stamps and now contains more than 13 million items. Geared toward children and stamp collectors, this museum offers a very interactive history of postal service in America. Beginning with an exhibit on the Pony Express that takes place in a colonial wood, it goes on to give visitors a chance to sort the mail, create their own land and sea mail routes, ride a stagecoach, land an airmail biplane via a computer game (it's quite difficult), and create their own postal imprint on a postcard, which they can send on to friends and family.

In addition, there is an extensive exhibit on the printing and history of stamps, as well as a complete master collection of the entire history of American stamps (copies are on view in plastic pull-out displays). The museum also features a gallery on the art of letter writing, using examples from wartime correspondence from WWI to Operation Desert Storm. There are a number of vehicles

The Story of the National Zoo's Pandas

When President Nixon opened diplomatic relations with China in 1971, the nations exchanged gifts. China gave the United States two giant pandas, Ling-Ling ("Darling Little Girl") and Hsing-Hsing ("Shining Star"), which became two of the four giant pandas living outside of China at that time.

Ling-Ling died at age 23 in 1992, and Hsing-Hsing died in 1999.

used to deliver the mail on view, from 1911 biplanes based on the designs of the Wright Brothers to a 1931 Ford Model A mail truck.

There are two gift shops on the premises, One offers posters, T-shirts, and various items from the general Smithsonian collection. In the stamp store across the hall, you can buy stamps for the postcards you create in the museum, as well as rare and special edition stamps.

Renwick Gallery of the National Museum of American Art

Pennsylvania Ave. at 17th St. NW, one block west of the White House. Farragut West Metro station.

Near the White House and not far from the Corcoran Gallery, this museum, in an Empire-style mansion (designed by James Renwick, of course), is one of my favorite little museums in Washington, D.C. The building itself was once the site of the Corcoran Gallery (and the exterior features the inscription "Dedicated to Art" and an etched portrait of Corcoran), and it was used as a courthouse until Jackie Kennedy convinced the Smithsonian Institution to take it over.

When you enter its lush interior, restored in late-nineteenth-century grandeur, you enter the Grand Salon that features mauve walls, carved wainscoting, and a large skylight that makes you feel like you've stepped back in time to the Victorian era. There are a number of minor nineteenth-and twentieth-century paintings on the walls and two colossal Centennial urns on top of the plush velvet banquettes, but just sitting in this room will make you understand how some once called it the American Louvre.

Across the hall from the Grand Salon is an archway that was built to showcase Hiram Powers's highly controversial sculpture *Greek Slave*, a nude woman in chains that was so scandalous in the nineteenth century that it was shown to groups of men and women on different days of the week. Now Wendal Castle's trompe l'oeil *Ghost Clock* is displayed in this space (the *Greek Slave* sculpture is on display in the Corcoran Gallery of Art) and it too is a masterpiece, its brilliantly carved wood, painted white to resemble a sheet draped over a grandfather clock.

The Curse of
the Hope Diamond

Many people say that the reason the Hope diamond lies behind glass in the Smithsonian is because the curse on the diamond can't harm anyone from there.

According to legend, the diamond was once the eye of an Indian idol, which was stolen, smuggled into Paris, and later turned up as the Blue diamond, part of the French royal jewels. Everyone who came in contact with the jewel was said to have met with tragedy, from Louis XIV's oldest son to his oldest grandson and his great-grandson. There's even a rumor that the stone was used as a bribe to get Louis XVI and Marie Antoinette out of France, and we know what happened to them.

The diamond disappeared for a while (some think it appears on the neck of Queen Maria Louisa of Spain in a Goya painting) and resurfaced in Amsterdam where it was recut. The jeweler died penniless because his son stole the gem, and the jeweler's son committed suicide after his father's death. It was purchased by Harry Hope in London in 1830 (from whom we get the name), whose son and daughter-in-law inherited the stone and died penniless.

An Eastern European prince bought the stone and gave it to a Folies Bergere actress, whom he later shot. A Greek owner and his family were killed in a horrible car accident. The stone is also said to have then turned up in Russia in the hands of Catherine the Great, who did not have a happy ending to her life.

A wealthy Turkish sultan bought the diamond and gave it to his favorite wife, who was later murdered after he was dethroned. Evelyn Walsh McLean, wife to the heir of the *Washington Post* fortune, had seen the blue stone while on her honeymoon in Turkey, bought it, and, knowing about its legend, supposedly had a priest bless it before she wore it. However, that did her no good because her only son was killed in a bizarre car accident right outside his home, her husband was committed to a mental institution after his involvement with the Teapot Dome scandal was revealed, and her daughter committed suicide.

New York jeweler Harry Winston bought the stone in the early 1950s and gave it to the Smithsonian on permanent loan, some say because his wife kept begging him to let her wear it. Winston sent the diamond to the museum by registered mail and there's a story that after the mailman handled the package his life was cursed: his leg was mangled in a car accident, his wife died of a heart attack, his dog died and his house burned down.

Other rooms in the museum feature outstandingly quirky pieces of American craft and design such as Larry Fuente's *Game Fish,* made from bright pieces of beads, buttons, coins, game pieces, blocks, magnetized letters, light bulbs, paintbrushes, and even a yo-yo. It is a surprisingly fun museum in an exquisite setting.

The gift shops features a rich selection of scarves and glass pieces, as well as unique jewelry.

The National Zoological Park

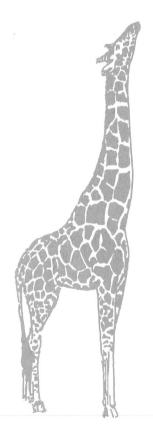

Connecticut Ave. NW (3000 block between Cathedral Ave. and Devonshire Pl.) Woodley Park/Zoo Metro station, and then a ten-minute walk. Grounds are open from 8:00 A.M. until 6:00 P.M., open until 8:00 P.M. from April 15 until October 15. There is limited pay parking on the zoo grounds, which fills up in the summer by 10:00 A.M. Stroller rentals are available.

This is a deceptively small zoo in appearance, but is actually 163 acres. It certainly feels like it if you walk the whole thing, which you have to do to see everything. Wear comfortable shoes! It will take you a minimum of four hours to do the zoo justice.

The zoo's highlights include the new Amazonia tropical rainforest, as well as a good display of lions, a white tiger, elephants, rhinos, and a wonderful aviary. Children find the exhibit of mole rats in the small mammals buildings particularly fascinating.

The zoo was designed by Frederick Law Olmsted, the ingenious landscape architect who also designed New York's Central Park and Boston's Public Gardens. There are currently eighteen major animal exhibit areas along Olmsted Walk. The first national zoo was originally housed on the Mall in downtown Washington, D.C. outside the Smithsonian Castle, where six American bison roamed until the turn of the century.

The National Zoo is also the home of one of the few Komodo dragons ever bred in captivity.

During the summer months, three exhibits are often crowded: Amazonia, The Invertebrate Exhibit, and the Reptile Discovery Center. Amazonia, the new tropical rainforest and the zoo's largest exhibit, features a steamy habitat for free-roaming amphibians, small mammals, and birds, as well as an aquarium to hold tropical fish.

The Reptile Discovery Center has a number of interactive exhibit areas for children to learn about the biology of reptiles and amphibians. The Invertebrate Exhibit features a giant octopus, which is fed several times a day. The museum director claims that the octopus has been able to open a screw-top jar with a shrimp inside by itself! The Pollinarium, a glass-enclosed addition, illustrates the mechanics of pollination and the role insects play.

The recently renovated monkey house features the Think Tank, where orangutans play on computers. The elephant house has a wonderful indoor exhibit on the anatomy of the elephant in comparison to dinosaurs that will leave any child fascinated, as well as the giraffes, rhinos, and hippos. The small mammal house features everything from small cats to mongooses. The Great Flight Cage, a wonderful aviary with 150 species of birds, is particularly well done, as is the neighboring exhibit on the wetlands, which contains five wading pools featuring waterfowl and wading birds. The lion and tiger exhibit is also quite interactive with many displays for children to learn about these animals' jungle instincts and preservation of the species. Other exhibits include Otters in the Valley, a fun-to-watch habitat when the animals are active (there's a glass wall in their den, so you can even see them sleeping) and the American Prairie where descendants of the zoo's famous bison still roam.

There are two restaurants on the premises—a full-scale main restaurant and an outdoor cafe. A fabulous indoor gift shop features all sorts of zoo-related toys, books, plates, scarves, and jewelry with an animal motif. If you forget to buy something here, there are smaller zoo stores at Union Station and Reagan National Airport.

Smithsonian Sites

Just about every major attraction and museum in Washington, D.C. has a Web site of its own that will provide helpful information and a program of upcoming events.

Smithsonian (*www.si.edu*). This is a comprehensive Web site that gives you the history of the Smithsonian, access to all its museum links, a calendar of events, and an archive of topic areas for research. In addition, each of the Smithsonian museums have their own Web sites. These are:

Anacostia Museum—*www.si.edu/anacostia/*
Arthur M. Sackler Gallery and the Freer Gallery of Art—
   www.si.edu/asia/
Arts and Industries Building—*www.si.edu/ai/*
Hirshhorn Museum and Sculpture Garden—
   www.si.edu/organiza/museums/hirsch/start.htm
National Air and Space Museum—*www.nasm.edu*
National Museum of African Art—*www.si.edu/nmafa/*
National Museum of American Art—*www.nmaa.si.edu*
National Museum of American History—*www.si.edu/nmah/*
National Museum of natural History
   www.mnh.si.edu/nmnhweb.html
National Portrait Gallery—*www.npg.si.edu*
National Postal Museum—*www.si.edu/postal/*
National Zoo—*www.si.edu/natzoo/*
Renwick Gallery of the National Museum American Art—
   nmaa-ryder.si.edu
S. Dillon Ripley Center—*www.si.edu/ripley/start.htm*
Smithsonian Castle—
   www.si.edu/activity/planvis/museums/aboutsib.htm

Chapter Seven

Memorials and Monuments

While Washington is full of statues, parks, and buildings erected in tribute to many of the country's presidents, there are only four commemorative memorials. Each of these presidential sites are awe-inspiring on their own, but the best way to see them is one right after the other on a night tour by bus or car when they are illuminated. It's also interesting to see them together so you can put their history into perspective.

The various war memorials are nearby those of the presidents, so a bus tour often views nine sites in a single four-hour period. Seeing these together also gives a different perspective to our nation's battle history and makes the Lincoln Memorial both a presidential and Civil War memorial.

Arlington National Cemetery is a surprisingly educational and somber experience with its acres of symmetrically arranged white crosses on the green hills and the various gravesites and memorials on the property. I never imagined that I could spend half a day in a national cemetery and say that it was one of the most moving and interesting travel experiences I've had.

The United States Holocaust Memorial Museum is a powerful educational experience that brings the horror of this twentieth-century crime directly in front of you with both sensory and visual stimulus. Because it is so thorough (you need four hours to see this site) and stirs such a strong reaction, I would find it very difficult to view anything else after this museum.

Washington Monument

900 Ohio Dr. SW, (202) 426-6841. Smithsonian Metro station. Open 8:00 A.M. till 5:00 P.M.; 8:00 A.M. to midnight April through September. You must have a ticket to get in, but they are free and you can get them at the ticket booth on 15th St. at the bottom of the hill. Closed Christmas Day and open only until noon on July 4.

The Washington Monument was the first memorial to be constructed in the nation's capital. It stands at the center of the National Mall between 15th and 17th Streets. The idea for the monument was around early in the city's history, and L'Enfant originally planned to erect a grand statue of George Washington on horseback. However, Congress failed to appropriate the necessary funds for the monument, and by the centennial of Washington's birth in 1832, a private society was formed to raise funds for a national monument to the first president and Revolutionary War general.

The plans for a mere equestrian statue seemed too meager for this great man, and in 1845 a competition was sponsored to create something different. Robert Mills's plans won the competition with his design for a Greco-Roman rotunda topped with an obelisk. It included a statuary group with Washington atop a chariot. Fortunately for posterity, they couldn't raise enough money for this grand scheme and only the obelisk was left.

The cornerstone was laid in 1848, but the Civil War interfered and the monument was dedicated in 1885, with various descendants of Washington present.

The monument is 555 feet 5⅛ inches high and is the tallest masonry structure in the world. There is a federal law on the books that restricts any building higher than the Monument. Years ago, you could climb the 897 steps to the top, but now you have to take the elevator up (hence the tickets). However, you can still walk down with a Park Ranger guide at 10:00 A.M. and 2:00 P.M. The view from the top is spectacular. There is a visitor's center inside, which offers videos and displays on the life of the president.

The Monument receives 800,000 visitors a year and is currently undergoing an exterior restoration, which will be completed by 2000. The ensuing scaffolding, covered in a clear plastic sheath by the architect Michael Graves, is oddly artistic in its own way.

The Lincoln Memorial

Twenty-third St. between Constitution and Independence Aves., at the western edge of the Reflecting Pool in Potomac Park. Foggy Bottom or Smithsonian Metro station, and then a long walk. Closed Christmas Day. Open 8:00 A.M. until midnight.

Even though the Jefferson Memorial was planned by L'Enfant when the city was designed, Lincoln's assassination so affected the country that his memorial became the second presidential

Restoring the Washington Monument

The renovation of the Washington Monument is the first in 80 years. Strong winds and tourist traffic have certainly taken their toll on this 110 year-old masonry structure. The interior stairways leading up to the top of the monument have been closed to public traffic since 1976, when the elevator became the only way to get to the top.

The renovation includes:

- Enclosing the entire structure in scaffolding designed by noted architect Michael Graves
- Sealing 500 feet of exterior and interior stone cracks
- Pointing 64,000 feet of exterior joints and 3,900 feet of interior joints
- Cleaning 59,000 feet of interior wall surface
- Sealing eight observation windows and eight aircraft warning lights
- Repairing 1,000 feet of chipped and patched stone
- Preserving and restoring 192 interior commemorative stones

commemorative site to be built in the nation's capital. It is the second most visited of the presidential memorials, with one and half million viewers annually.

The memorial's design, which we see every day on the back of the penny, is a neoclassical interpretation of the Parthenon from ancient Greece. Thirty-six Doric columns represent the states of the Union at the time of Lincoln's assassination, plus there are two at the entrance. Forty-eight decorative, wreath-like festoons above the columns symbolize the number of states at the time of the Memorial's completion in 1922. Hawaii and Alaska are included on a terrace inscription.

While the view of the Washington Monument across the Reflecting Pool from the front steps is serene, the power of the nineteen-foot-high seated white marble statue of Lincoln looking out onto the city makes you very aware of the loss that was the Civil War. The statue, designed by Daniel Chester French from a death mask, was carved over four years. The limestone walls of the memorial chamber feature the carved words of the Gettysburg Address and Lincoln's second inaugural address. There are also two murals by Jules Guerin depicting allegorical interpretations of Lincoln's achievements and beliefs on the north and south walls.

The Lincoln Memorial has become a shrine to civil rights in the twentieth century. While many know that Martin Luther King, Jr.'s famous "I Have a Dream" speech was delivered here in 1963, few are aware that as far back as 1939, the Lincoln Memorial was the site of a civil rights protest instigated by Eleanor Roosevelt, who offered the memorial as the location for a recital by Marian Anderson when she was refused the stage of the Daughters of the American Revolution Constitution Hall because she was black.

Roosevelt resigned her member-ship to the DAR over this snub. There is a gift shop and bookstore on the lower level of the memorial, and park rangers offer lectures every thirty minutes.

Daniel Chester French, Sculptor of the Lincoln Statue

Many art historians consider Daniel Chester French to be one of America's greatest sculptors of the Nineteenth century, but outside of Washington, D.C., his work is virtually unknown.

It was French's intention to depict Lincoln as "the war president" in the seated statue at the Lincoln Memorial. Lincoln sits in a curule chair like those used by Roman leaders with his arms resting on the chair arms that are adorned with faces that are classical symbols of authority. The Union flag is draped over the back of the chair.

Lincoln has one hand clenched in a fist and the other open. Some interpret this to suggest both his determination to preserve the Union and his compassion.

Legend also has it that the position of Lincoln's hands spell out "A" and "L" in American Sign Language fingerspelling. While many think this is coincidental, French did later sculpt Thomas Gallaudet, founder of Gallaudet University for the deaf in D.C., in which French did incorporate American Sign Language.

Other works by French in Washington, D.C. include:

- the statue of Samuel F. Dupont at Dupont Circle
- Butt-Millet Memorial (17th and E Sts.)
- First Infantry Division Memorial (State Place near 17th St.)

National World War II Memorial

Steven Spielberg's movie *Saving Private Ryan* inspired many World War II veterans to band together and support the creation of a national war memorial commemorating the Second World War to be constructed in Washington, D.C. They enlisted the aid of actor Tom Hanks, whose voice can be heard when you call the 800-639-4WW2 information and donation number.

You can also get information on this memorial and its fund by visiting the Website www.WWIImemorial. Donations are tax deductible.

The site for this memorial will be the east end section of the Rainbow Pool of the reflecting Pool between the Lincoln Memorial and the Washington Monument. A plaque now marks the site. Ground on the site is expected to be broken on Veteran's Day 2000.

The Jefferson Memorial

South side of the Tidal Basin on Ohio Dr. open 8:00 A.M. to midnight, except Christmas Day. Smithsonian Metro station, and then a long walk.

Although the concept of a memorial to the author of the Declaration of Independence and third president of the United States was planned in the L'Enfant city design, the actual location for the memorial was never laid out so the cornerstone for this commemorative site was not broken until 1939, after land was purchased on what is now the Tidal Basin. The memorial was dedicated in 1943, the 200th anniversary of Jefferson's birth.

The memorial's white marble colonnaded and domed design by John Russell Pope, who also designed the National Gallery of Art and the National Archives, is neoclassic in tribute to Jefferson's influences.

The bronze statue by Rudolph Evans, coated in wax to prevent ionization, depicts a standing Jefferson, in a pose intended to represent the Age of Enlightenment, holding a document symbolic of his role as one of the authors of America's founding democratic principles. In the vein, the surrounding marble walls of the memorial are inscribed with the words of the Declaration of Independence, as well as of excerpts of various letters and bills Jefferson authored that articulate his belief in the American citizenry's ability to govern itself.

The committee that drafted the Declaration of Independence is sculpted in bas relief above the entrance to the memorial. During April and May, when the Japanese cherry blossoms are in bloom, the Jefferson Memorial is one of the most beautiful and inspirational

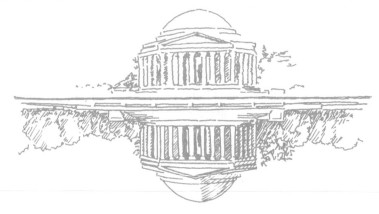

sites in the city. It is said that President Roosevelt, who was the guiding force behind the construction of this memorial, had a number of trees removed so that his view of the Jefferson Memorial would be unobstructed.

There is a gallery on Jefferson's life and works (he was also the founder of the University of Virginia and an amateur scientist) on the lower level of the memorial, and park rangers give talks every half hour. There is limited one-hour parking on the site.

The Franklin Delano Roosevelt Memorial

Between the Lincoln and Jefferson Memorials, in West Potomac Park on the west shore of the Tidal Basin. (202) 426-6841. Smithsonian Metro station, and then a very long walk. Open 8:00 A.M. to midnight.

The newest of the presidential memorials, this four-room, open-air memorial to President Roosevelt sits on a seven and a half acre site and is the most visited of the presidential memorial sites, with more than 3 million tourists a year. It is also the only presidential memorial that includes a tribute to a first lady.

The four "rooms" of the memorial represent Roosevelt's four terms in office from the Great Depression through WWII, 1933–1945. The first gallery represents his first term with a life-size statue of a poor Appalachian couple, the second room a bread line, the third a person listening to Roosevelt's fireside chats, and the fourth features a statue of Eleanor Roosevelt. There are also numerous fountains and green granite walls inscribed with Roosevelt's words, which are particularly moving when illuminated at night. A Social Programs mural depicts in images, writing, and Braille the fifty-four government programs implemented during Roosevelt's New Deal.

As with all commemorative works, there was some controversy associated with the FDR Memorial in that the images of Roosevelt do not portray him in a wheelchair, which he used from the age of thirty-nine until his death as a result of polio. However, a statue of Roosevelt in a wheelchair has been commissioned by President Clinton and it is to be displayed at the entrance to the memorial. A

FDR Memorial Quotes

The FDR Memorial features many of the quotations from the president etched in the polished green granite. While Roosevelt is best known for his statement that "we have nothing to fear but fear itself," his thoughts on war should also be remembered.

"I have seen war. I have seen war on land and sea. I have seen blood running from the wounded . . . I have seen the dead in the mud. I have seen cities destroyed . . . I have seen children starving. I have seen the agony of mothers and wives. I hate war."

Vietnam War
Memorial Controversy

An open national competition for the design of the Vietnam War Memorial was held in the late 80s and, to everyone's surprise, the winner was a twenty-one-year-old Yale architecture student, who was female and Asian-American as well. Her stark design of a simple black granite wall bearing the names of the American soldiers who died in Vietnam was so different than all the war memorials in Washington that it immediately received criticism from just about every veterans group, as well as special interest groups and some politicians.

Critics cast aspersions on her vision, her ability, her talent, her age, and her gender. Some called it "dishonorable" and "a scar." But Maya Lin stayed firm to her vision for "the wall" and refused to change her design. "I believed that this was going to help people," she said of her work.

Her entry described her vision for the wall as follows: "walking through this park, the memorial appears as rift in the earth. A long, polished, black stone, emerging from and receding into the earth. Approaching the memorial, the ground slopes gently downward and the low walls emerging on either side, growing out of the earth, extend and converge at a point below and ahead. Walking into this grassy site contained by the walls of the memorial, we can barely make out the carved names upon the memorial's walls. These names, seemingly infinite in number, convey the overwhelming numbers, while unifying these individuals into a whole. The memorial is composed not as an unchanging monument, but as a moving composition to be understood as we move into and out of it."

Today the Vietnam War memorial is the most visited war memorial in Washington, D.C. and many feel it is the most powerful.

Maya Lin has gone on to became a successful monumental architect. Other works she has completed include a Civil Rights memorial in Montgomery, Alabama, which consists of sheets of water running over a granite table bearing the words of Martin Luther King, Jr. "We are not satisfied and we will not be satisfied until justice rolls down like water of righteousness like a mighty stream."

She has also designed the *Women's Table* at Yale University which is a granite table with an ever-widening spiral of zeroes for each year that Yale was not coeducational, until 1969, when Yale admitted women, and other numbers begin appearing in the spiral.

In 1996, she completed the *Wave Field* on a two and half acre site in Michigan which is a landscape sculpture made of soil covered with grass that looks like a grass wave. It took more than two years to seed and grow.

replica of Roosevelt's wheelchair is also on view in the memorial's gift shop.

Although the memorial had been in the works for more than fifty years, Roosevelt himself had said that he never wanted one. He told his close friend, Supreme Court Justice Felix Frankfurter, that should posterity decide to erect a memorial to him, it should be no bigger than his White House desk. Until 1997, when the FDR Memorial was built, the only Roosevelt commemorative marker was a desktop-sized granite stone outside the National Archives building.

Vietnam Veterans Memorial

Constitution Ave. and 23rd St. NW, in Constitution Gardens, just northeast of Lincoln Memorial. Foggy Bottom Metro station.

Known as "the Wall," this is the most visited of the war memorials in Washington, D.C. and certainly one of the most powerful war images ever created. It is impossible to walk by the sloped black granite, 492-foot wall carved with the 58,196 names of those who were killed during this war (the earliest recorded casualty is 1959, the last in 1975) and not feel overwhelmed by the loss of lives. There is a black bound book at the start of the memorial that lists the names of the dead. It is the size of the Manhattan telephone book.

This memorial is usually crowded, as viewers pass by the reflective wall in a single file. Relatives and friends of those whose names are inscribed on the wall often leave flowers, flags, and tokens or make a charcoal rubbing of the loved one's name.

The design for the Wall was considered highly controversial in 1982 when it was erected. Yale architecture student, Maya Ying Lin, then only twenty-two, won the competition sponsored by a private organization, and many were disturbed that the memorial did not follow more traditional war motifs, such as the statue of the raising of the flag over Iwo Jima or the Civil War Memorial, both in Arlington National Cemetery. However, in the nearly twenty years since the memorial was erected, it has been accepted as a brilliant memorial to the sorrow and loss that most Americans feel when looking back on this war.

In the neighboring Constitution Gardens, there are two traditional sculptures to the soldiers of Vietnam and the women Vietnam veterans.

Korean War Memorial

Between 21st and 23rd Sts., directly across the street from the Lincoln Memorial. Foggy Bottom Metro station, and a long walk.

Within walking distance from the Vietnam Veterans Memorial and across from the Lincoln Memorial, this privately funded commemorative space to the soldiers who fought in the Korean War of the 1950s is more traditional (as were the cold war politics of that war) and yet a powerful counterpoint to the Wall. Like life-size chess pieces, nineteen statues of American servicemen, some wearing ponchos, are posed in various stages of advancement towards an imaginary hill where an American flag and a reflecting pool wait.

Like the Vietnam Veterans Memorial, the Korean War Memorial also has a black granite reflective wall, at the top of which are the words, "Freedom is not Free." Etched on the surface of this wall are the faces of soldiers, chaplains, and war personnel, and around the perimeter of the memorial is a raised, gray granite curb that lists the twenty-two nations that sent men to this conflict. Though much shorter in duration (1950–53), this war had almost as many casualties as the Vietnam War.

U.S. Navy Memorial and Naval Heritage Center

701 Pennsylvania Ave. NW. Heritage center open Mon.–Sat. 9:30 A.M. to 5:00 P.M. Admission free. (202) 737-2300. The Center is

National Law Enforcement Officers Memorial

National Law Enforcement Officers Memorial, bet. 4th and 5th Sts. and E and F Sts. (202) 737-3400. Open 24 hours. There is a visitors center at 605 E St. NW., which is open Mon-Fri. 9:00 A.M.- 5:00 P.M., Sat. 10:00 A.M.–5:00 P.M. and Sun. noon–5:00 P.M. Judiciary Sq. Metro station. This is memorial commemorates federal, state, and local officers who have died in the line of duty. Fifteen thousand officers' names are engraved on this marble wall.

closed Thanksgiving Day, New Year's Day and Christmas Day. National Archives Metro station.

This memorial to the men and women who served in the Navy is an outdoor circular plaza on an etched map of the world on which sits fountains and waterfalls flowing with the collected waters from the seven seas.

A bronze statue, *The Lone Sailor,* with a signature navy blue coat, flared jeans, and a duffel bag, stands watching over the map on the plaza. The statue was cast from the remains of eight Navy ships from the Revolutionary War through WWII and even a nuclear submarine.

Nearby is the Naval Heritage Center, which is a database, research center, and museum for the Navy. There are informative displays on the history of the Navy, its personnel, and ships, as well as the President's Room, which profiles the six presidents who were navy officers. There is also a Navy Memorial Room, which houses the computerized record of Navy personnel, both past and present (with more than 200,000 entrees including a young Tony Curtis in Hawaii in 1943 when he was still named Bernie Schwartz) and the showing of the film *At Sea* on a fifty-four-foot screen that tells the story of today's Navy. There is also a Ships' Store which sells Navy and nautical memorabilia.

Free concerts are held in the plaza in the summer months, and dramatic wreath, laying ceremonies are staged on Memorial and Veterans Days. Call for further schedules.

Arlington National Cemetery and Arlington House

Just over the Memorial Bridge, across from the Lincoln Memorial in Arlington, Virginia. (703) 607-8052. Open 8:00 A.M. to 5:00 P.M.; April–Sept. open until 8:00 P.M. There is public fee parking, but the Tourmobile is the best way to get there. Arlington National Cemetery Metro station.

The 614 acres of this national cemetery for the military is visited by four and a half million people a year. The many important sites on the grounds include the Kennedy gravesites, the former home of General Lee, the Tomb of the Unknown Soldier, the mast

Other Cemeteries

Other historic cemeteries that you can also visit, are *Congressional Cemetery* on 18th and E St. (202) 543-0539, Potomac Ave. It contains the remains of John Philip Sousa, J. Edgar Hoover, and Civil War photographer Matthew Brady.

Rock Creek Cemetery, Rock Creek Church Rd. and Webster Ave. NE (202) 829-0585. This is the oldest cemetery in Washington, D.C., established in the early eighteenth century on the grounds of St. Paul's Episcopal Church. People visit this graveyard to see the famous sculpture of "Grief" by Augustus Saint-Gaudens. Notable graves include Upton Sinclair, Alice Longworth Roosevelt (Teddy's daughter) and D.C. brewing legend Christian Heurich.

Georgetown's Oak Hill Cemetery was established in 1849. Lincoln's twelve-year-old son who died in the White House is buried here.

of the USS Maine, and the statue commemorating Iwo Jima, so expect to spend at least two, if not three, hours here. If you don't take the Tourmobile, make sure you wear comfortable shoes because there are a lot of hills.

When you enter the gates of the cemetery grounds, you will pass the newest war memorial in D.C.—the Women in Military Service Memorial—which honors the nearly two million women who have served in the armed forces. This memorial, which was designed by a husband and wife architect team and dedicated in October of 1987, features a round reflecting pool within a semicircle of a curved granite wall. Arched entries in this granite wall lead to an upper terrace, which offers a sweeping view of the cemetery and the city of Washington. Etched glass panels within the memorial include quotes about women's experiences in the military. Beneath the memorial is an education center where the Hall of Honor traces the history of women in the military, as well as a computerized database of personnel and a shop.

The Visitor's Center shows a video on the history of the cemetery, plus there is a shop, bathrooms and water fountains, and the ticket booth for the Tourmobile, which is the only authorized transportation service on this national park grounds.

Once out the door of the Visitor's Center, you should head to the grounds of the Curtis-Lee mansion, where the history of the cemetery begins. The property was owned by the adopted grandson of George Washington (George Washington Parke Curtis, who is buried on the property), who built the mansion

to house his Washington memorabilia and left it to his daughter, who married the man who would later lead the South against the North in the Civil War.

When the Lees left Virginia during the war, the Union took over the grounds and, some say out of spite, began burying the war dead on the property (1,800 casualties of Bull Run are buried in front of the house). Their son did try to retain the property after the war, but the many graves on the grounds made it an unattractive home, and he eventually sold it back to the government.

In front of the Arlington House is the sarcophagus of Pierre Charles L'Enfant, the man who designed Washington, D.C. His marble tomb sits on a hill overlooking the city.

The Kennedy gravesites are within walking distance to Arlington House. Many who remember the assassination of John F. Kennedy pass by the eternal flame, lit by Jacqueline Kennedy Onassis, who is now buried beside her first husband and the two babies they had who died in infancy. A short distance down the hill is the gravesite of Robert Kennedy, which is composed of a reflecting pool.

The Tomb of the Unknown Soldier, near the center of the cemetery, is one of the most visited sites on the grounds. The tomb honors the unknown soldiers of WWI, WWII, and the Korean War. The remains of the soldier who was interred in the Vietnam Tomb were identified in 1998 through DNA technology.

The tomb is guarded twenty-four hours a day by the Third Infantry Division (the Old Guard). The sentinels who guard the tomb perform a changing of the guard every half-hour in the warm months, every hour during the winter. There are also many wreath-laying ceremonies at the Tomb of the Unknowns.

Iwo Jima, the memorial to the United States Marine Corp., is a powerful tribute to the Marines and WWII. Through an optical illusion, if you can manage to drive around the monument it will appear that the flag is being raised by the marines. An Air Force Memorial and Museum is being planned for the future on this site. Nearby is the Netherlands Carillon, a gift of chimes from the people of the Netherlands, that has 50 bells.

Other sites of interest on the cemetery grounds include the Confederate War Veteran's Memorial, which was erected in 1912 and designed by a confederate war veteran who is buried beneath it, as well as the Civil War Memorial on the grounds of the Lee home. Also on the grounds of the Lee home is a former village for freed slaves, called the Freedman's Village, that thrived after the Civil War and even had its own hospital and a school with 900 students.

Other important memorial sites include a memorial to the crew of the Space Shuttle Challenger, two of whom are buried there;

African American Civil War Memorial

One of the newest of the nation's war memorials, this stone and bronze tribute to the more than 200,000 African-American soldiers and their white officers who fought for the Union in the Civil War was unveiled off U St. N.W. in September of 1996. The visitor's center offers a database for researching regiments and battle action.

Lockerbee Memorial Cairn for the 259 people killed on Pan Am Flight 103; an Iran Rescue Mission Memorial for servicemen killed in the hostage rescue attempt; a monument to Teddy Roosevelt's Rough Riders of the Spanish-American War; a memorial to the Hmong who helped the United States in the secret war in Laos; and the USS *Maine* Monument, which includes the actual mast and anchor of the ship.

Arlington National Cemetery is also the final resting place of some of America's most famous military leaders, as well as people who made an impact on the nation. Famous gravesites include:

- Thurgood Marshall, Supreme Court justice
- Audie Murphy, most decorated WWII soldier and actor
- Joe Louis (Barrow), WWII veteran and heavyweight boxing champion
- Oliver Wendell Holmes, Jr., Civil War veteran and Supreme Court justice
- Daniel "Chappie" James, Jr., the first African-American four-star general
- Richard Byrd, polar explorer and admiral
- William Howard Taft, president and chief justice of the Supreme Court
- Virgil "Gus" Grissom, astronaut
- Medgar Evers, WWII veteran and civil rights leader
- Samuel Dashiell Hammett, Army sergeant and Sam Spade author
- Lee Marvin, Marine Corps private and movie actor
- George Westinghouse, Civil War veteran and inventor

There are an average of twenty funerals at Arlington National Cemetery a day, and approximately a quarter of a million gravesites. In 1980 a Columbarium was erected to house cremated remains. Otherwise, it was estimated that at this present burial rate the cemetery would have been full by 2002.

Daniel's Story

Although there are many powerful exhibits in the United States Holocaust Memorial Museum, one of the most poignant is *Daniel's Story*, which is a walk-through exhibit on the first floor designed to attempt to explain the events leading up to the Holocaust to children over eight years old. This exhibit is a Jewish child's personal account of life in Germany during the Holocaust and takes viewers through his town, his home, the streets of his town in the aftermath of Kristalnacht, the ghetto he was sent to, the cattle car ride to a concentration camp and what happened to his family after the war.

Each room of the exhibit has sample diary entries in Daniel's own words. Daniel's diary entries chronicle the confiscation of his parents' store, the burning of their synagogue, being able to buy only from Jewish merchants, being taunted in school, and being forced to wear the Star of David. When his family is forced from their middle-class home and herded into a ghetto, both Daniel and his sister are made to work. His family is sent by cattle car to a concentration camp and a film ends the exhibit explaining what happened to the family after the cattle-car journey, where Daniel was separated from his mother and sister, who were killed in the camps.

For the young, and those who have never read *The Diary of Anne Frank*, this is as close to an interactive experience of what happened to those where were children during the Holocaust as one can come.

United States Holocaust Memorial Museum

100 Raoul Wallenberg Pl. (formerly 15th St. SW) off of the National Mall. (202) 488-0400. Open 10:00 A.M.–5:30 P.M. Closed Yom Kippur and Christmas Day. Smithsonian Metro station.

You need tickets (which are free, but given out in fifteen minute intervals) to see the main exhibits in this powerful memorial. Tickets are given out at the museum's information desk, or you can order them ahead of time from Protix, (800) 400-9373. The reason for the tickets is that the memorial receives 2 million visitors a year, and the gallery spaces of the museum itself are small.

This museum and memorial is not for young children. A thoughtful permanent exhibit on the life of a young Jewish boy in Germany (Daniel's Story: Remember the Children) is suitable for slightly older children (8–12 years old). The museum has a sign posted that recommends that children under twelve not view the material, but even teen-agers need to be prepared for this museum.

When you enter the main floor of the exhibit, it should be strikingly apparent that the interior architecture of red brick and painted steel beams is designed to resemble the railway stations and concentration camps themselves.

There are a handful of changing and permanent exhibits that you can view without a ticket (the above-mentioned Daniel's Story), as well as a brief orientation film on the history of the holocaust and the museum itself.

When you get in line to enter the elevator to the fourth floor, where the chronological history of the persecution and elimination of European Jews under Hitler begins, you are given a reproduction of an identity card from one of the holocaust's victims, two-thirds of whom were killed during this time. An estimated 12 million people were murdered by the Nazis during the holocaust, which include 6 million Jews, as well as gypsies, homosexuals, Jehovah's Witnesses, Soviet prisoners of war, the handicapped, and political dissidents.

The fourth floor tells the story of the Nazi's rise to power, with examples of their propaganda against the Jews. The third flour continues the story of the increasing ghettoization of Europe's Jews and includes an authentic cattle car that was once used to transport victims to the camps, which will make the hair on your neck stand as you pass through it, as well as a replica of the wrought iron sign over Auschwitz, "Work Will Make You Free." Here you will also see a disturbing documentation of the Nazi scientific experiments on the camp prisoners.

On the second floor, the story of the liberation of the camps and the end of the war is told. There are relics and a graphic display of the cost of human lives as seen by a room full of the shoes of victims and pictures of piles and piles of removed wedding rings and human hair that was used to stuff upholstery. Here, too, are actual pieces of the crematoriums and camps.

The final exhibit is a thirty-minute film called *Testimony*, where survivors tell their own stories. This leads to the solemn Hall of Remembrance, where an eternal flame burns to remember the victims of the holocaust.

The museum is also a research center and holocaust registry. There is a museum store that has a unique collection of books about the holocaust and its survivors, as well as a museum cafe that serves both kosher and non-kosher meals.

Chapter Eight

The Branches of Government and Government Agencies

T he three major branches of government—executive, legislative, and judicial—are all headquartered in Washington, D.C., and seeing them all gives you a real perspective on that social studies lesson in grade school about the balance of power inherent in our system of government as designed by the founding fathers. The other government agencies and service organizations give you a good idea about how those principles have evolved over the last 200 years.

However, everyone who comes to the capital wants to see some of these sites, but many require advance tickets and some are closed on the weekend. If you are in town for a long weekend, target your sites immediately and go about getting tickets (if you haven't done so already through your local representative or senator's office). In the summer months it is virtually impossible to see the White House without advance tickets (and it is closed to the public on Sunday and Monday). Also, the Mint and the FBI tour are both closed on the weekend, so head there first on a Friday or save them for the Monday (unless it's a federal holiday when government agencies are closed).

The White House

1600 Pennsylvania Ave. NW, (202) 456-7041. Open 10:00 A.M. till noon for the general public, 8:00 A.M.–10:00 A.M. for congressional tours, Tuesday–Saturday. Occasionally closed for official functions, so call ahead for scheduling. White House Visitor's Center, 1450 Pennsylvania Ave. NW, in the Dept. of Commerce Bldg. bet. 14th and 15th Sts. McPherson Sq. Metro station for the White House and Federal Triangle metro station for the Visitor's Center.

If you don't have tickets for a tour, your first stop will have to be the White House Visitor's Center, where tickets for the two hours a day that the presidential mansion is open to the public are given out beginning at 7:30 A.M. These 4,500 daily tickets go so fast in the summer months, that by 9:00 A.M. they are usually all gone. You can obtain up to four tickets at a time.

Since the general public tours begin at 10:00 A.M., you should consider having a leisurely breakfast at Old Ebbitt's Grill (see Chapter 5), which is almost across the street, or an exquisite breakfast in the Willard Room of the Willard Hotel, because nothing else is open that early.

White House Home Improvement

- The first interior bathroom was installed in 1883

- The first telephone line was installed in 1887

- The first electric light was turned on in 1891

- The entire White House was air-conditioned in 1909

Burning of the
White House in 1814

During The War of 1812, the British tried to take back the colonies they had lost during the Revolution. The only international war to be fought on American soil after the Revolution, The War of 1812 resulted in the British invasion of Washington and the burning of the White House in 1814.

The British redcoats landed in Maryland and made their way down to Washington. Legend has it that in 1813, British Rear Admiral Cockburn informed President James Madison that he "would make his bow" in the White House shortly.

The British arrived at the White House on August 24, 1814. Dolley Madison is revered for her determination to save the life-sized Gilbert Stuart portrait of George Washington, which she described in a letter to her sister she wrote while the British were approaching: "I insist on waiting until the large picture of General Washington is secured, and it requires to be unscrewed from the wall. This process was found too tedious for these perilous moments: I have ordered that the frame be broken, and the canvas taken out; it is done . . . and now, dear sister, I must leave this house, or the retreating army will make me a prisoner in it."

In addition to burning the White House on August 24, 1814, the British also torched the Capitol, the Library of Congress, and several military sites. A thunderstorm that evening saved the four walls of the East Room in the White House where the Stuart painting had hung.

The White House Visitor's Center has a number of displays itself, including a history of the mansion, its architecture, furnishings, and first families, as well as a thirty-minute film. There is also a small gift shop on the premises, as well as bathrooms (the public is not allowed to use the facilities in the White House).

The general public tour is self-guided, although Secret Service Tour Officers are available to answer questions. The congressional tour is guided by a Secret Service Tour Officer. The tours are otherwise identical. A total of 7,000 tourists pass through the White House each day. You will have to go through a metal detector and have your bags X-rayed before you enter the tour waiting area, and videotaping and photography are not allowed.

When you enter the visitor entrance, there are displays along a hallway looking out onto the Jacqueline Kennedy Gardens that explain the architectural and interior changes within the mansion over the past 150 years. These include such tidbits as the fact that the White House once had a Tiffany window that was sold in an auction in 1902 (Louis Comfort Tiffany was the interior designer during the Arthur administration!) and that the bed in the Lincoln bedroom was actually bought by Mary Todd Lincoln.

First stop on the tour is the Library where there are 2,700 books and a chandelier that once belonged to James Fenimore Cooper (author of *The Last of the Mohicans*). This is the site where the president holds private interviews. The next room on the tour is the China Room, where examples of the table settings from each presidential administration are on display. It is interesting to note that Nancy Reagan wasn't the only first lady to cause an uproar over her china pattern

White House Ghosts

By far the most famous ghost that is said to haunt the White House is that of President Lincoln, but ghost hunters and former White House personnel claim he's not the only one. According to various tales and legends, the presidential mansion is haunted by the ghosts of Abigail Adams, Dolley Madison, Lincoln's son Willie who died at age twelve in the White House, Presidents Jackson and Harrison, and a British soldier who was killed during the burning of the White House in 1814.

The ghost of Abigail Adams desires to hang her laundry in the grand East Room, and her ghost has been seen approaching the room with her arms out as if carrying a laundry basket. Some have said that they can smell a whiff of soap and damp cotton when her ghost is near.

Dolley Madison cared a great deal about the White House and planted her own garden where the Rose Garden is today. It is reported that when Edith Wilson attempted to tear up this plot of land, the ghost of Dolley Madison terrified the gardeners. Instead, the roses were planted to appease her and she has not reappeared since then.

The ghost of Lincoln's son is said to appear in the room where he died, and his mother reported that she felt him with her in the White House. A great believer in the spirit world, she also said she could hear Thomas Jefferson playing the violin.

The presence of Abraham Lincoln has been recorded throughout the White House ever since his assassination. He is said to walk through the halls and knock on the door of guests staying in the Lincoln bedroom.

Even before Lincoln's ghost was said to roam the halls, White House servants had said that they could hear laughter coming from the bed where Andrew Jackson slept in the Rose Room, and Mrs. Lincoln reported that she often heard his ghost stomping and swearing. President Harrison is said to haunt the White House attic.

White House History

The White House is the oldest public building in D.C. and has been the home of all presidents except Washington. It was designed by Irishman James Hoban, who won a competition in 1790, beating out fifty-one designers including Thomas Jefferson, who used a pseudonym for his entry. Originally called the "presidential palace," it acquired the nickname "the White House" after continuous applications of whitewash had been painted on the exterior. During the War of 1812, it was burnt nearly to the ground by the British, who left a burnt-out shell and the four walls of the East Room standing.

It was rebuilt between 1815 and 1817 under the guidance of the original architect, adding space for the presidential staff. In 1902 a west wing with the Oval Office was added under Teddy Roosevelt's administration as well as the Rose Garden. The third floor was added in 1927 to provide more living space for the first family. The entire White House was rehabbed in 1948 after the leg of the piano Margaret Truman was playing crashed through the dining room ceiling. The Trumans lived at Blair House, the presidential guest house, for four years, during which time the East Wing, an air raid shelter, an interior movie theater, and a balcony on the south portico were added.

choice. Mary Todd Lincoln's pattern uses a bright purple, which many thought was too royal, and caused quite a stir at the time.

The gold and white East Room on the second floor has been the site of many of the mansion's biggest events, including the wedding receptions of Nellie Grant, Alice Roosevelt, and Lynda Bird Johnson. It has also been the viewing room for seven president's funerals, the site of Susan Ford's senior prom, and the site of Nixon's resignation speech. It is the largest room in the White House and our secret service guide told us that in the nineteenth century it was the room where Abigail Adams hung the presidential laundry to dry because she didn't want people to see it hanging on the lawn. During the Civil War, Union troops were housed in this room.

The famous life-size painting of George Washington by Gilbert Stuart that was saved by Dolley Madison as the White House burned in 1814 is also on display here. Even though Stuart made many Washington portraits, the best will be traveling when the National Portrait Gallery is closed for renovation, so this is the only one you can catch in Washington during this time. Our guide told us that Dolley took an ax to the frame and rolled the portrait up. The four walls of the East Room are the oldest items left in the White House after the fire.

The Green Room, which once served as Jefferson's dining room, is now a parlor room with green silk walls from the Monroe administration. It is furnished in the Federal style of the early 1800s. There's a marvelous painting by Georgia O'Keefe of Bear Lake, New Mexico, as well as a street scene of Philadelphia that was purchased by an antique dealer for $10 and turned out to be one of the original White House paintings.

The Blue Room is the most formal room in the White House, where presidents often receive guests and where the largest Christmas tree in the mansion is on display. This was also the site of President Cleveland's marriage to Frances Folsom—Cleveland, incidentally, was the only president to get married while in office. The blue silk chairs from the Van Buren administration were being regilded by hand while I was there.

The Red Room, where the first lady traditionally does her entertaining, features red walls and red satin chairs, as well as a painting by Albert Bierstadt of the Rocky Mountains. This was also the room

Jackie Kennedy's White House Legacy

In 1961, First Lady Jacqueline Kennedy decided to make the White House the showplace it once was. She sent out a worldwide request for original furnishings from the house, and restored many of the rooms to their earlier splendor. Later she led the nation on the first-ever televised tour of the White House.

To preserve the historical decor and historical continuity now finally established in the White House, Congress passed an act declaring all furnishings and decorations used by the first family during their stay to be the property of the White House.

Ladybird Johnson furthered Jackie Kennedy's legacy by establishing a Committee for the Preservation of the White House with a permanent office of curator.

in which Abraham Lincoln rescinded Confederate President Davis's citizenship during the Civil War.

The State Dining Room, which seats 140 people, is also the site of the G.P.A. Healy portrait of Lincoln, which was given to the White House by his heirs. Carved above the fireplace mantel are the words of President John Adams from his second evening in the White House: "I Pray Heaven to Bestow the Best of Blessings on THIS HOUSE and All that shall hereafter inhabit it."

There ends the public tour. The second and third floor of the White House are the private domain of the first family. The Oval Office and the Lincoln Bedroom are not open to the public.

The United States Capitol

E and 1st Sts., at the east end of the Mall. (202) 225-6827. Open from 9:00 A.M.–8:00 P.M. in warm weather; 9:30 A.M.–4:30 P.M. in winter. Closed Thanksgiving Day, Christmas Day, and New Year's Day. You need timed tickets for the self-guided tour, which you can pick up on the east side of the building. Guided tours are given throughout the day. Capitol South or Union Station Metro stations.

The House and Senate galleries are open to all visitors, but you must obtain passes when Congress is in session (call (202) 224-3121). If you haven't received passes from your representative or senator ahead of time, you can get these by presenting a passport at your senator's office on the Constitution Ave. side of the building or your representative's office on the Independence Ave. side of the building. When either the House or the Senate is in session, a flag flies over the respective side of the building. The *Washington Post* also lists the schedule in its Today in Congress section.

Aside from being the seat of our government where the daily business of legislation is enacted, the Capitol building itself and the many artworks inside are incredible. Designed by William Thorton and amended by Benjamin Latrobe, the cornerstone was laid by

Washington in 1793, ready for Congress in 1800, and burned down by the British in 1814. The famous dome was actually added during the Lincoln administration. The capitol's east front is where most of the recent presidents have taken their Oath of Office.

From its domed ceiling (180 feet high and 96 feet wide) above the rotunda through its north and south wings, the Capitol is jam-packed with over 800 works of art, as well as artifacts as important as the Magna Carta, which is currently on loan from England and on display in a case in the rotunda.

The rotunda's bronze doors are a bas relief that depict the life of Christopher Columbus. On the walls are eight giant oil paintings by John Trumball depicting events in American history, such as the signing of the Declaration of Independence and the presentation of Pocahontas to British royalty. On the dome's ceiling is a fresco by Constantino Brumidi, who has been called the "Michelangelo of the Capitol" for this painting, *Apotheosis of Washington*. It's an allegorical portrait of the first president surrounded by Roman deities who are watching the development of the nation.

The rotunda also has a number of statues including the controversial group sculpture of the three leaders of the women's suffrage movement—Elizabeth Cady Stanton, Susan B. Anthony, and Lucretia Mott—which had been kept in the crypt until women's groups campaigned successfully to have it moved to a more prominent position in the building.

Beyond the Rotunda is the National Statuary Hall, which was the original chamber for the House of Representatives. Each state was invited to send two statues of important regional leaders, and the hall is now so full that statues spill out into adjoining halls and corridors and even show up haphazardly throughout the building. Some of the more prominent figures whose statues are on display include Ethan Allen, Daniel Webster, and Henry Clay; some of the more unusual works of art and personages that can be found elsewhere are Utah's sculpture of Philo Farnsworth, the father of television, and Colorado's painted bronze statue of Jack Swigert, Jr., an Apollo 13 astronaut.

The vaulted ceilings of the first floor of the Senate wing have paintings and panels celebrating American democracy, progress, and technology painted by Brumidi. Known as the Brumidi Corridors, they are based on the Loggia of the Vatican. This tradition continues

Who Designed the U.S. Capitol?

With its large dome looming over the city, the U.S. Capitol building is one of the signature landmarks of Washington, D.C. The original design was by William Thorton, but when the British burned the Capitol in 1814, Benjamin Latrobe redesigned it.

The cornerstone of the original building was laid by George Washington in 1793 and the building finished for Congress by 1800. After the burning, work began immediately to rebuild the Capitol building. The first dome was erected in 1826, but it collapsed during the Lincoln administration. The rebuilding of the Capitol continued through the Civil War under the direction of Charles Bulfinch. President Lincoln felt that if the Capitol were complete it would give the nation a sense of continuity. The second giant dome was completed in 1863.

throughout the halls and galleries in the House wing by other artists (after Brumidi's death) and depict such events in American history as the Boston Tea Party, the Women's Suffrage Movement, the signing of the Declaration of Independence and the burning of the Capitol in 1814. These scenes continue to the present and include a panel on the Space Shuttle *Challenger* disaster.

The south and north wings of the Capitol are the House and Senate chambers. The House of Representatives chamber is the largest legislative body in the world and the site of the president's annual State of the Union address.

There are also two museums on site. The original Supreme Court chambers, which have been restored to their original appearance with red velvet upholstery (the Supreme Court moved out of the Capitol to its own building in 1935), and the old Senate chamber, which has also been restored to its original nineteenth-century appearance.

Supreme Court

1st St. NE, between E. Capitol St. and Maryland Ave. (202) 479-3000. Open Monday through Friday 9:00 A.M.–4:30 P.M. Closed weekends and all federal holidays. Capitol South or Union Station Metro stations.

Over one million people visit the Supreme Court building a year. It was built in 1935 and features a classical Corinthian design of sixteen marble columns topped by a sculpted pediment (the building was nicknamed the Marble Palace). The court originally met in the Merchants Exchange building in New York City and moved a number of times until it was housed in the Capitol. This highest court of the judicial branch of our government is besieged

Supreme Court Facts and Trivia

The first bill introduced in the United State Senate was the Judiciary Act of 1789, which established the Supreme Court, originally composed of five Associate Justices and a Chief Justice. The first Supreme Court assembled was held in the Merchant's Exchange building in New York City, then the nation's capital.

For the first 101 years of the Supreme Court's existence, the justices were required to "ride circuit," which means they traveled throughout the country holding court in various jurisdictions.

There are eight Associate Justices and one Chief Justice today. Members of the Supreme Court are appointed by the president subject to approval by the Senate.

by close to 7,000 requests a year for retrial of controversial cases that bear on issues affecting the nation, but it hears only about 100 cases annually.

The court is in session Monday through Wednesday from 10:00 A.M. until noon, beginning the first Monday in October and ending in late April; brief sessions are held in May and June. The *Washington Post* regularly publishes the Supreme Court's calendar, or call (202) 479-3211 for case information. There are only 150 public seats, so arrive early if you want to get in. No cameras or videotaping allowed.

The Court's Great Hall features a twenty-minute film on how the Supreme Court works, as well as its history and some of its more famous cases. There's a gift shop on the premises, as well as two restaurants.

Library of Congress

1st St. SE between E. Capitol St. and Independence Ave. (202) 707-8000. Closed Sunday and all federal holidays. Jefferson Building open Mon.–Sat. 10:00 A.M.–5:30 P.M.; Madison Building open 8:30 A.M.–9:30 P.M., Sat. until 6:00 P.M. Capitol South Metro station.

This is the world's largest library, with more than 17 million books as well as manuscripts, letters, prints, photographs, recordings, movies, personal papers from scholars and celebrities (Jefferson to Groucho Marx), and musical instruments. The total collection has more than 131 million items. Of course, only a fraction of this material is on display at any given time, so there are constantly changing exhibits.

The Library of Congress was created by John Adams in 1800, "for the purchase of such books as may be necessary for the use of Congress" and was originally housed in a boarding house and later the Capitol, where the entire collection was torched by the British in 1814. Thomas Jefferson sold his personal collection of close to 7,000 books to the government to restart the library.

The first permanent home of the library—the Jefferson Building—was erected in 1897 and was expected to house the growing collection for decades, but it filled up in a mere thirteen years. Two additions have been added: the John Adams Building in 1939 and

American Treasures at the Library of Congress

American Treasures is a permanent, rotating exhibit of the rarest, most interesting and significant objects in the Library of Congress's vast collection.

Among the items on display are:

- The contents of President Abraham Lincoln's pockets the night he was shot (opera glasses with case, eye glasses with case, and a pocket knife)
- Jefferson's handwritten draft of the Declaration of Independence
- Maya Lin's original drawing for the Vietnam Veterans Memorial
- The earliest known baseball cards
- The first motion picture deposited for copyright
- Alexander Graham Bell's lab notebook
- Mary Pickford's palm print
- The Original comic book of Wonder Woman (1947)
- Bob Hope's joke file

the James Madison Memorial Building in 1980. The Jefferson Building underwent a major twelve-year renovation and reopened to the public in 1997.

The exterior of the Jefferson Building was designed to look like the Paris Opera House and has a very European fountain with a bronze statue of Neptune outside its front doors (this is my favorite statue in all of the city). The Great Hall of the Jefferson Building features a domed interior and a stained glass ceiling plus paintings, sculpture, and mosaics by fifty artists.

In the southwest gallery and pavilion of the Great Hall is the permanent "Treasures of the Library of Congress" exhibit which includes historic and rare pieces from the collection, such as a Gutenberg Bible and the Giant Bible of Mainz, which are on permanent display, and rotating exhibits from the collection. Other items that have been on display in the "Treasures of the Library of Congress" exhibit include Jefferson's handwritten draft of the Declaration of Independence with notations from other signatories, Jelly Roll Morton's early compositions, Maya Lin's original drawing for the Vietnam Veterans Memorial, Alexander Graham Bell's notebooks, and George Gershwin's orchestral score for *Porgy and Bess*.

The John Adams Building has murals illustrating scenes from *The Canterbury Tales* painted on its interior walls and the Madison Building is the home of the Library's restaurants and theater that shows rare films.

There is a twelve-minute orientation film shown in the Visitor's center in the Jefferson Building, which gives you an overview and history of the Library. The gift shop is also located here.

Anyone over eighteen may use the Library, but works do not leave the premises. You have to obtain a user card, which is available by showing a valid driver's license or passport or by filling out an information sheet.

The Library of Congress is celebrating its bicentennial in 2000 and will schedule a number of special events and exhibits to honor its history and legacy throughout the year, with special events on April 24, including a birthday party and the opening of an exhibit on Thomas Jefferson. A bicentennial gala is also scheduled for October 3. Publication of bicentennial posters, stamps, and coins will become available for purchase in the gift shop.

National Archives

On the Mall between 7th and 9th Sts. on Constitution Ave. (202) 501-5000. During warm weather the archives are open from 10:00 A.M. until 9:00 P.M. After Labor Day open until 5:30 P.M. Closed on Christmas Day. National Archives Metro station.

The National Archive Exhibition hall houses the originals of our nation's most precious documents—the Declaration of Independence, the Constitution, and the Bill of Rights—which are collectively called the Charters of Freedom and are on permanent display in glass cases where air has been replaced by helium.

Surrounding these cases are documents, photos, and artifacts that tell the story of our nation's history from the colonies to the present, from the Emancipation Proclamation to the Japanese surrender in WWII.

Although built in 1932, the building keeps the Greek revival style of so many federal buildings with its colonnade facade topped by a pediment and a dome. It was designed by John Russell Pope, who also designed the National Gallery of Art and the Jefferson Memorial. The National Archive collection includes more than 3 billion items.

On the walls of the Exhibition Hall are two murals by New Yorker Barry Faulkner. The mural on the left shows Jefferson passing the Declaration of Independence to Hancock for his signature, and the mural on the right shows Madison submitting the Constitution to Washington at the Constitutional Convention. The bronze design on the floor represents the four winged figures of legislation, justice, history, and war and defense.

A rotating collection of items from the permanent collection is on view in the rotunda in the American Originals panels. These have included the Louisiana Purchase, signed by Napoleon, and Greta Garbo's driver's license. A gallery on the lower level features themed exhibits from the collection.

Where's George?

Everyone knows that a dollar bill travels extensively in its lifetime, but now there's a Web site that tracks where a buck stops.

If you log onto *www.wheresgeorge.com* you will be able to enter the series number of a bill currently in your possession, and they will e-mail you back its travel history. One sample dollar bill was tracked at traveling 193 miles in six months.

Copies of the documents, as well as books, can be purchased in the museum shop on the premises.

Bureau of Engraving and Printing

14th and C Sts. SW, (202) 874-3188. During the winter, tours are given from 9:00 A.M. to 2:00 P.M., Monday through Friday. In the summer, afternoon hours are added from 4:00 to 7:30 P.M. Closed weekends, federal holidays, and the week between Christmas Day and New Year's Day. Smithsonian Metro station.

Timed tickets are required during the busy season and can be obtained at the Visitor's Center in front of the building or by writing to your representative or senator ahead of time. Once you have a ticket, you can wait a while for your thirty-minute tour, but it is fascinating to see the bills, stamps, and White House invitations being printed (coins are minted in Texas and Philadelphia).

Again, you must pass a security checkpoint before entering. While you wait in line for your tour to begin, you will see a brick of $20 bills that totals one million dollars and TV displays of interesting facts about our currency, such as it's not made out of paper but is 75 percent cotton and 25 percent linen, or that the average lifespan for a $1 bill is a year and a half.

The tour begins with a brief film about the history of the bureau (in 1862 it consisted of six employees who separated $1 and $2 bills printed by a private company; the staff is currently about 3,000), the printing of money, and the changing design of all U.S. currency, which will include a watermark portrait, like some European bills, that you can hold up to the light and see. These changes are being implemented to make counterfeiting more difficult.

The "money factory" prints 38 million notes a day totaling approximately $541 million.

The tour leads you through the actual printing process. You witness the giant presses roll behind a plexiglass wall and smell the paintlike odor of the green and black inks. The production process of U.S. currency involves 65 steps including examining the bill sheets, overprinting, slicing the sheets, and shrink wrapping the bills.

After the tour you are let out into the shop, which sells such novelties as bags of shredded money and imperfect sheets of currency. It has a number of interactive displays for kids, as well as a photo booth where kids can have their picture imprinted on a $20 bill.

U.S. Dept. of Treasury

15th St. and Pennsylvania Ave. NW. (202) 662-0896. Metro Center or Federal Triangle Metro station. Public tours are given only on Saturdays, and you must reserve ahead of time, giving your name and Social Security number.

Once money is printed and bundled, it is sent off to the U.S. Treasury where it is dispersed to banks. The white granite building of the U.S. Treasury Department should be familiar to all Americans as it appears on the back of the $10 bill. The building itself is a prime example of the Greek revival architectural style that swept the nation in 1800s (it is the third oldest Federal building in the city, after the White House and the Capitol), with a facade full of Ionic columns and topped by a pediment.

The tour takes you through the restored interior of both the east and west wings, which features vaulted ceilings, chandeliers, and period furniture that includes some chairs with dollar signs on their backs.

The burglarproof vault room is now an office, but you can see its metal walls and federal symbols on its exterior. Another treasury room was the office of Andrew Johnson for six weeks while Mary Todd Lincoln prepared to move from the White House.

The best reason for visiting the Treasury Department and going through the annoying tour request bureaucracy is the Cash Room. Once a U.S. Treasury-operated bank until the mid-1970s, this small marble room (thirty-two by seventy-two feet) with chandeliers was the site of President Grant's inaugural reception. Six thousand invitations were sold and the crowd was so tight that people passed out.

Federal Bureau of Investigation

E St. between 9th and 10th St. in the J. Edgar Hoover Building, 935 Pennsylvania Ave. (202) 324-3447. Monday through Friday 8:45 A.M.–4:15 P.M. Closed federal holidays, Christmas Day, and New Year's Day. Metro Center or Federal Triangle Metro stations.

During the summer of 1999, the FBI building was closed to the public to increase security measures (so expect to encounter security precautions when entering the building), and make sure you call before you head out for tickets because there may not be tours available. You can also get tickets from your representative or senator's office in advance.

More than half a million people take the FBI tour a year (especially kids, who love the ballistics demonstration). The tour begins with a short film about the FBI's history and departments. There's a weapons collection that includes some of the most notorious firearms in crime history such as the guns used by Bonnie and Clyde, Al Capone, and John Dillinger (as well as his cigar, hat, and glasses). The FBI's ten Most Wanted criminals is always a fascinating exhibit (and can be followed at home on the TV show *America's Most Wanted* and at the FBI's Web site at www.fbi.gov).

The tour includes a visit to the FBI lab where DNA testing is explained, as well as the Firearms Unit, where agents explain how a bullet can be matched to the weapon it was fired from, and the material analysis unit, which examines fragments from everything from paint chips to rug fibers and matches them. There is also a display of items seized from drug dealers and a demonstration by an agent on the FBI's firearms policy and gun safety.

Years ago the FBI used to give out bullet casings after the demonstrations, but that is no longer the general practice. However, you can write to the FBI to request a bullet casing or a used target, if you so desire, at: FBI, Tour Unit, Room M-956, J. Edgar Hoover FBI Bldg., 935 Pennsylvania Ave. NW, Washington, D.C. 20535.

There is an FBI store on the premises that sells memorabilia.

Chapter Nine

Other Museums

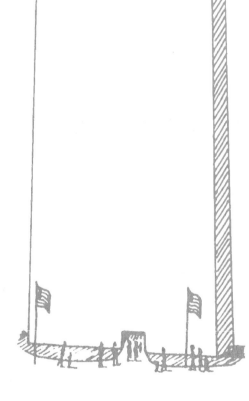

Art Museum Security

Because of so many recent destructive acts aimed at artworks, none of the city's art museums will allow backpacks into the museums. You must check them in the coat check areas.

Washington, D.C. has the largest number of museum items per capita of any city in the world. It has twenty art museums.

As if the national monuments and the Smithsonian museums and galleries weren't enough to keep you busy, the capital also has a number of fabulous private museums, which means you have to pay to get in, but it's worth it. There is also the National Gallery of Art, which is free (but not part of the Smithsonian).

National Gallery of Art and Sculpture Gallery

Constitution Ave., between 3rd and 7th Sts., on the north side of the Mall. (202) 737-4215. Open Monday–Saturday 10:00 A.M.–5:00 P.M., Sunday 11:00 A.M.–6:00 P.M. Inquire about free tours, special exhibits, concerts, and films. National Archives, Judiciary Sq., or Smithsonian Metro station.

This monumental museum of art takes up two city blocks and continues across the street with a new outdoor sculpture garden. Half a day is hardly long enough to see everything.

The original neoclassical West building was designed by John Russell Pope (who also designed the Jefferson Memorial and the nearby National Archives building). The newer East Building is connected via an underground passageway that includes a gift shop and restaurant. Its H-shaped facade and signature skylights were designed by Chinese-American architect I.M. Pei, who also designed the controversial glass pyramid addition at the Louvre museum in Paris.

The gallery was created by Congress after financier Andrew Mellon donated his world-renowned art collection to the nation, which includes two of the Raphaels on display. The National Gallery has one of the finest collections of Renaissance art outside of Italy, and it houses the only painting of Leonardo da Vinci in the United States. His *Ginevra de Benci*, a noblewoman's portrait, is a

double-sided wooden panel, and it is believed he painted the museum's *Madonna and Child with a Pomegranate* while apprenticing in Verrocchio's studio. The Renaissance collection is extensive and takes up fifteen rooms of the West building. Highlights include five Botticellis, Raphael's *St. George and the Dragon*, a number of Fra Angelicos and Filippino Lippis, as well as a room of Italian frescoes that is the only one of its kind in the United States.

The Flemish and Dutch collections are equally stupendous, with some of the finest Rembrandts, Vermeers, Halses, Rubenses and Van Eycks in America. The eighteenth-and nineteenth-century galleries displaying French works include some marvelous rococo Watteaus and Bouchers, as well as David's *Napoleon*, Georges de La Tour's *Repentant Magdaleine,* and fourteen paintings by El Greco, and Jean Baptiste Siméon Chardin's (boy with) *Soap Bubbles,* a classic work.

In the nineteenth century English paintings galleries there are marvelous landscape paintings by Turner and Constable, as well as portraits by Thomas Gainsborough.

My favorite colonial American painting on display in the American collection—John Singleton Copley's *Watson and the Shark*—tells the story of fourteen-year-old Watson's fall into Havana harbor where a shark ate his right foot, but he survived to become a successful British merchant and politician.

Other American classics include a terrific selection of early American paintings by unknown artists, especially *Strawberry Girl;* Augustus Saint-Gaudens' life-size sculpture of the Shaw Memorial; a tribute to the Buffalo soldiers of the Civil War; and Thomas Coles's four paintings of the stages of man's life. The nineteenth-century American collection also includes a number of Homers, Sargents, Eakinses, Bellowses, and Hassams.

The indoor sculpture collection downstairs spans the fifteenth to nineteenth centuries and includes a fabulous Rodin collection, including studies for his *Kiss* and *Thinker*, as well as some ballerinas by Degas. This floor also features furniture, tapestries, and ceramics.

Break for lunch after you've seen the West Building and eat in the full-service Terrace Cafe, which offers a good selection of sandwiches, pastas, and hot meals. You can even enjoy a glass of wine and use your credit card to pay. Then head through the ground

The Shaw Memorial

Augustus Saint-Gaudens created the Shaw Memorial, a larger than life-size bronze relief, which is a tribute to Robert Gould Shaw and the Buffalo Soldiers of the Massachusetts 54th Regiment, which is on display at the top of Boston Common. The full scale plaster cast of the memorial can be seen at the National Gallery of Art. The memorial is considered one of the most powerful pieces of art dealing with the American Civil War. Saint-Gaudens took extreme care to depict the individual faces of the African-American soldiers, who ranged in age from sixteen to old men. He hired African-Americans to pose for him and in all made forty studies for the heads of the soldiers. The Shaw memorial took Saint-Gaudens fourteen years to complete.

The Washington Architecture of James Renwick

One of the most influential architects of Washington in the 19th century was James Renwick, who brought an American sensibility to the neoclassic style that was prevalent at the time. He designed the Smithsonian Castle, the original Corcoran Gallery (now the Renwick Gallery), the gate house in Georgetown's Oak Hill Cemetery, as well as St. Patrick's Cathedral and Grace Church in New York City, and Vassar College.

floor gift shop, which features mainly prints, scarves, and posters, and look at the twentieth-century art housed in the East Building.

The East building features an impressive number of large-canvas moderns from the abstract expressionist movement including Robert Motherwell's gigantic black and white painting *Reconciliation Elegy*, Pollock's *Number 1*, and Mark Rothko's *Orange and Tan*. Alexander Calder's orange and black finned mobile hangs above you. Barnett Newman's *Stations of the Cross*, as well as works by pop artists Roy Lichtenstein, Claes Oldenburg, and Andy Warhol are also on display. Early twentieth century works include thirteen Picassos and paintings by Braque, Kandinsky, Mondrian, Rene Magritte and Edward Hopper.

The outdoor sculpture garden on 8th Street features about thirty works from the late twentieth century and is a wonderful marriage of large-scale art and public space. A large circular fountain shoots jets of water in the center of the garden (during the winter its an ice skating rink) and there is an outdoor cafe. People flock to the giant typewriter eraser by Claes Oldenburg and Lichtenstein's *House I*, a two-dimensional primary color sculpture that plays with the spatial illusion of the house, as well as the metaphorical. Other artists represented include David Smith, Alexander Calder, Sol LeWitt, and Lucas Samaras.

Corcoran Gallery of Art

500 17th St. NW, between E St. and New York Ave. (202) 639-1700. Closed Tuesdays. Open MWF 10:00 A.M.–5:00 P.M., open until 9:00 P.M. on Thursday nights, Sat. and Sun. 10:30 A.M.–12:30 P.M. (Sunday Gospel brunch is $18.95 for adults, $8.50 for children). Closed Christmas Day and New Year's Day. Suggested donation for adults is $3, $5 for a family. There are fees for special exhibits. Farragut North Metro station.

An incredible private collection in a beautiful beaux arts museum building, the Corcoran was Washington, D.C.'s first art museum. Originally housed in what is now the Renwick Gallery, the collection outgrew its space and moved to its current location in 1897.

The collection was amassed by William Corcoran, a Washington banker who realized how important it was to begin collecting

American art, not just the European masters that everyone else with money was buying. Highlights of his personal collection include Bierstadt's *Last of the Buffalo* and Frederick Church's *American Falls Niagra*, as well as Healy's portrait of Abraham Lincoln (a second one is in the White House) and the controversial sculpture of the naked female *Greek Slave* by Hiram Powers.

There are a number of important works by European artists here as well such as Rubens, Delacroix, Renoir, Monet, Corot, Degas, and Turner. You can also see a working clock that once belonged to Marie Antoinette.

Newer works by American artists include almost all the members of the Hudson River school, as well as paintings by Mary Cassatt, Thomas Eakins, Mark Rothko, and Helen Frankenthaler. In the lower level of the gallery, near the cafe, is a changing exhibit of works by African-American artists (the Corcoran has the largest collection of works by African-American artists in any American art museum and includes 350 works dating back to 1806) that has featured Kara Walker's powerful silhouette works, photos by Gordon Parks, and paintings by Jacob Lawrence, Romare Bearden, and Sam Gilliam.

The Corcoran regularly features special exhibits from the sculpture of Roy Lichtenstein to the photos of Annie Leibovitz.

The museum restaurant, Café des Artistes, offers a wonderful lunch that is often tied to the show. When I was there, the menu echoed the work of Roy Lichtenstein. On the walls above the restaurant is a copy of a frieze from the Parthenon.

The museum shop offers an eclectic mix of clever art-related items, from Warhol glasses to traditional posters and mouse pads. Because the Corcoran has an art school, it often supports the work of local artists. Recently featured were a banner and posters by the thirty-one-year-old D.C.-based artist Alan Simensky, whose work is reminiscent of Lichtenstein's.

Phillips Collection

1600 21st St. NW at Q St. (202) 387-2151. Admission: $7.00 for adults; $4.00 for seniors and students. Includes audio tour. Free for children under eighteen, but without the audio tour (audio tour

The Hudson River School of Artists

The Hudson River School is the first style of art born in the United States by painters who celebrated the beauty and splendor of the American landscape. The name of this style of painting was given to it by art critics because the most famous members of this group of New York artists painted views of the Hudson River just around the turn of the century.

Hudson River School artists include Frederick Church, Asher Durand (both of whom have work hanging in the White House), Jasper Cropsey, George Inness, John Kensett and John Trumball Peale.

The Ashcan School of Art

The Ashcan School of art is another purely American style of art born just after the turn of the century. It was created by New York artists who primarily painted dark, gritty city scenes. An art critic did not appreciate the subject matter of their work—tenements, alleys, and city slums—and dubbed this group of artists "the Ashcan School."

This group of artists were also referred to as "the Eight" because they once banded together in a group exhibit against the traditions of the National Academy of Art. These artists include Robert Henri, the leader of the group, Arthur B. Davies, Ernest Lawson, George Luks, Maurice Prendergast, William Glackens, Everett Shinn and John Sloan. George Bellows, Albert Maher, Edward Hopper, and Guy Pene du Bois were also considered to be members of the Ashcan School.

alone $3). Suggested contribution during the week. Wednesday free admission. Closed Mondays. Open Tues.–Sat 10:00 A.M.–5:00 P.M., late on Thurs. until 9:00 P.M.; Sun, noon–7:00 P.M. Closed Fourth of July, Thanksgiving Day, Christmas Day, and New Year's Day. Dupont Circle Metro station (Q St. exit) and then a short walk.

This incredible private museum, with works bought by a collecting couple that span the twentieth century, rivals any modern art museum in the world. The Phillips Collection was the first modern art museum in the country and was shown to the public in two rooms of this Georgian mansion of steel fortune heir Duncan Phillips and his wife Marjorie Phillips. Marjorie was an artist herself, and her American impressionist work is on display in the museum.

Highlights of this incredible personal collection include Renoir's *Luncheon of the Boating Party*, which you can buy on handbags, mouse pads, and umbrellas in the gift shop, as well as the Rothko room, which features four works in a small room.

This collection of more than 2,500 works is known throughout the world for its breadth of European impressionist and postimpressionist works, which the Phillips felt started with El Greco because he was "the first impassioned expressionist" and Chardin because he was "the first modern painter." There are also works by Van Gogh, Monet, Degas, Gauguin, and Cezanne, as well as Pissarro, Bonnard, Vuillard and thirteen Braques. American painters in the collection include O'Keeffe, Marin, Dove, Hartley, many of the Ashcan school artists, and four striking works by Jacob Lawrence from his *Migration of the Negro* series.

Sometimes when a museum benefactor is also an artist, the work is included to appease the family, but Marjorie Phillips's *Night Baseball* is an American classic. Using post-impressionistic techniques for its very middle-American subject, it deserves the treatment it receives as one of the icons of this museum.

The museum gift shop is small but clever, featuring many reproductions from the collection as well as unusual modern art items such as a Man Ray tea pot. The cafe, located on the lower level, serves a good selection of sandwiches and homemade soup.

On Thursday nights the museum hosts "artful evenings" with music, gallery talks, and a cash bar. On Sunday nights during the fall and winter the museum hosts free concerts in the music room at 5:00 P.M., although you do have to pay the price of admission.

Kreeger Museum

2401 Foxhall Rd. NW, (202) 337-3050. Tuesday through Saturday on docent-lead tours at 10:30 A.M. and 1:30 P.M., which take an hour and a half. You must call for a reservation as tours are limited to fifteen people at a time. Closed Monday and Sunday and the entire month of August. Five dollar donation. Children under twelve not permitted. Parking available. There is no public transportation, but a taxi cab ride from downtown will run about $5.

The Kreeger Museum is one of those incredible places that you can't believe everyone in the world doesn't know about. It is one of Washington, D.C.'s best kept secrets. This museum and the Pope-Leighy House designed by Frank Lloyd Wright (see chapter 11) are my two favorite sites in the city.

Off the beaten track in the city's exclusive suburbs, the Kreeger houses a breathtaking collection of nineteenth-and twentieth-century modern art. The Kreeger is located in a private mansion built by noted architect Philip Johnson in the late '60s when he was at the beginning of his postmodern style. The architecture and the art complement each other so well that it's hard to decide which is the more impressive.

The Kreeger Museum, a private home until 1994, was designed along a module system. Every room and public space (including the stupendous pool) is constructed on some variation of the 22 x 22 x 22 foot box (sometimes two modules, sometimes half) and often topped by a dome. The entire structure is composed of beige limestone, and the museum's acoustics (both indoor and outside in the sculpture garden) are wonderful.

Although there are more than 180 works in this collection, the most memorable room is the dining room where nine paintings by Monet catch the sunlight through glass door panels that overlook the sculpture terrace.

The husband and wife team of the Kreegers were responsible for amassing the collection and it is said that they agreed on every

Women Artists at the Kreeger Museum

Although there are over 180 pieces in the art collection of the Kreeger Museum, only one piece, an African sculpture, was created by a woman. The art field was so heavily dominated by male artists and critics that the essential art historical reference text for all art historians, J.W. Hanson's *History of Art*, featured no female artists until it was revised in the 1970s.

Today the trustees of the Kreeger Museum are trying to remedy this disparity, so the two contemporary large outdoor sculptures recently acquired are both by female artists.

The Peale Family
of Artists

The Peale family dominated American art from 1770 through 1870, producing a total of 10 artists who chronicled the personalities and times of early America.

The head of this painting family was Charles Willson Peale, who left us more than 1,000 portraits, which included some of his friends, such as George Washington and Thomas Jefferson, as well as many of the other founding fathers. Peale also founded the first museum for arts and science in Philadelphia more than 200 years ago, as well as the Philadelphia Academy of Fine Arts.

Following in their father's footsteps as both painters and museum founders, Peale's son, Rembrandt, founded the Baltimore Museum in 1815, and another son, Rubens, created a museum in New York City in 1825.

Charles Willson Peale named ten of his seventeen children after artists and believed that anyone could learn to paint. His sons Raphael, Rembrandt, Rubens, Titian, and James all became professional artists. Three of James' daughters—Anna, Margretta, and Sarah Miriam (she is considered one of the first American women to have a career as an artist)—also became painters (their work can be seen at the National Museum of Women in the Arts), as did a nephew, Charles Peale Polk.

piece they purchased, though Carmen was more partial to nineteenth-century works and David liked those of the twentieth century. The collection begins with French masters of the nineteenth century, such as Corot, Courbet, and Renoir and continues through every modern art movement from the cubists to the symbolists to pop. The Kreegers also collected African art, from masks to sculpture, and the presence of it here certainly helps reveal the connection between the influence this art had on the art of the twentieth century.

Artists in the collection read like a who's who in modern art, from thirteen Picassos that span his entire career to Braque, Cezanne, Man Ray, Kandinsky, Degas, Bonnard, Van Gogh, Léger, Mondrian, Munch, Stella, Rodin, and Chagall, to name only a fraction. It is truly amazing that all these wonderful works once hung on the walls of a private home, which itself is a work of art, and that the owners had the generosity and vision to leave it all to the public.

National Museum of Women in the Arts

1250 New York Ave. NW at 13th St. (202) 783-5000. Open Mon.–Sat. 10:00 A.M.–5:00 P.M., Sun. noon–5:00 P.M. Closed Thanksgiving Day, Christmas Day, and New Year's Day. Metro Center Metro station.

Another gem of a museum, the National Museum of Women in the Arts is housed in a restored Masonic temple. Here you will find the work of two of the Peale sisters who were as talented as their father and brothers (nineteenth-century portrait painters Charles, James, and Rembrandt) but whose work is virtually unknown. The permanent collection also features early Italian Renaissance and Flemish works by female artists, as well as seventeenth century female silversmiths. Rosa Bonheur, considered the best animal painter of the nineteenth century, had to dress as a man to paint in public. Also on display are works by Elizabeth Lebrun, who was the court painter to Marie Antoinette and one of the few known female portrait painters of her time. Mary Cassatt's Japanese-inspired prints are all on view here, as are two Frida Kahlos, including her *Self-Portrait Dedicated to Leon Trotsky*, which some art historians believe was a visual love letter between the painter and the communist philosopher. Other works on display include those by Georgia O'Keeffe, Lee Kranser, and Helen Frankenthaler, as well as Alice

B'nai B'Rith Klutznick National Jewish Museum

1640 Rhode Island Ave., NW. (202) 857-6593. Sun.–Fri. 10:00 A.M.–5:00 P.M. Closed Saturdays. Farragut North Metro station. The permanent collection includes a display of antique Judaica and artifacts. The Center for Jewish Artists showcases contemporary art.

Mies van der Rohe in D.C.

The Martin Luther King Jr. Library is the main city library of Washington, D.C. and an architectural landmark. It is the only building designed by the founder of the International style of architecture, Ludwig Mies van der Rohe, in the city. Most Washingtonians don't even know that Mies van der Rohe, one of this century's most influential architects, was responsible for the design of this building, even though it is an excellent example of his glass and steel style. It is a stark black and glass panelled rectangle on the street facing the Museum of American Art and the American Portrait Gallery.

Neel's powerful *T.B. in Harlem*. There's a quirky sculpture on the landing outside the second floor elevator near the restaurant that caught my eye and stayed with me: Petah Coyne's dripped pink and white wax ballerina costume suspended from the ceiling.

The museum's small restaurant has a surprisingly good and clever selection of sandwiches such as the Frida Kahlo, a toasted cheese, havarti, and spinach sandwich, or the Mary Cassatt, tuna with Swiss. The gift shops features a terrific collection of books and posters about women artists, as well as a creative jewelry display. There are special exhibits all year round, so call for information.

National Museum of Health and Medicine

6825 16th St. NW, Bldg. 54, in the Walter Reed Army Medical Center, accessible via the Elder St. NW gate off of Georgia Ave. NW, (202) 782-2200. Open 10:00 A.M.–5:00 P.M. Guided tours are available. Closed Christmas Day. Silver Springs or Tacoma Metro stops, with a short bus ride.

A little off the beaten track, but certainly one of the most interesting and unusual museums in existence, the National Museum of Health and Medicine is one of the nation's oldest medical museums. Where else could you find the bullet that killed Lincoln or see Civil War surgical tools? You can also see centuries-old Inca skulls that show the results of head surgery and Paul Revere's dental tools.

It will take about two hours to fully explore this unusual museum. Its four permanent exhibits include To Bind Up the Nation's Wounds, which focuses on medicine during and after the Civil War, Living in a World with AIDS, Human Body Human Being, which offers a look at a smoker's lung and the opportunity to touch a human brain, and the Billings Microscope Collection, which features the world's most comprehensive collection of microscopes from the earliest in the 1600s to the first electron microscopes of the 1930s.

The museum also has a number of special exhibits, so call for information.

More Museums

American Red Cross Headquarters and Museum, 17th and E Sts. NW., (202) 639-3300. The Board of Governors building was turned into a memorial building to honor the heroic women of the First World War in 1930 and can be recognized by the giant white banner with the red cross on the outside of the beaux arts building.

In 1996, three Tiffany windows from 1917 were relit after having been dark since the black-outs of WWII. Funds for the windows were raised by the Women's Relief Corps of the North and the United Daughters of the Confederacy, two organizations of Civil War women. The Museum features regular exhibits on the Red Cross' efforts worldwide, as well as a history of this organization started by Clara Barton after the Civil War.

There is a gift shop on the premises which features such unusual items as a Fabergé style Red Cross egg pendant and earrings modeled after a Fabergé Red Cross egg presented by Czar Nicholas to his wife Alexandra and his mother on Easter 1915; a plate with the replica of the Tiffany windows; Red Cross Christmas ornaments; as well as mugs, scarves and ties. Needless to say, these items make wonderful gifts for nurses.

Art Museum of the Americas, 201 18th St. NW. (202) 458-6016. Free admission is just one reason to check out this museum, located a stone's throw from the White House and just behind the House of the Americas 9see the listing under "Walks and Tours"). In keeping with the international theme set down by that home to the Organization of American States, the museum is dedicated to Latin American and Caribbean art. See contemporary works on all kinds of themes by artists and sculptors from Mexico, Venezuela, the Galapagos Islands, and more. Hours are Tuesday through Saturday from 10A.M. to 5P.M.

Art, Science, & Technology Institute, Holography Museum of the 3rd Dimension, 2018 R St. NW. (202) 667-6322. Dupont Circle Metro station. Tours by appointment only. This is a museum of holography, with art that literally jumps off the walls. There are extensive explanations of the medium and its applications for both art and science. There are museum-lead tours. A gift shop is on the premises.

National Building Museum

401 F St. NW. (202) 272-2448. Mon.–Sat. 10:00 A.M.–5:00 P.M., Sun. noon–5:00 P.M. Judiciary Sq. Metro station. Housed in the giant U.S. Pension building, the museum is dedicated to the architecture and technology of American building. The first major exhibit here was on air conditioning.

College Park Airport Museum, 1909 Corporal Frank Scott Dr., College Park, MD; (301) 864-6029. The world's oldest operating airport was established here in 1909, when two guys by the names of Orville and Wilbur brought their "aeroplane" to this field. It led to the creation of the first Army Aviation School, one of many firsts to occur at this site; and, through it's in history books, the airport continues to operate today.

Much newer is the museum, filled with displays and artifacts on these and other important contributions to aviation. Admission is free. And don't miss the annual "Air Fair," held each fall, with stunt shows and historical aircraft on display. Call the above number to request a copy of their newsletter, "The Wright Flyer," for more info. Museum hours are 11 A.M. to 3 P.M. Wednesday through Friday's, 'til 5 P.M. on weekends.

Decatur House Museum, 748 Jackson Pl. NW (202) 842-0920. Decatur House is an interesting part of the historical landscape of the District. It has been the home of a naval hero, three secretaries of state, several members of Congress, and a vice president. World leaders have dined and danced here. The ground floor preserves the Federal-era style of the original occupants, the Decaturs, while the second floor shows the Victorian decor of its later residents, the Beatles.

The museum is open to the public Tuesdays through Fridays from 10 A.M. to 3 A.M., and Saturdays and Sundays from 12 noon to 4 P.M. Admission is $3 for adults, $1.50 for students and seniors, and free for members of the National Trust.

Daughters of the American Revolution Museum, 1776 D St. NW, (202) 879-3241. This is the museum of the National Society of the Daughters of the American Revolution. It houses a collection of American decorative arts from the 17th to the 19th centuries in period rooms organized around 33 states. All objects in the museum's extensive collection were donated by members. Tours are lead by a docent. Open Mon–Fri. 10:00 A.M.–2:30 P.M. and Sun. 1:00–5:00 P.M. Closed Sat.

National Archives, Seventh St. & Constitution Ave. NW, (202) 501-5205. You've heard about them in history class; now see the real things, up close and personal. The Declaration of Independence, the Constitution, and the Bill of Rights—collectively known as the Charters of Freedom—are on display here, in all their aged glory. They're sealed under glass in helium-filled cases; at night they are lowered some twenty feet into a 55-ton vault below. Hey, when you build a nation, you don't want to lose the instructions.

But there's lots more. This rotunda also houses tons of documents, maps, photographs, movies, and sound recordings created by the government over the past 200 years or so—all available for reference and research. There's even a copy of the Magna Carta, the early British document that is the basis for our own Bill of Rights. (It's on loan from Ross Perot; no wonder he wants he wants to work in Washington.)

Admission to the National Archives is free; you can visit between the hours of 10 A.M. and 9P.M. from April through Labor Day, and until 5:30 P.M. September through March. For recorded information, call (202) 501-5000

National Geographic Explorers Hall, 1145 17th St. NW, (202) 857-7588. Like a science project come to life, "Geographica" is filled with fun ways to explore the geography and ecology of th earth. Appropriately, it is located in the Explorers Hall on the first floor of the National Geographic Society's headquarters. Geographica is an interactive exhibit where you can touch a tornado, explore the solar system, gaze at the stars, and check the weather.

Space buffs shouldn't miss Earth Station One, a 72-seat amphitheater that takes you into orbit 23,000 miles above the earth—well, at least it feels that way. Earth Station One is also home to National Geographic's 11-foot, freestanding globe. Explorers Hall is open Mondays through Saturdays from 9 A.M. to 5 P.M., and Sundays 10 A.M. to 5 P.M. Admission is free.

Society of Cincinnati, 2118 Massachusetts Ave. NW, (202) 785-2040. Dupont Circle Metro station. This museum features many international art treasures of historic significance. It is housed in the Gilded Age Anderson House, the former home of an ambas-

Navy and Marine Corps Museums

9th and M Sts. SE. (202) 433-3534. Navy Museum is open Mon.–Fri. 9:00 A.M.–4:00 P.M., Sat. and Sun. 10:00 A.M.–5:00 P.M. Marine Corps Museum is open 10:00 A.M.– 5:00 P.M. daily, except Tuesday. Sun. noon–5:00 P.M. Navy Yard Metro station. Housed in the old Naval Gun Factory, the Navy Museum features a rigged fighting top from the frigate *Constitution* and a Gulf War Tomahawk missile. The Marine Corps Museum features memorabilia from the Marines history, going back to 1775. Outside, the USS *Barry,* a decommissioned Navy destroyer from 1955, allows visitors a peak into life at sea.

sador to Japan. The house was donated to the Society of Cincinnati in 1937, which was founded by Continental officers who had served in the American Revolution (George Washington was its first president). There are fifty rooms in the mansion, full of furnishings, paintings and tapestries, as well as artifacts from the American Revolution. There are regular special exhibits. Open Tues.–Sat. 1:00–4:00 P.M., closed Sunday and Monday, free admission.

National Museum of American Jewish Military History, 1811 R St., NW. (202) 265-6280. Mon.–Fri. 9:00 A.M.–5:00 P.M., Sun. 1:00–5:00 P.M. Closed Saturday. Dupont Circle Metro station. This museum documents the experiences of Jewish men and women in the U.S. armed forces through photos and memorabilia.

Textile Museum, 2330 S St. NW, next to the Woodrow Wilson House. (202) 667-0441. Open Mon.–Sat. 10:00 A.M.–5:00 P.M., Sun. noon–5:00 P.M. Examples and samples of textiles and fabrics from all over the world can be found at this museum. On the fourth floor, there is an interactive exhibit on textile making for children.

Chapter Ten

Sites of Historical Interest

Lincoln Artifacts

Although the Lincoln Museum at the Ford Theatre has a wealth of items from Lincoln's assassination, such as the gun Booth used, other artifacts from that night can be seen at different locations throughout the city.

• The Health & Medicine Museum has the bullet that killed Lincoln

• The Library of Congress has the contents of Lincoln's pockets from the night he was killed

• A blood-soaked pillow can be seen at the Peterson House

Washington, D.C. is one of the oldest cities in the nation, and since it was planned as the nation's capital, it is full of historic places that tell its story. Unlike other cities in the country, much of these historic moments were preplanned; their importance was known from the onset, and preservation was in mind at the time of the occurrence.

Washington, D.C. is also a city that has expanded outward, around the Potomac, so that the older, original part has not been continuously torn down and rebuilt for the next generation. This is only one of the reasons why a neighborhood like Georgetown, which was established before the city itself, can remain so full of the restored historic homes and sites we see today.

Though only one Civil War battle took place in Washington, D.C., it is amazing how much of the city's history, from the Arlington House and Arlington National Cemetery to Ford's Theatre and the Peterson House, was shaped by those four years.

Ford's Theatre

517 10th St. NW. (202) 426-6924. Self-guided tours 9:00 A.M.–5:00 P.M., except during rehearsals and performances. Closed Christmas Day. Metro Center Metro station.

Less than a week after General Lee had surrendered, the actor and Confederate sympathizer John Wilkes Booth shot President Lincoln at close range in the back of the head while he watched the play *Our American Cousin* in 1865. Ford's Theatre has kept the second story balcony booth draped in Presidential bunting.

From the time of Lincoln's death until the 1930s, Ford's Theatre was used as an office building and storage space, but when the Lincoln Museum was opened there in 1932, funds were raised for its restoration, and it has been managed by the National Park Service since then. The theatre was beautifully restored and now hosts a full season of theatrical performances.

Washington During the Civil War

Although no battles were fought in Washington, D.C. during the Civil War, the city became a virtual military camp, with armed troops housed everywhere from the White House to the alleys of the Foggy Bottom neighborhood, which was referred to as "camp-town." D.C. was the main storage area for military supplies for the Union Army, as well as a medical center. Many of the city's buildings, such as the U.S. Patent Building now the National Museum of American Art and the National Portrait Gallery were transformed into make-shift hospitals.

The population of the city swelled from 60,000 to 120,000 almost overnight. Many of the new residents were freed slaves who came to the city for protection (and many made their home on the grounds of the Arlington House, where they formed their own town, known as the Freedman's Village).

Five days after the city was celebrating the end of the Civil War, President Lincoln was assassinated, and the country went into mourning. The city itself was in chaos, both from the over-burdening of its resources with so many new residents, and the political upheaval. Many of the city's slums were created during this time, and the neighborhoods remained slums until well into the twentieth century.

Downstairs there's an extensive Lincoln Museum, which exhibits artifacts from the night Lincoln was shot such as the gun Booth used, the clothes Lincoln wore when he was shot, blood-stained pillow cases and towels, mourning memorabilia collected from throughout the nation, a cast of Lincoln's face and hand, as well as photos of the other conspirators in the assassination.

There is an extensive bookstore that includes videos, biographies and even puzzles of Abraham Lincoln.

Peterson House

516 10th St. NW. (202) 426-6924. Metro Center Metro station.

Lincoln died in a first floor back bedroom of the home of William Peterson, a tailor. Doctors knew immediately after he was shot that the head wound was mortal, and they did not dare move him to a Civil War hospital less than two blocks away (now the National Portrait Gallery on 10th St.).

The bed he lay in was too short for him, and he lay sideways for part of the night until the end piece was sawed off so his feet could hang out. Blood from his head injury is said to have soaked through seven pillows. A park ranger told me that a psychic who visited the room said she could see a mist rising from one of the blood soaked pillows.

Dumbarton Oaks

1703 32nd St. NW (between R and S Sts.). (202) 339-6401. Tues.–Sun. 2:00–5:00 P.M. Closed Monday, federal holidays, and Christmas Eve. No Metro access.

Dumbarton Oaks was the site of an international conference that lead to the creation of the United Nations in 1944. Today, the original Georgian mansion is the site of a museum of Byzantine art, and a newer addition designed by Philip Johnson houses a pre-Columbian art collection.

Lincoln Dreams of His Own Death

According to White House legend and John Alexander's *Ghosts; Washington Revisited*, one evening Lincoln dreamed that he heard crying throughout the White House. When he left his bedroom to see what was going on, he saw a crowd of people around a coffin. When he asked who had died, he was told, "The assassinated president." It is reported that when he looked in the open casket he saw himself.

Assassination Ghosts

Stories of the ghosts of those responsible for Lincoln's assassination are also told in Washington. There are those in the White House who swear that on the anniversary of the night of Mary Surratt's death, the ghost of her daughter appears at the front door, knocking and begging for her mother's life to be spared. In real life, Anna Surratt did knock on the door of the White House and pleaded for her mother's life the night before she was hanged. Some believe that Mary Surratt was unjustly tried and sentenced because it was her son who was a Booth compatriot and she owned the boarding house where the conspirators met and rented a room to the actor Booth.

Although some actors who have performed in the restored Ford's Theatre have said that they thought they had felt the presence of John Wilkes Booth as he made his escape from the theater (and one said he had seen Lincoln's face in the presidential booth), neither Booth nor Lincoln have been reported to be the most commonly seen ghosts of the assassination. Mary Surratt's ghost has been sighted at four locations: the Old Brick Capital where she was briefly imprisoned; on the grounds where she was hanged; inside her rooming house on 10th St., which is now a Chinese restaurant; and at her farm in Maryland.

Historic Houses

Hillwood Museum, 4155 Linnean Ave. NW (202) 686-8500. Open Tues.–Sat. 9:00 A.M. –4:30 P.M. Closed Sunday and Monday and entire month of February. $10 donation. Children under 12 not admitted. Former residence of the cereal heiress Marjorie Meriweather Post features a large collection of French and Russian art, greenhouse and formal gardens.

This Georgetown mansion is on a sixteen-acre plot that features some of the most beautiful gardens in Washington, D.C., which are open to the public in warm weather as part of the house tour. The historic music room, where the Dumbarton Oaks conversations took place, has a sixteenth-century stone fireplace as its focal point and also features French tapestries on the walls and El Greco's *Visitation*.

Woodrow Wilson House

2340 S St. NW. (202) 387-4062. Tues.–Sun. 10:00 A.M.–4:00 P.M. Docents lead tours beginning every half-hour, and you cannot wander the house on your own. Admission is $5 for adults, $4 for children. Closed on federal holidays, Thanksgiving Day, Christmas Day, and New Year's Day. Dupont Circle Metro station.

The Wilson House is the only museum of a former president in Washington, D.C. After Wilson left the presidency, private groups of friends and benefactors bought him this house, and a car, to make sure that he lived the remainder of his years in comfort.

Wilson and his second wife Edith lived here from 1921 until his death in 1924. The house offers a wonderfully preserved glimpse into the 1920s, with an antique phone, Victrola, radio consoles, and even an early GE refrigerator. The parlor still holds wedding presents the couple received, such as a tapestry from the ambassador to France. Long after Wilson left the presidency rules were passed to prevent presidents from taking official gifts and memorabilia, but the Wilson House is peppered with bits and pieces from his days in the White House, such as his White House desk chair and even presidential china.

Rumor has it that Wilson's ghost haunts the house, shuffling up and down stairs with the aid of his cane (which he used after a stroke), still disgruntled that his plans for the League of Nations did not come to fruition in his lifetime.

Special events at the Wilson House include a preservation Garden party in May and a spot on the annual Kalorama and Embassy tour in September. There is a small gift shop on the premises that sells Wilson memorabilia, including replicas of the Wilson china pattern.

Decatur House

748 Jackson Place, NW (corner of H St. on Lafayette Sq.). (202) 842-0920. Docents lead tours every half-hour. Tours are $4 for adults; $2.50 for students and seniors. Farragut West or Farragut North Metro stations.

This red brick Federal-style home was considered one of the first "decent" homes in the city when it was built in 1817. A War of 1812 naval hero and commodore Stephen Decatur hired Benjamin Latrobe, who also contributed to the design of the U.S. Capitol, to design his home. It quickly became a gathering place for the city's uppercrust until Commodore Decatur was killed in a duel only fourteen months after moving in.

His widow moved to Georgetown and quickly sold the house, which over the years has been home to Henry Clay, Martin Van Buren, and George Dallas. In was bought by a California family in the 1870s who furnished it with the Victorian taste of the time.

There is a large gift shop with an excellent selection of Americana and Victorian gifts. Special events include a showing of quilts with architectural themes in January and February; Mother's Day Open House in May; participation in the Federal City walking tour and Lafayette Sq. Open House in September, and a three-week long nineteenth-century Christmas display in December.

The Octagon

1799 New York Ave. NW. (202) 638-3221. Tues.–Sun. 10:00 A.M.–4:00 P.M. Closed Mondays. Guided tours are offered every half-hour at $3 for adults and $1.50 for students and seniors.

One of the oldest houses in the city (1789–1801), this was the temporary home of Dolley Madison and the president when they lived here while the White House was rebuilt after it burned down.

Historic Houses

Sewall-Belmont House, 144 Constitution Ave. NE, (202) 546-1210. Tues.–Fri. 11:00 A.M.–3:00 P.M., Sat. noon–4:00 P.M. closed Sundays and Mondays. Donation requested. This is a feminist museum and library in the home of suffrage leader Alice Paul, founder of the National Women's Party and drafter of the Equal Rights Amendment. It is the oldest house on Capitol Hill, with some parts dating back to 1680. Artifacts on view include the roll-top desk of Susan B. Anthony on which she is said to have drafted the nineteenth Amendment.

Black History Sites

Starting with its role as the mecca for freed slaves during and after the Civil War, and continuing through this century as the site of many major Civil Rights demonstrations, Washington D.C. has one of the nation's most extensive groupings of sites of historic significance to African-Americans. However, most of them are not close together.

Madison signed the Treaty of Ghent, ending the War of 1812, in the circular room at the circular desk on the second floor. The Madisons could watch the White House being constructed from the windows of this six-sided house (the children of its first occupants gave it its current name).

The townhouse was designed by Dr. William Thorton, one of the many architects of the U.S. Capitol building. It was built for the wealthy Tayloe family, who lived here with their fifteen children and slaves, and has a number of unique design features such as a three-story oval staircase and hidden doors. The English basement features a working kitchen and the servants quarters, which offer a glimpse of what life was like for servants during this time.

After the Tayloes moved out, the house became a girls school and eventually became a boarding house. The museum is now run by the American Architectural Foundation, which features changing exhibits about American architecture.

Heurich House

1307 New Hampshire Ave. NW (corner of 20th St. and New Hampshire Ave.). (202) 785-2068. Open Wed.–Sat. 10:00 A.M.–4:00 P.M. Admission is $3 for adults, $1.50 for students and seniors. Docent-guided tours are $5. Dupont Circle Metro station.

Even if you do not like meandering around old houses, the Heurich house is a one-of-a-kind experience and should not be missed. It was built at the turn of the century by eccentric beer magnate Christian Heurich, whose grandson has revived the family business and now offers a Foggy Bottom Ale on sale throughout the city.

The house is a unique combination of German beer garden and ornate Victorian flourishes. From the outside it looks like a castle, with a tower and arched portico doorway and a handful of gargoyles, human heads, and animals thrown in for design elements.

Inside it is crammed full of the carved wooden panels, wainscoting, and matching furniture that was popular to the nouveau riche of this time but that rarely survives today. The front parlor's ceiling is a painting of blue sky with angels of the seasons. The dining room is wall-to-ceiling carved oak and mahogany with matching fireplaces; carved wooden tables and chairs feature berries, fruit, and animals. The hallway is mauve with a stencilled gold fleur-de-lis-pattern. On the lower level, where the kitchen is, is a tavern room where Heurich had eight German drinking mottoes painted as frescos on the walls, offering such wisdom as "there is room in the smallest chamber for the biggest hangover."

Heurich had suffered two fires in his beer factories, so he ordered that his home be fireproof. As a result, this house on Dupont Circle is one of the first private residences in the country that used poured concrete as a foundation and is the first fireproof building in the city. Heurich was ahead of his time in many building innovations as well. His was one of the first homes to use electricity throughout the house (because of his fear of fire) as well as a "speaking tube" to communicate from one floor to the other and an electric bell system. He also used a coal-burning steam boiler to heat the house.

Special events at this museum include an annual Octoberfest in late September, with all you can eat and free beer for $3, and visits from the Heurich's grandchildren. The house is also done up in Victorian splendor for Christmas.

There's a small shop on the premises that sells old postcards of Washington, D.C., Victorian tea items, as well as a section for children. There is also a Victorian garden that is open to the public.

Cedar Hill

1411 W St. SE. (202) 426-5961. Open daily 9:00 A.M.–4:00 P.M., except Thanksgiving Day, Christmas Day, New Year's Day. National Park Ranger tour is $3 for adults, $1.40 for seniors. Anacostia Metro station and then the B2 bus, which stops in front of the house.

This last home of Frederick Douglass—freed slave, author, civil and women's rights orator, and U.S. Marshall of the District of Columbia in 1877—is far off the beaten track, but the tour is well worth it. Douglass bought Cedar Hill, a twenty-one-room mansion on a hill overlooking the Capitol, for $6,700 as a bankruptcy fore-closure and broke the neighborhood's "whites only" barrier.

Historic Houses

Tudor Place, 1644 31st St. NW. (202) 965-0400. Open Tues. –Sat. 10:00 A.M.—4:00 P.M. Guided tours all day. Donation of $6 for adults; $5 for seniors; $3 for students. Hourly tours available on the hour. The former home of Martha Washington's grand-daughter, Martha Parke Custis Peter, this 1805 Federal mansion was designed by William Thorton. It houses six generations of Washington memorabilia and furnishings. The house has an extensive garden which features a knot garden, period plants and old rose plants. There is a gift shop on the premises.

Banneker Circle & Fountain

L'Enfant Plaza near Maine and Water Sts. SW. This is a commemorative tribute to the African-American mathematician and astronomer Benjamin Banneker, who worked with Pierre L'Enfant to create the original design for the city of Washington D.C. in 1791.

• • •

Family Tree of Life Statue

16th & Colorado Sts. NW. In Rock Creek Park, this red oak fifteen-foot totem monument represents an African-American family.

Douglass moved into the house at the age of sixty, and walked the two miles to the Capitol every morning. He lived here with his first wife and five children for years. When she died, he married his white secretary, which many considered scandalous; his response was that his first wife was the color of his mother and his second the color of his father.

The house is furnished with the memories of a long career in public service. He was a close friend of Harriet Beecher Stowe and Abraham Lincoln, and Mrs. Lincoln had given him one of the president's canes. He had served as the U.S. Ambassador to Haiti, and a prized possession in the house is a leather rocking chair from the people of Haiti. He also had an extensive library and built himself a small brick house in the back of the property where he liked to work alone. Family members dubbed it "the Growlery" because he growled at anyone who bothered him there.

There is a half-hour movie of Douglass's life that plays in the Visitor's Center, which is extremely well done. There is also a gift shop that sells copies of his famous autobiography.

Mary McLeod Bethune House

1318 Vermont Ave. NW, (202) 673-2402. Mon.-Sat. 10:00 A.M.–4:00 P.M. McPherson Sq. Metro station. Every July 10th there is a birthday celebration the Victorian residence of Mary McLeod Bethune. Bethune, the child of freed slaves advised FDR and three other presidents, and created the National Council of Negro Women. She was also the founder of Bethune-Cookman College in Daytona, FL. The visitor's center shows a brief film on Bethune's life. This is also the site of the National Archives for Black Women's History, which is open by appointment. There is a treasure hunt through the council house for children.

Martin Luther King Jr. Library

901 G. St. N.W. (202) 727-1126. The main branch of the Washington D.C. library, and an architectural landmark, The Martin Luther King Jr. Library was designed by International style architect Ludwig Mies van der Rohe. It also serves as a memorial to the

slain Civil Rights leader and contains a large mural by Don Miller on the life of Martin Luther King, Jr. that rivals any of the WPA murals of the 30's. The library often hosts events related to the life of Martin Luther King, Jr., as well as special events during black history month.

Freedom Plaza

On Pennsylvania Ave., is a national park that lies between the Ronald Reagan Building, the National Theatre, the Warner Theatre and the J.W. Marriott Hotel near the Federal Triangle Metro station. It is named after the freedom rally in which Martin Luther King, Jr. delivered his "I Have a Dream" speech. In the summer, there are frequent concerts and performances. It is a favorite hangout for the city's skate-boarders.

Lincoln Park

E. Capitol St. between 11th and 13th Sts. N.E. Although the park honors Abraham Lincoln and features a statue of him commissioned in 1876, the real draw here is the Emancipation Statue. This statue, which was built from funds raised by freed slaves, depicts Archer Alexander, the last slave captured under the Fugitive Slave Law, breaking the chains of slavery while President Lincoln reads the Emancipation proclamation. There is also a statue of Mary McCleud Bethune in the Park, which was erected in 1974.

Sumner School Museum and Archives

1201 17th St. NW. at M. St. (202) 727-6812. Open Mon.–Fri., but call to make sure the school is open to the public. Local legend has it that Sen. Charles Sumner petitioned for this school for freed slaves to be taxed so that it could be accredited. It opened in 1872 and became the city's first public school for African-Americans. Today it is also the archive center for the D.C. public school system, as well as a museum on Martin Luther King, Jr., Frederick Douglass and Washington, D.C. history. In the permanent collection

Historic Churches and Places of Worship

Franciscan Monastery, 1400 Quincy St. NE. (202) 526-6800. Mon.-Sat. 9:00 A.M. –4:00 P.M., Sun. 1:00–4:00 P.M. Located on forty-four acres of land, it is dotted with replicas of Holy Land shrines surrounding a turn-of-the-century Byzantine-style church. Tours of Roman-style catacombs are given on the hour.

St. John's Church, 16th & H Sts., NW. (202) 347-7866. Called the Church of Presidents, this nineteenth-century Episcopalian church has seen every president from James Madison to Bill Clinton worship here.

St. Matthew's Cathedral, 1725 Rhode Island Ave. NW. (202) 347-3215. Open Sun.–Fri. 6:30 A.M.–6:30 P.M., Sat. 7:30 A.M.–6:30 P.M. Guided tour Sunday at 2:30 P.M. Most Washingtonians pass this red brick church without realizing it was the site of JFK's funeral in 1963.

Important Black Churches

Calvary Baptist Church
755 8th St. NW (202) 347-8355. One of the oldest black churches in Washington and one of the stops on the underground railroad, this church was attended by General Oliver Howard, one of the founders of Howard University.

• • •

Ebenezer Methodist Church
420 D St. SE. (202) 544-1415. Open Mon.–Fri. 8:30 A.M.–3:00 P.M. Capitol South Metro station. The site of the first public school for African Americans. in 1975, the church was designated as a landmark by the D.C. government.

there is an 1877 diploma from one of the first graduates, which was the first class of black high school graduates in the city.

African-American Civil War Memorial

10th and U Sts. N.W. (202) 667-2667. U St. Cardozo Metro station. A stone and bronze commemorative statue grouping created by Paul Devoraux, Jr. to the more than 200,000 African-American Union soldiers and their white officers who fought during the Civil War. There is a visitor's center with a database where you can look up the history of those honored by the memorial.

Howard University

2400 6th St. N.W. (202) 806-6100. Howard University was founded in 1866 as a liberal arts college and university to educate the nearly four million emancipated African Americans of the time. It was named after white Civil War General Oliver O. Howard, Commissioner of the Freedman's Bureau, and one of the university's founders and third president. His home, on Georgia Ave., is a historic landmark.

The Gallery of Art in the College of Fine Arts features the permanent Alain Locke African collection and changing exhibitions. The Moorland-Springarn Research center houses the country's largest collection of information on the history and culture of African-Americans.

Black Fashion Museum

207 Vermont Ave. NW, (202) 667-0744. By appointment only, but group tours are welcome. A private museum started by Lois K. Alexander-Lane, a former president of the National Association of Fashion and Accessory designers and a member of the National Association of Milliners, Dressmakers, and Tailors, this features the designs of Anne Lowe, Elizabeth Beckley, Patrick Kelley, Thony Anyiam, Edward Burke, Bill Washington and others. It also displays a collection of bridal gowns from the slave era to the present.

Who Was
Frederick Douglass?

Frederick Douglass was the first African-American nationally renowned Civil Rights leader. After he escaped from slavery (and purchased his freedom), he wrote and published his autobiography, *Life of Frederick Douglass*, which became an international best-seller. He traveled extensively throughout the north and the world telling first-hand of the injustices and horrors of slavery in the South.

When he returned to the United States, he printed an abolitionist newspaper out of Rochester N.Y., and oversaw the Rochester activities of the underground railroad. When he attended the first women's rights convention in 1848, he also became an ardent supporter of women's rights.

He became a confidante to Presidents Abraham Lincoln and Andrew Johnson regarding black suffrage, but turned down Johnson's offer to be the head of the Freedman's Bureau. Instead he became the first president of the Freedman's Bank, where he thought he could do more good.

He served the country as U.S. Marshall, recorder of deeds in Washington, D.C., and the American consul-general to Haiti. When he died in 1895, thousands attended his funeral.

Georgetown Walking Tour

Georgetown is the oldest part of Washington, D.C. and was a town, founded in 1751, before there was even a nation to build a capital city for. It was named after King George II and featured cobblestone streets, some of which still exist around Georgetown University, where Bill Clinton went to school (he is the only president to have gone to college in D.C.). Many of the houses are very narrow (a pink one-bedroom on M St. that is only 9$\frac{1}{2}$ ft. wide recently sold for $375,000) because houses in the colony were taxed by width.

Georgetown has always been the home to the city's influential and well-known, and houses here have belonged to Alexander Graham Bell, Louisa May Alcott, Elizabeth Taylor when she was married to Senator Warren, Sylvester Stallone, Arnold Schwarzenegger, and countless politicians such as Kennedy and Kissinger (3026 M St.).

A number of movies have been filmed in Georgetown as well. The most famous are *The Exorcist*, *St. Elmo's Fire*, *The Pelican Brief*, and *No Way Out*.

Start your walking tour at the Old Stone House (3051 N St.), considered to be the oldest building in the city. It was built in 1765 by carpenter Christopher Layman, who had his workshop on the first floor. This four-room museum is now furnished in eighteenth century decor and open free to the public Wednesday through Sunday from 9:00 A.M.–5:00 P.M.

Walk down Jefferson Street to the Chesapeake & Ohio Canal Lock (between M and K St.) where you can see this important link to the shipping history of Georgetown. The C&O Canal was supposed to link with the Ohio River so that products could be shipped a total of 185 miles, but railroad use made this method of transportation a thing of the past. Visitors can still travel on barges (mule drawn ones at that) and canoes on the canal.

Walk down K St. until it intersects with Wisconsin Ave. and you should find a fence, inside of which is a worn plaque identifying this site as Suter's Tavern, where George Washington and Pierre L'Enfant are said to have planned the city of Washington in 1790. No one knows for sure exactly where the tavern was situated.

Up Wisconsin Ave. and on the corner of Grace St. you will find the C&O Canal Commemorative Marker. This granite stone is the only record of the canal in existence today, and it commemorates the completion of the canal in 1850. It lies right outside The Shops at Georgetown, a four-story mall that features a food court, Benihana, and Clyde's restaurants, and everything from bead stores to barber shops.

At 1066 Wisconsin Ave. is the Vigilant Firehouse, the oldest volunteer firefighter brigade in Washington, which was founded in 1817. The firehouse was built in 1844 and is now a restaurant that still bears the large "V" for Vigilant near its roof.

Further along M St. is the City Tavern (3206 M St.). Built in 1796, this tavern was the main terminal for the stagecoach line in Georgetown and once hosted President John Adams for dinner on his inspection of the new city.

It's hard to believe that a city that has preserved so much of its history allowed Francis Scott Key's house to be torn down to make way for a freeway exit ramp. All that is left is the Francis Scott Key Memorial Site (3518 M St.), which is a public park and a marker for the former home of the author of *The Star-Spangled Banner*.

Further along M St., turn at 35th St. and you will reach Prospect St. Here you will find the site of *The Exorcist* stairs, which were built on the site of Southworth Cottage (3600 Prospect St.), the former home of a Victorian novelist. There are now two townhouses and the long stairs (to Canal St.) where the movie *The Exorcist* was shot. This is a favorite haunt of the university crowd around Halloween.

Walk up 35th St. to N St. and on the corner of 33rd St. you will find The Marbury House (3307 N. St.) where Senator and Mrs. Kennedy lived before they moved into the White House in 1961. It had been built for William Marbury in 1812.

Walk up 33rd St. and turn right at Q St. and you will come to Tudor Place (1644 31st St., (202) 965-0400). William Thorton, who designed the Octagon and had a hand in the design of the U.S.

Clinton's First Electoral Defeat

According to Georgetown University records, in 1967, as a junior at the school of Foreign Service, William Jefferson Clinton ran for president of the East Campus Student Council but lost to a classmate. GU legend has it that he lost to a much lesser-known candidate over his willingness to unite all five of G.U.'s undergraduate schools. Many felt he had collaborated with the university's administration, who wanted the unification.

Capitol, designed this home for Martha Washington's granddaughter, who married the mayor of Georgetown. The house is now a museum of Washington memorabilia. Open Tues.–Sat. for guided tours only with admission.

Walk Along Q St. until you get to 29th St. and then head to R St., where you will come to the large, fenced Victorian Oak Hill Cemetery, which was established by William Corcoran, who is also buried here, in 1850. The chapel was designed by James Renwick (Smithsonian Castle and original Corcoran Gallery architect), and even the gatehouse (3001 R St.) is quite beautiful. If you stroll the grounds, you will see some beautiful pieces of Southern Victorian mourning sculpture such as winged angels. You can get a map of the gravesites at the gatehouse, and the cemetery is open 10:00 A.M.–4:00 P.M. on weekdays. Other gravesites of note include Lincoln's twelve-year-old son, Willie, Lincoln's Secretary of War Edwin Stanton, presidential candidate James Blaine, and former Mayor of Washington John Peter Van Ness.

Just around the corner from the Oak Hill Cemetery is Evermay (1623 28th St. NW), a huge, quirky red brick mansion that looks like something out of an Edgar Allan Poe story. You can't enter, but you can walk along its brick wall and peer in at this home of Scottish bachelor Samuel Davidson who once took out an ad about his property that warned his neighbors to avoid "Evermay as they would a den of evils, or rattlesnakes, and thereby save themselves and me much vexation and trouble." When he died, his will forced his nephew to change his name to Davidson in exchange for the estate.

On Q and 28th St. is The Gun Barrel Fence, which stretches about a half a block and looks wholly unspectacular until you realize that is was made from the guns and recovered metal from the Old Navy Yard after it was burned by the British in 1814.

Walk back down 28th St. to N St. until you get to 30th St. and you will be standing in front of The French House (3017 N St.), which is where Jacqueline Kennedy lived for a year after her husband's assassination in 1963.

Chapter Eleven

Other Important Attractions

Washington D.C. MAP

Not only is Washington, D.C. a great city for museums and historical and government sites, but it has some truly fabulous buildings and arts centers that compete with those of other major cities, some that are truly unique.

John F. Kennedy Center for the Performing Arts

New Hampshire Ave NW (at Rock Creek Parkway at the tip of F St.). (800) 444-1324 for information or tickets. Free performances daily at the Millennium Stage. The Center is open daily for tours 10:00 A.M. until midnight. Guided tours are given Mon.–Fri. 10:00 A.M.–6:00 P.M., Sat. and Sun. 10:00 A.M.–2:00 P.M. Foggy Bottom Metro station (three's a free shuttle from the metro station).

The John F. Kennedy Center for the Performing Arts is a living memorial tribute to President Kennedy and is our nation's premier performing arts center. It houses five theaters and is home to the National Symphony Orchestra, the Washington Opera, and the American Film Institute.

The Kennedy Center is built on seventeen acres of land overlooking the Potomac. It was designed by Edward Stone (who designed the GM building in New York) in the International architectural style of the 70's, with lots of marble and glass. The free fifty-minute guided tour starts at the Hall of Nations, where the flags of the countries that the United States has diplomatic relations with are on display in alphabetical order. Throughout the Kennedy Center are gifts sent by various nations, such as the Swedish modern chandeliers, the Belgian mirrors, and the marble itself, which was contributed by Italy.

The next stop on the tour is the Grand Foyer, where free concerts are given and the signature giant bronze bust of President Kennedy's head by Robert Berks is on view. It is also the reception area for all three theaters on the main floor.

The tour will take you through the Israeli Room, where panels from the Old Testament adorn the walls, and the African Room, which displays beautiful tapestries donated by various African nations. The tour leads you through the Concert Hall, which is the largest auditorium in the building with 2,700 seats, where the National Symphony Orchestra performs and the Opera House, which has 2,200 seats and an interior decor of red and gold. There is also a smaller Eisenhower Theatre, which seats 1,100 and is wood-panelled, and the newer Terrace Theatre, which was donated by Japan as a Bicentennial gift, where chamber concerts are performed. There are also two smaller theaters: the Theatre Lab, which seats 380 people, and the American Film Institute's theatre, which seats 200. You will end your tour in the Hall of States, where the flags of the fifty states and four territories are displayed in the order they joined the nation.

The view from the roof terrace is stupendous. If there are no performances, you will be allowed to visit. There are also two excellent restaurants on the premises.

You can obtain free tickets for performances by writing to your representative or senator before your arrival.

Folger Shakespeare Library

201 E. Capitol St. SE. (202) 544-7077. Mon.–Sat. 10:00 A.M.–4:00 P.M. Closed federal holidays. Free guided tours at 11:00 A.M. Capitol South Metro station.

This incredible collection of Shakespearean plays, memorabilia, and artifacts was amassed by an Amherst student after hearing Ralph Waldo Emerson lecture on his love of the Bard. Henry Clay Folger began the collection by buying a cheap set of Shakespeare's plays and from there went on to put together the world's largest collection of Shakespeare's printed works, now housed in the Folger Shakespeare Library.

On the exterior of the marble building are nine raised Art Deco reliefs depicting scenes from Shakespeare's plays. A statue of Puck, from *A Midsummer's Night Dream*, stands in the west garden, and there are quotes from Shakespeare and his contemporaries etched onto the facade.

On the east side of the building is an Elizabethan garden, with flowers and herbs from Shakespeare's time. In warm weather the garden is included in the Library tour.

The Millennium Stage at the JFK Center

The Millennium Stage at the JFK Center for the Performing Arts features free concerts every evening at 6:00 P.M. (they are also broadcast on the Internet) for 400 people. It was started in 1997 as part of the Performing Arts for Everyone Initiative, and has been so successful that a mirror project was started in 1998 on the grounds of the U.S. Capitol during the summer months.

The Library is an active research center for both Shakespearean scholars and those who wish to research English and Renaissance history and literature. There are more than a quarter of a million books on hand, many of which are very rare, such as early editions of Shakespeare's plays. The collection also features a number of rare Renaissance manuscripts, musical instruments, costumes, and paintings. The Reading Room, which is only open to the public in April during the Library's annual celebration of Shakespeare's birth, houses a replica of the bust of Shakespeare on view at Stratford's Trinity Church. At the other end is a stained glass window showing the seven ages of man from *As You Like It*.

The interior Great Hall is chock full of Shakespeare-related decor, from the wood-paneled walls with a carved relief of the Bard to the painted plaster ceiling depicting Shakespeare's coat of arms to the tiled floor inlaid with the masks of Comedy and Tragedy.

Special exhibits on the works of Shakespeare, as well as other Renaissance interests, are on view throughout the year. The Library also hosts PEN-Faulkner readings, poetry readings, and a concert series.

There is a performance space designed to resemble an Elizabethan theatre with a three-tiered gallery, carved oak columns, and a sky balcony at the end of the Great Hall. Performances are given here throughout the year.

There is also an extensive gift shop on the premises.

Union Station

50 Massachusetts Ave. NE. Open twenty-four hours, but most restaurants and the movie theaters close by 11:00 P.M. Union Station Metro station.

Built at the turn of the century during the great railroad age, Union Station was once the largest railway station in the world and an important center of Washington, D.C. life for many years (Roosevelt's funeral train left here amidst thousands of mourners). It later fell into disrepair and became a place that people avoided. In 1981 it was renovated to the tune of $160 million and has once again become an important part of Washington's bustling life. It is now even the site of a number of charity events and gala evenings in the station's Main Hall beneath its ninety-six-foot-high gilded vaulted ceiling.

The station was designed by Daniel Burnham, who incorporated a number of neoclassical design elements, as well as American motifs. The design was based on the ancient Baths of Diocletian and the Arch of Constantine in Rome, featuring arches, and Ionic columns, and 100 eagles on the white granite facade. In front of the building is a replica of the Liberty Bell, and a huge statue of Columbus greets visitors as they disembark and grab a cab. Above the arched entry way are six carved figures representing Fire, Electricity, Freedom, Imagination, Agriculture, and Mechanics.

Inside the Main Hall are a total of forty-eight statues of Roman soldiers designed by Augustus Saint-Gaudens (one each for the states that were in existence at the time of the station's construction). The East Hall, with its marble walls, a hand stencilled skylight, and bright murals, is now a shopping arcade that features more than 135 stores from Ann Taylor to The Gap.

A number of very good restaurants are featured in the Main Hall of the Station (America, B. Smith, Thunder Grill), as well as a food court on the lower level that supplies more than forty varieties of faster food from burgers to sushi. The lower level also features a nine-theater movie complex, where films are shown in the carved-out underground passageways of the former train station.

Both Amtrak trains and Greyhound buses come and go from the station.

Washington National Cathedral

Massachusetts and Wisconsin Aves. NW (202) 537-6207. Open daily from 10:00 A.M.–4:30 P.M., the nave level is open weeknights until 9:00 P.M. Daily evensong service at 4:00 P.M., noon service Mon.–Sat., 11:00 A.M. service on Sun. Tenleytown Metro station, then a long walk along Wisconsin Ave. or hop on a bus.

Designed to be Your Church in the Nation's Capitol, (it is an Episcopal church with a nondenominational congregation), Washington National Cathedral stands higher than the Washington Monument and crowns a fifty-seven-acre plot of land at the capital's highest point. It is

Philip Randolphe Statue at Union Station

This larger-than-life-sized bronze statue that greets visitors to Union Station when they arrive by train at Gate C depicts the founder of the Sleeping Car Porters Union and the Civil Rights Activist who organized the famous 1963 March on Washington.

the sixth largest cathedral in the world and took a total of eighty-three years to complete (in 1990).

Its exterior and interior feature an incredible collection of gargoyles from the traditional to Darth Vader, which was designed by a twelve-year-old boy in an annual competition. New gargoyles are added every year.

This church is designed in the fourteenth-century English Gothic style, complete with flying buttresses. It has many beautiful stained glass windows, but the one that draws the most attention is the "space" window commemorating *Apollo 11*, which contains a chunk of moon rock.

In the crypts on the lower level lie the sarcophagi of President and Mrs. Wilson, as well as Helen Keller and her companion, Anne Sullivan.

There is an observation gallery that you get to by elevator where you can see a panoramic view of Washington, D.C. from a very different perspective.

There is also a lovely garden and an extensive gift shop that offers many gargoyle-related items, tea services, and cookbooks. The selection of jewelry for sale is quite comprehensive.

Guided tours are given all day and highlight many of the different and offbeat aspects of the cathedral, from a gargoyle tour to a behind-the-scenes tour that takes you up slender staircases. Tours suggest a donation of $2 per adult, $1 per child.

There is also an incredible medieval arts and craft workshop for children every Saturday from noon–4:00 (see especially for children) and afternoon tea on Tuesday and Wednesday afternoons (see Chapter 5 on dining in D.C.).

Pentagon

Off I-309 or take the Metro to the Pentagon station. (703) 695-1776. Guided tours Mon.–Fri. 9:30 A.M.–3:30 P.M. every thirty minutes. Closed weekends and federal holidays.

The five-sided headquarters of the U.S. military is the world's largest office building and houses more than 24,000 employees. It is huge in every sense of the word, from the 583 acres of land it occupies on to the $17\frac{1}{2}$ miles of interior corridors, about a mile of which you will have to walk through on the hour and a half tour, so wear very comfortable shoes.

You have to pass through airport-quality security before you begin the tour, which starts at the Concourse area of the Metro station. There is a short film about the development of the Pentagon, which was built just after WWII in sixteen months on former swamp land for $83,000 and consolidated seventeen buildings of the War Department. Tours were opened to the public in 1976 and were expected to be discontinued after the Fourth of July, but they turned out to be very popular so the Pentagon has continued the service.

The tour includes visits to the Air Force Art Collection, which includes some of Walt Disney's early cartoons that he did while he was an ambulance driver in WWI, as well as more traditional art depicting historic events in Air Force history. You then pass the executive offices of the Air Force and the POW Alcove, where paintings of POW camps are hung. Next you will pass the Marine Corps Corridor and then the Navy Corridor, where models of ships and submarines are on display in glass cases. Next is the Army Corridor where the army command and divisional flags and 172 army campaign streamers from just after the Revolutionary War to the present are on display.

Next up is the *Time-Life* Corridor, where civilian artists' paintings of war commissioned by *Time-Life* during WWI hang. The MacArthur Corridor honors General MacArthur's fifty-two-year military career. The hall of heroes commemorates the 3,409 Medal of Honor recipients. The Military Women's Corridor tells the story of women in the military. The Navajo Code Talkers Corridor honors the 400 Navajo marines who created an indecipherable-to-enemies communication code based on the Navajo language to use during WWII. The two newest additions to the Pentagon tour are the African-Americans Corridor and the Hispanic Heroes Corridor. The Flag Corridor displays state and territorial flags throughout the nation's history.

The Pentagon cafeterias are not open to the public, but there is a mall inside the Pentagon with two banks, an Amtrak station, and a post office.

Newseum and Freedom Park

1101 Wilson Blvd. (at N. Kent St.). (703) 284-3544. Wed.–Sun. 10:00 A.M.–5:00 P.M. Closed Monday, Tuesday, and federal holidays. Rossalyn Metro station.

Facts about the Pentagon

- The Pentagon contains enough cable to circle the globe three times?
- There are 4,200 clocks and 691 water fountains in the Pentagon
- 200,000 phone calls a day are made here
- 250 light bulbs are replaced every day

This is an interactive museum dedicated to journalism, its history, and changing technology. The heart of the Newseum is a 126-foot-long Video News Wall where breaking news is broadcasted from around the world. The global reaction is also on display.

Below the video wall are the front pages of newspapers from fifty states and foreign countries, so you can see how the stories are played in different regions.

Kids love the chance to make their own newscast or radio announcement, which can be purchased for $7. There are also touch-screen exhibits to test your investigative reporting, photojournalist, or news editor skills and decide what stories make the front page.

In the News History Gallery visitors learn how news evolved from an oral tradition to the printed page to the satellite feed and the Web. Included in this exhibit are interesting artifacts such as a Gutenberg Bible and Charles Dickens's pen. There is also a collection of newspapers, magazines, and vintage newscasts from major events in history.

There's a snack bar for lunch and a shop that sells news-related merchandise.

The nearby Freedom Park, which is open from dawn till dusk, is dedicated to the spirit of freedom throughout the world. There's a chunk of the Berlin Wall on display here, a toppled, headless statue of Lenin, a bronze casting of Martin Luther King, Jr.'s Birmingham, Alabama jail cell door, stones from the Warsaw ghetto, and a casting of a South African ballot box.

At the center of Freedom Park is the glass and steel Freedom Forum Journalists Memorial, which honors journalists who have died while trying to report the news. The monument bears 1,000 names, dating back from 1812.

Ronald Reagan Building and International Trade Center, 1300 Pennsylvania Ave. NW, (202) 312-1300. Federal Triangle metro station. Open seven days a week. The food court is open until 8:00 P.M. but the building itself is open until midnight. Guided tours are given Mon., Wed., and Fri. at 11:00 A.M. One of the newest Federal buildings in the city (and certainly the newest on Pennsylvania Ave.), the Reagan Trade building was designed by James Ingo Freed, who was the architect for the U.S. holocaust Museum and memorial. There is a giant slab of the Berlin Wall covered with graffiti when you enter from the Federal Triangle side and an underground food court that caters to office workers. The walls are lined with contemporary artworks and there is a gift shop selling Reagan memorabilia. By using the Federal Triangle entrance, the Trade Center is also a great shortcut to the mall on an extremely hot or cold day.

Old Post Office Pavilion, 1100 Pennsylvania Ave. NW, (202) 606-8691. Free tours daily 8:00 A.M.–11:00 P.M. Federal Triangle Metro station. Built in 1899, the Old Post Office Pavilion was once the largest government building in Washington. It was the first public building with a clock tower and electric power. Only eighteen years after it was built, it started to be referred to as "old," because a new post office has been built at Union Station. It was slated for demolition in the 1920's, but the depression saved the building, which many now appreciate for its beaux arts design. A statue of Benjamin Franklin stands outside the building to remind us that he was our first postmaster general. The building now houses a number of shops, a food court and the office of TICKETplace (202TICKETS) where you can buy half-price tickets for concert and theatre events the day of the show. The Clock Tower is open for tours and offers a splendid view of the city.

House of the Temple Library, 1733 16th St., NW (202) 232-3579. Open Mon.–Fri. 8:00–3:45 P.M. Free tours Mon.–Fri. 8:00 A.M.–2:00 P.M. Dupont Circle Metro station. This was the site of the first public library in the city and is now the headquarters for the Scottish Rite of Freemasons. The neoclassical building is guarded by stone sphinxes. There is a museum, archives and a research library on the premises.

The Washington Post Newsroom

Tours of the inner workings of the *Washington Post* are available by appointment on Mondays at 10:00 and 11:00 A.M. and 1:00, 2:00 and 3:00 P.M., but they are free. Because this is a working newspaper, children under 12 are not permitted on the tours. Call (202) 334-7969 for appointment. The tour is lead by a specially trained *Post* guide who will take you through the newsroom, where you can see reporters gathering information and writing their stories. Stops include pre-press production, and a visit to the presses, which print the day's papers. You will also be taken to the circulation department and the hot type museum, where you'll see how newspapers were once produced.

Chapter Twelve

Especially for Children

Washington, D.C. is a city that has been hosting family vacations for generations, so it's not surprising that there are so many attractions and museums that are geared to children or the young at heart. It is also a place where countless school children have been taken on class trips and is therefore very child friendly, from the restaurants in the Smithsonian to those around the Mall. The following listings may extend beyond the Beltway, but all are in easy reach by Metro or car.

MCI National Sports Gallery

601 F St. NW, on 7th St., on the third floor of the MCI Center, (202) 661-5133. Open 11:00 A.M.–6:00 P.M. daily, open until 10:00 P.M. if there is an evening game. Admission is $7 for ten tokens and exhibits; $15 for one hour's worth of play and exhibits; $32 family rate includes one hour of play and exhibits. General admission without tokens is $5, children under five are free. Gallery Place Metro station.

A child or grown-up who is at all into sports (everything from football to golf) will never want to leave this place. Aside from an interesting two-floor collection of sports memorabilia, there are hundreds of challenging interactive sports games to be played here. Local kids hold their birthday parties here.

The highlights of the sports artifacts collection on display are Babe Ruth's bat (which you can touch) and the only ball Ruth ever signed, the 1909 T206 Honus Wagner card; the only known Joe Jackson autographed bat; the last touchdown ball thrown by Joe Montana; the first baseball (from 1839); Muhammad Ali's boxing gloves and red velvet shorts; Rocky Marciano's robe; Washington Bullets' 1978 NBA trophy; Joe Louis's heavyweight belt; Ty Cobb's uniform; Oksana Baiul's dress from the 1994 Olympics, and one of Arnold Palmer's drivers. There is a special exhibit that features Mark McGwire's 1987 rookie card and baseball jerseys worn by Sammy Sosa and McGwire in 1998.

One of the most interesting exhibits is a recreated Redskins huddle, where you can place your head in a football helmet and hear Joe Theisman call the famous play for fullback John Riggins who scored the game-breaking touchdown against the Miami Dolphins in Super Bowl XVII.

The Sports Center is also the home of the American Sportscasters Hall of Fame, where interactive displays feature the sportscasting legends of Red Barber, Mel Allen, Jim McKay, Harry Caray, Howard Cosell, and Curt Gowdy. Fans can recreate early radio broadcasts or dial up their favorite sportscaster's most famous call in this exhibit area on the top floor.

Interactive games (for which you need tokens) include a basketball H-O-O-P-S shootout, a baseball batting and pitching game, a hockey goal-shooting game, a soccer game against an on-screen goalkeeper, a golf game that replicates the eighteenth hole at the MCI Heritage Classic in Hilton Head, a football game where you get to be quarterback, a downhill skiing experience, and the opportunity to be a sportscaster. There are also indoor tennis courts.

The Discovery Channel Store

601 F St. NW, in the MCI Sports Center. (202) 639-0908. Open 10:00 A.M.–9:00 P.M. Mon.–Sat., noon–6:00 P.M. Sun. *Destination D.C.* film is $2.50 for adults, $1.50 for children and seniors. Gallery Place Metro station.

This four-floor store is designed like a museum where you can buy things. I imagine it would be virtually impossible to come here with kids and not buy something, but the experience is worth it and there are many items on sale (most between 30 and 50 percent off), so you don't have to dent your wallet too hard.

When you enter the store, you're in Paleo World where there's a replica of a T Rex skeleton that the kids can get much closer to than in a museum. In this same area you have the opportunity to buy a mammal skull for $4,300, mammoth molars for $4,000 or dinosaur eggs for $15,000. There's also a good selection of geodes and fish fossils embedded in rock for you to purchase (or just look at).

The second level features Ocean Planet where you can experience a shipwreck staring up through a virtual ocean created with a ceiling of cracked glass and colored light. There's also a display on famous shipwrecks, including the *Titanic*.

The third floor is devoted to animal habitats and there's a giant ant colony, as well as interactive computer displays on various creatures. The fourth level features the environment with many instructive displays such as tornadoes and astronomy.

The fifth floor is devoted to space, with a model of a B-52 bomber that you can walk through and a flight simulator game. The top floor allows you to peer through telescopes and visit the Hubble Observatory to see its most recent findings about the stars. There are also interactive displays on weather, medicine, engineering, and biology.

On the top floor is the DC Theater, which features the film *Destination D.C.*, a fifteen-minute, high-definition tour of the city.

National Geographic Society's Explorer's Hall

17th & M Sts. NW, (202) 857-7588. Mon.–Sat. 9:00 A.M.–5:00 P.M., Sun. 10:00 A.M.–5:00 P.M. Closed Christmas Day. Farragut North or Farragut West Metro stations.

Kids love this place almost as much as the huge National Museum of Natural History, and it's much smaller. There are many interactive exhibits, such as giant slides in a microscope, and an exhibit in which they can touch a tornado. Everyone comes here to see the *Aepyornis maximus* egg from the extinct elephant bird. Other objects on display include a replica of a giant Olmec stone from 32 B.C., the dog sled from Admiral Perry's trek to the North Pole, and a full-scale model of Jacques Costeau's diving craft.

There's a geology exhibit where you can see inside the Earth and another where you can explore Martian terrain. A circle in the round theater explains the earth's weather and ecology.

The Explorer's hall always has new and interesting exhibits that change monthly. The museum store has an extensive display of books, science-related toys, and ecological items for children.

Capital Children's Museum

800 3rd St. NW, (202) 675-4120. $6 per person, children under two free, seniors $4, AAA members $5. Union Station Metro station.

A hands-on education complex right near Union Station, the Capital Children's Museum has a number of intriguing permanent exhibits, as well as special exhibits. The Chemical Science Center features interactive experiments with "scientists" in lab coats for children over six. The Cityscapes exhibit area gives kids a chance to slide down a fire pole, drive a Metro bus, navigate a maze, and stand inside a bubble. Kids can also put on their own puppet show and have their faces painted. There's also the opportunity to explore an Ice Age cave.

Another popular exhibit is on animation, in which an interactive exhibit teaches children how cartoons are made from start to finish. There are old-fashioned animation machines, as well as sound effects machines, and kids can create their own cartoons and view their work.

There are two exhibit areas on the culture of Mexico and Japan. In the Mexican exhibit area, kids can make and taste chocolate and tortillas, and they can make arts and crafts to take home. There is also a replica of a Mayan pyramid and a Yucatan beach. The Japanese exhibit features a contemporary Japanese home, including a Tatami Room where kids can sit at the traditional low table (Kotatsu) and learn to use chopsticks. They can also try on Japanese school children's uniforms, examine kimonos, and learn about the Japanese language and alphabet. The exhibit also features a simulated ride on a Bullet train and a Japanese shopping street, where children can put together their own Bento box lunch with plastic items.

Discovery Creek Children's Museum

5125 MacArthur Blvd. (202) 364-3111. Sat. 10:00 A.M.–3:00 P.M.; Sun. noon–3:00 P.M. $4 for children; adults are free.

Located in the only remaining one-room schoolhouse in Washington, D.C., this children's museum's focus is on interacting with nature, since it lies in the beautiful Rock Creek Park. The museum's events change seasonally, especially since so much of the program is based on interacting with nature.

Kid Fun at Mount Vernon

There are a number of activities and experiences geared toward children at George Washington's home in Virginia (see chapter 13). Kids can learn to build a colonial fence, play a variety of eighteenth century games and harness a fiberglass "mule." There's also a special "treasure hunt" for kids, which you can pick up at the main gate. If you've brought a camera, there's an opportunity to have the kids dress up in colonial garb for a picture.

American Girl Doll Program at the Heurich House

This quirky turn-of-the-century mansion of a Washington Beer magnate offers an American Girl doll program for girls. You can tour the Victorian mansion led by a costumed guide, make paper fans, and then have tea and petit fours in the conservatory, or, if you've packed a picnic lunch, have your meal in the secluded Victorian gardens. Call (202) 785-2068 for more information.

Washington Dolls' House and Toy Museum

5236 44th St. NW, (202) 363-6400. Tues.–Sat. 10:00 A.M.–5:00 P.M.; Sun. noon–5:00 P.M. $4 for adults, $3 for seniors, $2 for children. Friendship Heights Metro station.

A small museum that's a bit out of the way, but if you or your children are interested in antique toys, this is a charming short trip. Every corner of this museum is packed with old dolls, toys, games, and doll houses from all over the country, as well as Europe and Mexico.

National Aquarium

In the Department of Commerce Building. Mon.–Fri. 9:00 A.M.–5:00 P.M. Closed weekends. $3 for adults, $1.75 for children. Federal Triangle Metro station.

This aquarium is small by big-city standards, but that's one of the things that makes it so nice (it's also old and less high-tech than many of those around the country, which again, makes it very child friendly). There's a tidal pool where kids can touch horseshoe crabs and rather large snails, and there is a fairly large and ominous looking electric eel.

The absolute kid pleaser is the daily shark or piranha feeding, which takes place at 2:00 P.M. (sharks are MWF; piranhas TTh) The day we were there the guide told the story of how when President Teddy Roosevelt visited South America and saw a school of piranha eat a cow that was lowered into the waters, the fish had not been fed for a month and are usually not that vicious. To prove his point, a filet of flounder was lowered into the piranha tank, and it took a good ten minutes for the rather small fish to eat the whole thing.

You can visit the aquarium in the morning and have your hand stamped to go back for the feeding in the afternoon.

Washington National Cathedral's Medieval Arts and Crafts Workshop

(202) 537-2934. $4 per child materials fee. Tenleytown Metro Station.

Every Saturday from noon until 2:00 P.M. (until 4:00 in July), the cathedral holds an arts & crafts workshop for kids. I've been to many medieval castles, cloisters, and cathedrals throughout the world (including Notre Dame in Paris and the Cloisters in New York) and no other like institution has anything as wonderful for children. Here they can make their own gargoyles out of fast-drying gray clay (most kids try to make a replica of the Cathedral's famous Darth Vader gargoyle), rub raised etchings with wax, hammer copper like a blacksmith (although they can't take their hammered piece home because they are reused, which can be disappointing), chisel stone (while wearing goggles), put together a stained glass window, and try their hand at manuscript illumination.

And Don't Forget

Uncle Beazley

On the National Mall on Madison Dr. Smithsonian Metro station.

This twenty-five-foot fiberglass sculpture of a triceratops has fascinated children for years. It was created for the 1964 New York World's Fair and is based on the children's story *The Enormous Egg* by Oliver Butterworth.

Smithsonian Carousel

On the National Mall across the street from the Arts and Industries Building. $2 per ride. Open 11:00 A.M.–5:00 P.M. on weekdays, 10:00 A.M.–6:00 P.M. on weekends, weather permitting. Smithsonian Metro station.

This nineteenth century carousel features beautiful horses for the kids to ride when the weather is nice. It reminds me of the many merry-go-rounds in Paris that are near all the major sights.

Rock Creek Park Nature Center

5200 Glover Rd. (202) 426-6829. Wed.–Sun. 9:00 A.M.–5:00 P.M. Friendship Heights Metro station, then take the E2 or E3 bus to Military Rd.

Located in Rock Creek Park, the nature center has a number of child-related activities such as a weekend planetarium show for kids over four, arts and crafts, and live animal demonstrations. Call for schedule.

Textile Museum

2320 S St. NW. (202) 667-0441.

The top floor features a loom where kids can weave their own material. For children interested in fashion and design, this can be a fascinating interactive exhibit.

A Likely Story Children's Bookstore

1555 King St., Alexandria, VA; (703)836-2498. This bright, cosy bookshop, between downtown Alexandria and the Metro station, has a variety of activities to entertain the most rambunctious of kids. There are storytelling hours for all ages, and many popular authors and illustrators come to talk about their work. If your little ones won't sit still that long, watch for one of Likely's well, more, *active* activities. These include a rubber stamp demonstration and a quilt-style ornaments workshop.

The store even holds seminars for parents, on topics like child care, early learning, and more. Some workshops charge a small fee, usually to cove the cost of materials, and they often require reservations. Call ahead to secure your spot. Store hours are Mondays through Saturdays 10 A.M. to 6 P.M., and Sundays from 1 to 5 P.M.

Adventure Theatre, Glen Echo Park

7300 MacArthur Blvd., Glen Echo, MD; (301) 320-5331. Washington's longest-running children's playhouse, Adventure Theatre offers magical stories in a style that all kids can enjoy. The seating is especially designed for little ones, and shows last no longer than an hour—about the max in tots' attention spans. What's more, even classic fairy tales get a new spin.

Tickets to weekend plays are $5, and a variety of discounted subscriptions are available. Shows are at 1:30 and 3:30 on Saturday and Sunday afternoons.

Bethesda Academy of Performing Arts Imagination Stage

White Flint Mall, 11301 Rockville Pike, Rockville, MD; (301) 231-7467. If you can't bring the kids to the theater to the mall! The Bethesda Academy of Performing Arts Imagination Stage features professional actors in an intimate setting that encourages audience participation. Kids will love performances like The Frog Prince or The Witch and the Magic Mountain. Some shows, like The Sorcerer's Apprentice and Kids' Clubhouse, feature BAPA's Deaf Access Company, which performs in both voice and sign language.

Ticket's are just $4.50 each; $3.50 for groups of ten or more. Showtimes are Saturdays and Sunday's at 3 P.M.

The Children's Theatre

Thomas Jefferson Community Theatre, 125 S. Old Glebe Rd., Arlington, VA; (703) 548-1154. The Children's Theatre offers plays by and for children, giving kids the opportunity to work with stage professionals.

Tickets to these magical journeys are a mere $5 apiece. All shows feature young actors (ages 9-14) and crew (high schoolers). They're appropriate for audiences from age three up.

Each summer, the Children's Theatre also runs a young adult (14 and up) company called "ACT III." They present a modernized version of a classic Shakespeare play. Tickets are $8 for adults and $6 for students and seniors.

Discovery Theater

900 Jefferson Dr. SW. (202) 357-1500. Located in the Arts and Industries Building of the Smithsonian Institution, the Discovery Theater features live actors performing informative and entertaining shows for young and old alike. See adaptations of children's books,

short plays that bring museum exhibits to life, dances, puppet representations of dinosaurs, and more.

Tickets are generally $4 each, or $3.50 for groups of ten or more.

FCS Family Concert Series

6201 Belcrest Rd., Hyattsville, MD; (301) 927-6133. Held at First United Methodist Church, this annual concert series offers a variety of shows, every two months from fall to spring. They are oriented toward families and have featured such diverse performers as an African-American storyteller; mime and musician Mark Jaster; a rhythm and blues singer/songwriter; and an area dance and theater company's renditions of Aesop's Fables and other stories for youths.

"They're meant to be for children, although I've invited adult friends who have really enjoyed themselves," says an organizer.

Tickets for each hour-long show are a mere $4. You can call the Friends Community School, which organizes the series, at (301) 699-6086. The church seats about 350, and it usually fills up.

Now This! Kids!

Omni Shoreham Hotel Marquee Lounge,2500 Calvert St. NW (202) 745-1023. If you think improv comedy is strictly for grownups, think again. Now This!, a professional comedy troupe, performs "totally improvised, interactive children's musical theatre" every Saturday at 12:30 P.M. Kids love it because they become part of the show, and parents love it because tickets are just $8 for them and $6 for the half-pints.

The Rainbow Company

Burke Village Center II, 9570 Burke Rd., Burke, VA (703) 239-0037. You've probably heard "interactive" used to describe a zillion video games. You may also despair of ever finding activities your kids can enjoy without sitting in front of the tube. The Rainbow

Company has an alternative with its "interactive children's theater." Kids in the audience volunteer to become a part of the show, which doesn't begin until a selected child counts to three and the whole crowd chants, "Once upon a time . . . ."

Although the performance is largely improvised, professional actors guide the young participants through the story. They are well-trained to deal with any situation—handy skills in a room full of excited youngsters. After "the end," everyone is invited to come up on stage and try on costumes, examine the sets, and chat with the actors. Its great fun for everyone—even parents—and it's a great way to introduce kids to *live* entertainment. Tickets are just $3.50, and free for children under two. Performances are given on Saturday, Sunday, and Monday afternoons.

The Rainbow Company is located off Exit 5 of the Capital Beltway, about half an hour from downtown Washington.

Gardens and Parks in Metropolitan D.C.

While there aren't many playgrounds for kids in downtown Washington, the city is full of green spaces, gardens, and parks, all of which have plenty of outdoor activates for kids.

Enid A. Haupt Garden

10th St. and Independence Ave. NW. in the inner courtyard of the Smithsonian museums on the Mall. Open daily 7:00 A.M.–9:00 P.M. in the summer, 7:00 A.M.–5:45 P.M. during colder weather.

Enid Haupt, the donor after whom this garden was named, was an avid horticulturist, who also has a conservatory named after her at New York's Botanical Gardens. These four acres of gardens, enclosed by the National Museum of African Art, Smithsonian Castle, the Arts & Industries Building, the Sackler/Freer galleries and the Ripley center, are a wonderful respite for kids to explore after a long day of museum going. While most children won't appreciate the central floral bed that copies the rose window design of the Smithsonian Castle, they will enjoy the fountain garden outside the

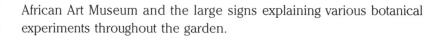

African Art Museum and the large signs explaining various botanical experiments throughout the garden.

U.S. Botanic Garden

100 Maryland Ave. at First St. SW (at the east end of the Mall). (202) 225-8333.

The Botanic gardens will be closed for renovation through 2000. When it reopens in late 2000, there will be much for kids, such as a Jurassic plant recreation, a tropical rain forest, and many exhibits on endangered plant species.

Visitors to the reopened Botanical Gardens will find new exhibits, upgraded interiors, an enlarged gift shop and an entrance on Independence Ave. Themes within the newly renovated glass house will focus on plant conservation and endangered species, plant discoveries, orchids and tropical medicinal plants. Case exhibits will explore how plants have influenced the development of civilization, their therapeutic value, and how plants are represented in the arts.

Exhibits in the east half of the conservatory will focus on the ecology and evolution of plants. There will be exhibits on primitive plants in a reconstructed Jurassic landscape (which is sure to be of interest to kids who are serious about dinosaurs), an oasis, and plants of the desert.

The former Palm House is to be reborn as a jungle, representing the reclaiming of an abandoned plantation by the surrounding tropical rain forest. The former subtropical House will become an expanded exhibit of economic plants focusing on plants that are used to make cosmetics, fiber, food, and industrial products.

The National Garden is set to reopen simultaneously with the Conservatory and will feature a First Ladies Water garden, and a Lawn terrace for outdoor events. The Showcase garden will display native plants in ecological settings, such as a wet meadow bog, stream pool, and woodland habitats.

Bartholdi Park, across the street from the Botanic Gardens at Independence Ave., is currently open and features the Botanic Gardens home gardening demonstration landscape which displays plants that are suitable for urban growth. Among the displays are:

- The all-seasons garden where plants that have four seasons are on display.
- The heritage garden, which features North American plantings.
- The romantic garden, which features beautiful roses and a secluded park bench
- The rock garden, which features unusual plants in raised rock beds.
- The American parterre is the entrance to the Bartholdi Fountain, which displays the sculptor of the Statue of Liberty, where Columnar Japanese holly and Justin Boxwood provide the framework for interlaced perennials and annuals

U.S. National Arboretum

3501 New York Ave. NE. (202) 245-2776. Open daily 8:00 A.M.–5:00 P.M. Closed Christmas Day. Stadium Armory metro station, then take the B2 bus to Bladensburg Rd. and R St. NE. Free admission and parking, but there are fees for tours.

The National Arboretum is a 446-acre preserve dedicated to research, education and conservation of trees, shrubs, flowers and other plants. Among the highlights are the National Bonsai and Penjing Museum (open 10:00 A.M.–3:30 P.M.), which includes fifty-three miniature trees given to the U.S. by Japan as part of their bicentennial gift. The Arboretum also features a conservatory for tropical bonsai trees that includes a Japanese garden.

The largest planting of azaleas in the nation can be found at the Arboretum, as well as a historic rose garden and the Franklin tree, which is a species of tree now extinct in the wild discovered by a botanist friend of Benjamin Franklin in 1765. There is also a national grove of state trees.

Tram tours are available on Saturdays and Sundays only from April through October. The forty-minute, narrated, open-air tram tour of the entire site is available at 10:30 A.M., 11:30 A.M., 1:00 P.M., pm 3:00 P.M. and 4:00 P.M. and you can buy tickets at the ticket kiosk in the administration building. Tours are $3 for adults, $2 for seniors and $1 for children 4–16.

The Arboretum also has a lovely gift shop with all sorts of books on plants, as well as planting and gardening-related parapher-

Water Fun in D.C.

You can rent a paddleboat at the Tidal Basin for $7 an hour for a two-seater, and $14 an hour for a four-seater. Kids also love the mule barge rides at the C&O Canal, where boat guides, dressed in costumes from the 1870s, often have a box of old-fashioned toys for kids to play with.

nalia. If you call ahead, you can inquire about special workshops and lectures on the day of your visit.

Potomac Park

Potomac Park consists of the 722 acres of land around the Tidal Basin surrounding most of the Presidential Memorials, where you will find all the lovely Japanese Cherry Blossom trees. It is divided into East Potomac and West Potomac Park.

West Potomac Park includes Constitution Gardens, the Vietnam, Korean, Lincoln, and Jefferson Memorials and the reflecting pool.

East Potomac Park has picnic grounds, three golf courses, a large swimming pool, and biking and hiking trails overlooking the Potomac.

Rock Creek Park

Headquarters (202) 282-1063; Nature center and Planetarium (202) 426-6829; Pierce Mill (202) 426-6908; Old Stone House (202) 426-6851. Open 7 days a week during daylight hours. Nature Center and Planetarium open Wed.–Sun. 9:00 A.M.–5:00 P.M. Closed New Year's Day, Fourth of July, Thanksgiving, and Christmas Days. Old Stone House, same as above except closes at 4:00 P.M. Pierce Mill, same as above except closes at 4:30 P.M.

Nearest metro station is Friendship Heights, then take E2 bus to Glover and Military Rds.

Rock Creek Park is one of the oldest national parks in the country, established in 1890, and one of the largest forested urban parks in the United States offering an undisturbed 1,754, acre expanse of urban forest, open fields, and creeks with running water. According to some locals, parts of it are still so wild that you can occasionally see deer in the fall and winter.

The main visitor center is the nature center and Planetarium (5200 Glover Rd. NW) where much of the information on the history of the park is located such as exhibits on the park's wildlife, a hands-on discovery center for children, an observation beehive, as well as the site for many child-oriented workshops and activities. The Planetarium offers a daily showing on "Tonight's Sky" at 4:00 P.M., and a weekend showing of "the Night Sky" at 1:00 P.M. Programs last between forty and sixty minutes. From April through November there are meetings of the National Capital Astronomers, who hold a once-a-month evening star-gazing session.

Admission to the planetarium is free, but you must pick up tickets at the nature center in advance.

The park also contains the Old Stone House, the oldest house in Washington, and Pierce Mill, which was once an active gristmill where corn and wheat were ground into flour using water power from Rock Creek. The park grounds also contain remains of Civil War fortifications, including Fort Stevens, the site of the only battle within the District of Columbia during the Civil War.

The park's grounds contain a wealth of hiking and biking trails, picnic facilities, tennis courts, a skating rink, horseback riding and a golf course. Call ahead for fees and reservations.

Theodore Roosevelt Island

(703) 285-2598. Open seven days a week during daylight hours. Nearest metro station is Rosslyn, then walk across the pedestrian bridge at Rosslyn Circle. By car, take the George Washington Memorial Parkway exit north from the Theodore Roosevelt bridge.

Roosevelt Island is a memorial to the conservation efforts of President Teddy Roosevelt. Soon after his death in 1919, a memorial association was put together to purchase the ninety-one-acre island for this purpose.

Roosevelt Island is one of the locals' favorite places to picnic and just enjoy the wooded outdoors. There are a number of trails through the marsh, swamp, and forest where visitors can see birds and small mammals. There is also an outdoor memorial with a statue of Roosevelt, with quotes about his conservation beliefs. You can also rent canoes at Thompson's boat center.

Outdoor Activities

Below is a list of some of the places where you can hike; rent bicycles, canoes, and paddle boats visit swimming pools (if your hotel does not have one); play tennis and golf; and go skating in the winter.

Fort Dupont Park

Minnesota and Massachusetts Aves. at Randle Circle (202)426-7745. One of Washington's largest parks, Fort Dupont offers 376 acres of wooded land which serve as a friendly haven for picnics, nature walks, and various outdoor sports. Although the Civil War fort itself is no more, the former site is marked by earthworks and an explanatory plaque. Runaway slaves found safety within its walls; Dupont was one of 68 forts encircling Washington in the 1860s.

Today, the grounds feature a sizable garden, a skating rink, and a sports complex, among other amenities. A hiking-biking trail surrounds the park, while an activity center includes park rangers leading workshops and walks; nature studies; and Civil War exhibits. Most presentations are free; there is a small charge for the ice rink and sports complex activities. Summers feature weekend jazz concerts at an outdoor stage, free to all. The center's hours vary by season; it's open Tuesday's through Saturdays in the summer, weekdays only the rest of the year.

As for those other 67 forts, some of their ruins may be seen while walking the marked trails that make up the Fort Circle Parks. Maps are available showing the approximate location of the various forts in the ring; call the National Park Service at (202) 343-4747 for more information.

Kenilworth Aquatic Gardens

1900 Anacostia Dr. SE; (202)426-6905. Not far from the United States National Arboretum, Kenilworth Aquatic Gardens is a twelve-

Kids Stuff at
Grown-Up Museums

Sometimes it's hard to take the kids to adult museums, but most of the Smithsonian museums and the art museums have special kid-related programs or kid-friendly tours.

- National Gallery of Art has a Family Guide, which you buy at the book store for $2.50, which turns the museum into a treasure hunt where kids search for Napoleon, Gilbert Stuart's George Washington, and other recognizable faces and figures. Kids also love to eat in the underground cafeteria and watch the cascading waterfall.

- National Gallery of Arts Sculpture Garden. Kids love looking at Claes Oldenburg's giant *Typewriter Eraser* (and having you explain to them how you used to have to erase typing mistakes before computers), as well as Roy Lichtenstein's two-dimensional *House*. The outdoor fountain makes a nice place for a picnic or a sit-down snack at the outdoor cafe. In the winter, there's ice skating among the art.

- National Museum of African Art features African masks, drums and gongs that kids can handle.

- Both the Freer Gallery of Art and the Sackler Gallery have Interactive ImaginAsia programs that allows kids (and adults) to touch and explore materials used in the making of the art.

- The Hirshhorn Museum offers a free Family Guide which has kids search for Alexander Calder's Finny Fish, Giacometti's Dog, and various child-accessible works of art.

acre garden devoted to water-living plants. Over forty ponds are filled with water lilies, lotus flowers, and other aquatic flora. Cattails and yellow flag irises edge the ponds. Completing this watery world, the garden naturally attracts an interesting ecosystem of turtles, snakes, frogs, and ducks.

Bordering all this is the Kenilworth Marsh, the last remaining tidal marsh in the District. Walk the garden's River Trail for spectacular views of the marsh, the Anacostia River, and nearby wooded swamps.

Kenilworth Aquatic Gardens are open to the public, free of charge,. Visitors are welcome to picnic in designated areas. The gardens are open daily until late afternoon, but evening walks can be arranged. The best time to visit is June and July for hardy water lilies, and July into August for tropical plants and lotuses.

Hiking

There are many hiking paths throughout the urban area, and therefore, many local hiking clubs. The *Washington Post* weekend section always lists hiking activities of the local clubs, which you can usually join. In addition, the C&O Canal in Georgetown has an eighteen mile hiking path, which is fairly easy, so you can take slightly older children. Both Rock Creek and Theodore Roosevelt Island have extensive hiking trails, but they are slightly more rugged. The hiking paths along East Potomac Park are also fairly easy to navigate. There are also hiking trails in Mount Vernon.

Bicycles

Again, check *The Washington Post* weekend section for bicycling tours, or call one of the many organized bicycling tours (Bike the Sites 202-966-8662 is the most well known). If you just want to rent bikes and ride through a park, you can do so at Fletcher's Boat House at the C&O Canal (202) 244-0461) or at Thompson's Boat House (202) 333-9543 in Rock Creek Park. You can also rent bikes at Big Wheel Bikes, 1034 33rd St. NW in Georgetown, which is right near the C&O Canal and its extensive bike path. There is also a new seven-mile bike path that takes you from Georgetown to Bethesda MD along an abandoned railroad track on the Potomac known as the Capital Crescent Trail.

Canoes & Paddle boats

Thompson's Boat House (see phone number above) in Rock Creek Park rents canoes, kayaks, and row-boats, as well as paddle boats, but you must leave a photo I.D. and a credit card with your rental fee. Fletcher's Boat House on the C&O Canal also rents canoes and rowboats, and sells fishing licenses, with bait and tackle.

Tennis

There are public tennis courts at Rock Creek Park (202) 722-5949 and East Potomac Park (202) 554-5962, but you should call ahead for availability and fees. The D.C. department of parks and recreation (202) 673-7660 will also give you a list of other outdoor tennis courts in the district.

Golf

The only two public golf courses in D.C. are in Rock Creek Park (202) 882-7332 and East Potomac Park (202) 554-7600. Call for fees and information.

Skating

The newly opened National Gallery of Art Sculpture Garden (202) 737-4215 offers ice skating on the fountain pool in the winter. You can also skate on the C&O Canal in the winter (301) 299-3613, but you must bring your own skates. Pershing Park at 14th St. and Pennsylvania Ave (202) 737-6938 also features outdoor skating.

Horseback Riding

The stables at Rock Creek (202) 362-0117, near the nature center, offer a one-hour guided trail tour Tuesdays through Thursdays.

Tickets to Events

If you're a basketball fan or you want to catch the circus while it's in town, below is a list of where to get event tickets. However, I am told that it is virtually impossible to get football tickets unless you use a ticket broker, which can be quite pricey since regular price football tickets are around $50.

MCI Center is the home of Washington's basketball Wizards and hockey Capitals. Tickets can be purchased at the box office at 7th and F Sts. NW or by calling (800) 551-SEAT or (202) 296-2473. The MCI Center also hosts many rock concerts, so you can call these numbers for those tickets as well. The Ringling Brothers & Barnum & Bailey Circus comes to the MCI Center in late March/early April.

JFK Center for the Performing Arts—Call 800 444-1324 for information on performances.

Wolf Trap Theater—This is an outdoor theater. Call (703) 255-1868 for tickets and information.

National Shakespeare Company—Call (202) 393-2700 for information on performances.

Ford's Theatre—The theater where Lincoln was assassinated still holds regular theatrical performances. Call (202) 347-4833 for information.

Folger Shakespeare Library—There are regular performances of Shakespearean and Elizabethan plays. Call (202) 544-7077.

Chapter Thirteen

Day and Side Trips Outside Washington, D.C.

The surrounding towns and suburbs of Washington, D.C. are as old (if not older) than the city itself and offer a host of fascinating and interesting things to see and do, from visiting our first president's "gentleman farm" in Mount Vernon to enjoying later twentieth-century entertainments like amusement parks and outlet shopping malls.

If you have a car (you can go by bus, but then you are on someone else's time schedule) and you have the time (if you are staying in the city at last five days), you should try to see Mount Vernon and the spectacular Pope-Leighey house designed by Frank Lloyd Wright on the grounds of the neighboring Woodlawn Plantation. They are both worth the trip. You have to pass through Alexandria, Virginia to get there, so you might want to take a drive-through tour of this old Southern town as well.

Mount Vernon

Mount Vernon, Virginia. (703) 780-2000. Open 8:00 A.M.–5:00 P.M. April through August; March, Sept., and Oct. 9:00 P.M.–5:00 P.M.; Nov. through Feb. 9:00 P.M.–4:00 P.M. Admission: $8 for adults, $4 for children (under six free); $7.50 for seniors. *www.mountvernon.org*.

Getting There: By car it is a pretty direct trip from the city. Cross any of the memorial bridges and then take the George Washington Memorial Parkway (Rt. 1) going south, which ends at Mount Vernon.

By bus the Gray Line, (202) 289-1995, goes to Mount Vernon at 8:30 A.M. from Union Station. Adults are $24; children $12. They will drop you off at your hotel when the four-hour tour is over. There are evening tours in the summer.

The Tourmobile, (202) 554-5100, also goes to Mount Vernon, leaving from the Visitor's Center at Arlington National Cemetery at 10:00 A.M. and noon. Adults are $20; children $10 with admission to the estate included. Make reservation, in the summer months.

By boat, the Spirit Cruise Line, (202) 554-8000, leaves from the Washington waterfront and offers a five-hour cruise at $25.50 for adults and $17 for children, which includes the price of admission to the estate.

Mount Vernon is vast. It was once an 8,000-acre farm (Washington gave his adopted granddaughter some of his land as a wedding present, on which Woodlawn Plantation is now built), and the estate you see is a mere 500 acres of the former president's holdings. Even at one-eighth of its original size, Mount Vernon is at least a half day touring experience, plus there's a wonderful gift shop and a colonial restaurant nearby, so plan on making a day of this trip.

Washington lived at Mount Vernon for forty-five years, from the time he was twenty-two until his death. He and Martha are buried on the premises. He loved this place, and over the years he tripled the size of the mansion, redesigned the grounds and outbuildings, and bought neighboring lands. The present site was purchased by the Mount Vernon Ladies Association in 1858 from Washington's descendants for $200,000 and is almost unchanged in its appearance from 1799 when Washington died.

The Mount Vernon admission includes a tour of the mansion, which Washington made the center of his estate. Restoration on the mansion is meticulous from the color of the paint on the walls to the placement of many of the original furnishings (such as the leather chair in his study that he used for the eight years he was president to the bed he died in).

The property also includes a new forest trail where you can walk through Washington's wilderness grounds, see his cobblestone quarry, cross a footbridge, and learn about wildlife on the estate. Washington himself loved to ride around his grounds on horseback.

Washington considered himself quite a scientific farmer, and he oversaw all the plantings on his estate (some of his original tree plantings are still growing at the Bowling Green entrance to the estate). At the new Pioneer Farmer site, horses tread wheat outside the restored sixteen-sided barn and costumed workers participate in hands-on colonial farming activities and farm animal demonstrations.

A new museum on the grounds replicates Washington's presidential office. His last will and testament and the famous bust of Washington by Houdon are also on display. There's also a display on the archeology and restoration of the site, which shows how work was done and what has been found on the site over the years.

Mount Vernon also holds the Washington Tombs (where annual memorial services are held on his birthday and a daily wreath laying takes place at 10:00 A.M., April–October) four gardens, a slave memorial (Washington freed his slaves upon his death), a greenhouse, stables, slave quarters, and the original outbuildings throughout the estate.

The gift shop is large and offers a great selection of Washington-related memorabilia from a porcelain bust of Washington (a copy of the Houdon) to plates depicting Washington crossing the Delaware. The shop offers great gifts to bring home such as Mount Vernon wine (Virginia Blush), mulled cider, Martha's cake, and colonial toys for kids.

There are special events on the estate throughout the year, so call ahead or visit the Web site to help plan your trip.

Where to Eat: No food is allowed on the grounds, but there is a snack bar right outside the entrance that offers a fair selection of fast food.

Next door to the gift shop is The Mount Vernon Inn, (703) 780-0011, which serves both lunch and dinner in a colonial setting with costumed waitpersons. The food is moderately priced and features a colonial menu.

Nearby is also the Cedar Knoll Inn, which also serves lunch and dinner. The dinner menu offers a colonial meal at a prix fixe of $29.95 for dinner for two.

Seasonal Events at Mount Vernon

- *October*: Celebrate Virginia Archeology month with thirty-minute tours of excavation sites at 11:30 and 2:30 all month long.
- *December*: Holidays at Mount Vernon are commemorated with a special tour that includes costumed characters and a visit to the rarely opened third floor of the mansion. Hot

cider, cookies, and caroling around a bonfire are also on the program.

- *February*: All month long there is a thirty-minute walking tour on the slave life at Mount Vernon at 10:00 A.M., 11:30 A.M., and 1:30 P.M. Weekends in February include musical presentations and storytelling. On the weekend of Washington's birthday there are always special events, and Mount Vernon is open free to the public.

Woodlawn Plantation

9000 Richmond Highway, Mount Vernon, VA, (703) 780-4000. Open daily March through December. Guided docent-led tours are offered on the half-hour, $8 per person, but you can buy a joint tour ticket to see the Pope-Leighey house as well for $12. You can actually walk from Mount Vernon to Woodlawn, but take your car if you have one.

Woodlawn Plantation was the home of Washington's nephew, who married Washington's adopted granddaughter. Washington gave the couple the property to build their home from his holdings at Mount Vernon. The Georgian-style house was designed by William Thorton, one of the first architects of the U.S. Capitol building. You can see the Potomac from the back porch.

The house has much Washington-related memorabilia on its two floors as well as many early American works of art (two Rembrandt Peales and a Hiram Powers bust), but the item that I found most intriguing was a mourning embroidery by Anna Austin on the second floor that features a woman crying on a large memorial urn who disappears and reappears as an angel when you change perspective.

High tea is offered at the Plantation at 12:30 P.M. for $20, which also includes a tour.

There is a gift shop in the basement that offers many wonderful early American gifts and T-shirts (and you can see the old well, which was one of the first successful attempts at indoor plumbing). This is also the gift store for the Pope-Leighey House, so you can buy many Frank Lloyd Wright knicknacks as well, such as cups, a mouse pad, and canvas bags, with the decorative fret design from the house's windows.

Frank Lloyd Wright

Most architects consider Frank Lloyd Wright the greatest, and most influential American architect. His designs, which spanned nearly fifty years influenced American home to such an extent that we might not have the ranch house with its open living room space connected to the kitchen and the carport if it were not for his vision of the American home.

More than 500 of Wright's buildings were erected in his lifetime. These include a number of churches, skyscrapers and the Guggenheim Museum in New York, which many consider his crowning achievement.

He is also known for his simple, yet elegant and useful design of the furnishings for many of his homes. The Pope-Leighey House has most of the original furnishings designed by Wright.

Pope-Leighey House

Same hours and address as Woodlawn Plantation.

The Pope-Leighey house is one of Wright's earliest Usonian houses (designed for middle-income families), and one whose construction he personally oversaw (many of the later Usonian homes were built by associates of Wright). It was commissioned by newspaperman Loren Pope, who was so taken with a *Life* magazine profile on Wright that he wrote him a letter requesting he design him a house: "Dear Frank Lloyd Wright, There are certain things a man wants during life, and, of life. Material things and things of the spirit. The writer has one fervent wish that includes both. It is a house created by you." And Wright replied: "Dear Loren Pope, Of course I'm ready to give you a house . . ." Those were the days!

The small three-bedroom house was built in 1939 in Falls Church, VA (it has been moved twice by the National Trust, which now runs it) and has many of the signature Wright elements: a small utility center where the kitchen and bathroom are housed (the size of those in a small one-bedroom apartment), a cantilevered roof, horizontal lines, a repeating fret stencil pattern on the windows, and next to no closets.

Although Pope loved the house, his family outgrew it and it was sold to the Leighey family, who lived there until the 1980s, and opened to the public in 1996. Much of the original furniture and color scheme is preserved. When the house was commissioned, its purchase price of between $6,000 and $7,000 included the furniture.

During the month of December, a 1940s Christmas is on display at the house.

Alexandria, VA

Only about a ten-minute drive from downtown D.C. or a Metro ride, Alexandria is as charming as and older than Georgetown. It still has a lot of colonial character, such as its brick sidewalks, cobblestone streets, and many historic homes. Washingtonians refer to it simply as Old Town.

Getting There: By car take the Arlington Memorial or 14th St. Bridge to the George Washington Memorial Parkway south, which becomes Washington St. in Old Town Alexandria. If you go to the Visitor's Bureau, they will give you an all-day parking pass, or you can park in metered spaces on the street.

Alexandria is surprisingly easy to get to by Metro (whereas Georgetown is not). Take the yellow line to the King St. station, and catch an eastbound AT2 or AT5 to the Visitor's Bureau.

Alexandria is a small town and is easy to walk around in. The center of the grid is the intersection of Washington and King St. Many of the streets retain their original colonial names (King, Prince, etc.).

For information on special events and celebrations, call the **Alexandria Convention and Visitors Bureau,** (703) 838-4200, or drop in at their headquarters situated in the historic William Ramsay House on King and South Fairfax Street, where you can obtain a free map for a self-guided tour.

Alexandria was named after a Scottish tobacco merchant who purchased the land in 1669. The town was founded in 1749, and one of the surveyors who helped plan the streets was a seventeen-year-old George Washington.

Since its founding, Alexandria has always been a country retreat for prominent Washington families. George Washington had a town-house here, and many of the upper crust colonial families worshipped at the English style **Christ Church (Cammeron and N. Washington Sts.),** where Washington was a vestryman and had his own pew and where Robert E. Lee was confirmed.

Washington is also said to have held his last birthday party at **Gadsby's Tavern (N. Royal and Cammeron Sts., (703) 838-4242),** which features a museum and is still a restaurant where costumed waitpersons serve homemade colonial fare. Jefferson, Madison, and the Marquis de Lafayette are also said to have dined here.

Arlington House Oronoco St. at North St., (703) 548-8454, is another historic home in Alexandria. Lee lived here until he he in enrolled in West Point in 1825. He married one of Washington's great granddaughters and lived in the Arlington House, whose grounds eventually became Arlington National Cemetery.

Alexandria Visitors' Information

Most historic homes charge a $4 tour price and are closed on Mondays. However, you can buy a group admission ticket that will get you into most of the historic homes for a $12 adult price, $5 for children, at the Visitors Bureau or at any one of the historic homes.

On the south side of Oronoco St. is the **Lee-Fendell House, (703) 548-1789,** where more Lee descendants lived (a total of 37 over 118 years) and where there is an extensive display of Lee memorabilia.

Other historic homes in Alexandria include the **Caryle House (121 N. Fairfax St. at Cammeron St., (703) 549-2997,** where in 1755 Major General Edward Braddock met with five colonial governors to begin taxing the colonies to defend themselves against the French and the Indians. The colonists were not happy with this proposal and eventually drove him out.

City Hall and Market Sq. (bounded by King, N. Royal, Cammeron and N. Fairfax Sts.) is the site of a weekly outdoor market. Across the street on the south side of King St. is the **Stabler-Leadbeater Apothecary Shop and Museum, (703) 836-3713,** which was the second oldest drugstore in the nation until it closed in 1933. It was run for five generations by a Quaker family. It is now a museum and gift shop.

The Lyceum (201 S. Washington St., off Prince St.) is a museum that features changing exhibits on the history of Alexandria from the seventeenth century to the present.

The Torpedo Factory Art Center (105 N. Union St. between King and Cameron Sts. on the waterfront) is the shell of a former torpedo factory. Two hundred artists now show their works on the premises; an exhibition of Alexandria archeology, lets visitors see archaeologists at work in their lab.

King's Dominion

Doswell, VA, (804) 876-5000. Open only March (weekends only) through October. There are concerts and special events, so call for information. Adult admission $33.99, children ages three to six $24.99, fifty-five and over $28.99. There are two-day tickets available. Parking is an additional $6 per vehicle. Take Interstate 95 south to exit 98 and follow the signs.

An amusement park in the national Paramount Six Flags amusement park chain, King's Dominion is known for its roller coasters (four wooden ones) as well as the steel roller coaster, the Anaconda, and its newest roller coaster, the Volcano. It also features a sixteen-acre water park with Big Wave Bay, a 650,000 gallon wave pool; Surf City Splash, which has fifty water attractions; and many water slides.

Leesburg Corner

Leesburg, VA, (703) 737-3071. Stores open seven days a week. Mon.–Sat. 10:00 A.M.–9:00 P.M.; Sun. 11:00 A.M.–6:00 P.M. Take Rte. 267 (Dulles Toll Rd./Greenway) or Rte. 7 to Rte. 15 N. Follow signs, turn right on top of Ft. Evans Rd.

This sixty-shop outlet center just past Dulles Airport features popular designers such as DKNY and Tommy Hilfiger, a Gap outlet, as well as an Off 5th-Saks Fifth Avenue Outlet. There are also a number of specialty shops for children's clothing, shoes, and housewares.

Fort Ward Museum & Historic Site

4301 W. Braddock Rd., Alexandria, VA; (703) 838-4848

Fort Ward was taken under the wing of the City of Alexandria in 1961, and has since been both restored and preserved as befits an important Civil War site. Today, this fifth-largest of 162 forts built by Union forces features a completely restored Northwest bastion, and over 95% of its original walls. Both the fort and accompanying museum occupy a 45-acre park setting just east of Route 395.

Tour museum, open 9 A.M. to 5 P.M. Tuesday through Saturdays and 12–5 P.M. Sundays, and browse through artifacts, a research library, and a range of educational programs. One recent exhibition covered "Medical Care for the Civil War Soldier," full of the expected horrors of battlefield treatment; a gentler exhibit dealt with the "Art of the Artilleryman."

The historic site itself is open from 9 A.M. to sunset daily. A path runs along the earthwork walls and can take as long as 45 minutes to walk. Admission to the fort, and the museum, is free.

Black History in Alexandria

There is a Black History Resource Center in Alexandria, which is housed in the former Robinson Library, once a segregated library for Alexandria's black community. America's first sit-in against segregation was staged in Alexandria in 1939 to protest the exclusion of blacks from Alexandria's public libraries, which lead to the creation of the Robinson Library in 1940. The center presently displays objects and records of African-American history in the region, as well as special exhibits. There is also a research library on the premises. 603 N. Alfred St. (703) 838-4829. Open Tues.–Sat. 10:00 A.M.–4:00 P.M.

NASA/Goddard Space Flight Center

Soil Conservation Rd., Greenbelt, MD; (301) 286-3979

Named for the "Father of Modern Rocketry," the Goddard Space Flight Center was built by NASA back in 1959. Along with displays of rockets and spacecraft, the lab's visitor center has lots of fun hands-on stuff—like a gyro-chair that lets you experience the sensation of steering with no gravity, and a maneuvering unit that lets you try to retrieve a satellite in space.

Special events include model rocket launches, stargazing groups, lectures by scientist, and videos of new NASA projects. The visitor center is open daily from 9 A.M. to 4 P.M.; for a schedule of special events, call (301) 286-8981.

In addition to the exhibits, you can tour some of the actual laboratories—including stops at the Test and Evaluation Facility, NASA Communications Network, Flight Dynamics Facility, and satellite control centers for such spacecraft as the Hubble Space Telescope. Tours are offered Mondays through Saturdays.

Busch Gardens & Water Country USA

One Busch Gardens Blvd. Williamsburg, VA 23187 Phone: (757) 253-3584

An Anheuser Busch theme park with 17th century flair, Busch Gardens boasts more than 40 thrilling rides, dazzling shows, quaint shops and European cuisine. Open March-October. Group rates and meeting space available. Call for details.

College Park Aviation Museum

1985 Cpl. Frank Scott Drive College Park, MD 20740 Phone: (301) 864-6029.

Opened in 1998, the College Park Aviation Museum is a 27,000 sq. ft. state-of-the-art facility located on the grounds of College Park Airport—the world's oldest continuously operating airport. The museum includes an open, 1 1/2 story exhibit area for full-sized aircraft, as well as display and exhibition areas, a library, preservation and collection rooms, a lobby, The Prop Shop Gift Shop, offices and an auditorium. The deck off the second floor gallery, which is available for workshops and special events, offers a clear view of the airfield. The museum highlights many significant aviation achievements through its use of animatronics and interactive exhibits. Memorabilia, photographs, aviation-related books and manuscripts, oral histories, and information kiosks provide considerable information to visitors about College Park Airport's significance in aviation history. Architecturally, the facility combines brick and glass, and has a curved roofline reminiscent of an early Wright aeroplane. The facility is open to the public for self-guided tours and for a variety of special events, lectures and fun activities. Group tours are scheduled by appointment, and combine fun and education in an exciting environment.

The museum is open from 10 AM to 5 PM daily, except holidays.

Gettysburg, PA

Gettysburg, PA

Located about 1-1/2 hours from Washington, DC. Major sites include Gettysburg National Battlefield Park, Eisenhower home, plus 25 other attractions.

Luray Caverns

121 U. S. 211 West P.O. Box 748 Luray, VA 22835
Phone: (540) 743-6551

The largest and most popular caverns in Eastern America, this U.S. Natural Landmark is located 90 minutes southwest of Washington, just 10 minutes from Skyline Drive and Shenandoah National Park. Open daily 9 am-4 pm (to 6 pm March 15-June 15 & day after Labor Day-Oct. 31; to 7 pm June 15-Labor Day; to 5 pm weekends Nov.1-March 14). Admission: Adults $14, children (ages 7-13) $6.

Six Flags America

P.O. Box 4210 Largo, MD 20775-4210 Phone: (301) 249-1500

A family theme park offering 100 rides, shows and attractions, including the NEW Typhoon Sea Coaster and four roller coasters,

Other Washingtons in Virginia

In Fredericksburg, Virginia, you can find Kenmore Plantation and Gardens, the former home of George Washington's sister, Betty Washington Lewis, and his brother-in-law, Colonel Fielding Lewis. This stately mansion, built in 1755, is noted for its fine plaster ceilings. 1201 Washington Ave., Fredericksburg, VA (take I-95 fifty miles south of D.C.). (540) 373-3381. Open Mon.–Sat. 10:00 A.M.–5:00 P.M., Sun noon-4:00 P.M. Admission is $6 for adults; $3 for children. There is a gift shop on the premises.

including the New Roar Wooden Coaster and the world famous Mind Eraser, plus a variety of children's rides in the specially themed A Day at the Circus. Enjoy the 25-acre Paradise Island water park and Crocodile Cal's Outback Beach House, plus live shows, games, gift shops, restaurants and more. Open daily Memorial Day through Labor Day and weekends only in May, September and October. Closed November through April. Admission: adults $25, children 4–8 $19. Call for group rates.

Prime Outlets, Hagerstown

Hagerstown, MD, (888) 883-6288. Open Mon.–Sat. 10:00–9:00 P.M.; Sun. 11:00 A.M.–6:00 P.M. Closed Easter Sunday, Thanksgiving Day, and Christmas Day. Take I-495 to I-270, which leads into I-70, exit 29 will lead you to the Hagerstown outlet center.

This outlet center seventy-five minutes outside Washington, D.C. features about sixty outlet and discount stores, with many of the same stores as the Leesburg outlet, including a Gap outlet, DKNY, and Tommy Hilfiger. Among the many housewares, specialty, and children's apparel stores there is a KB Toys outlet here, which many Washington parents visit for their Christmas shopping.

Chapter Fourteen

Entertainment, Nightlife, and Art Galleries

Washington, D.C. has a lot to do after the museums close, from sporting events (football tickets are nearly impossible to get unless you go to a ticket broker) to theatre, concerts, and nightclubs. The city also has over 200 art galleries, featuring everything from local artists to old masters. Check out the *Washington Post*'s weekend guide, which is published every Friday, for a comprehensive list of events during your stay.

Washington's nightlife centers around Georgetown, Adams Morgan, Dupont Circle, and the U St. Corridor. Many of Washington's hotels also offer dancing or jazz performances in the hotel lounges.

Half-price tickets to the theatre and some comedy, opera, and ballet performances can be purchased on the day of the show at the Old Post Office Pavilion, 1100 Pennsylvania Ave. NW (202-TICKETS), Federal Triangle Metro station.

Full-price tickets for day of performance for most shows can be purchased from Ticketmaster (202) 432-SEAT or by calling (800) 551-SEAT.

Comedy Clubs

Chelsea's, 1055 Thomas Jefferson St. NW, (202) 298-8222, features the Capitol Steps, a musical satire troupe that spoofs current events. Dinner and show $50; show and $10 bar credit–$33.50.

The Improv, 1140 Connecticut Ave. NW, (202) 296-7008, a Washington, D.C. branch of this nationally known comedy club, features local and national comedians.

Gross National Product, Chief Ike's Mambo Room, 1725 Columbia Rd., (202) 783-7212, is a local satire troupe that pokes fun at national politics. $20 per person with $10 bar minimum.

Dance Clubs

Bar Nun, 1326 U St., (202) 667-6680, features hip hop, house, live jazz and "old school" music at a funky nightclub. Poetry readings are on Monday nights. Open seven days a week.

Chaos, 17th and Q St. downstairs, (202) 232-4141. Open Tues.–Sat. with different music every night and a drag show on Saturday.

Club Heaven and Hell, 2327 18th St. NW, (202) 667-HELL. Cover charge for heaven, Hell is free. Open Tues.–Sat. This two-story nightclub is an Adams Morgan mainstay. Upstairs is a psychedelic version of heaven with '80s pop; downstairs is a darker version of the same thing. Not particularly Goth, but it tries; youngish crowd.

Club 2:K-9, 2009 8th St. NW (in the U St. Corridor), (202) 575-2009. This dance club features a multicultural mix of music in a funky dance hall with bright colors. Open Thurs.–Sat. until 3:00 A.M.

D.C. Live, 932 F St. NW, (202) 342-7200, is mostly geared toward the college crowd, with a college night on Sunday and a live broadcast on KISS FM 93.9 on Saturday. Open Thurs.–Sun.

Decades, 10th St. (between E and F Sts.) next to Ford's Theatre, (202) 242-3648, is a large nightclub with three clubs featuring the music of the '70s, '80s, and '90s. You must be twenty-one with I.D. to enter.

Latin Jazz Alley, 1721 Columbia Rd., (202) 328-6190, is a popular Adams Morgan hangout devoted to Latin dance where you can mambo and merengue until 3:00 A.M. from Wed. through Sat. Dance lessons are offered in the early part of the evening.

Polly Ester's, 605 12th St. NW., (202) 737-1970, has a cover charge. Open Thurs.–Sun., this '70s nightclub has disco dancing and '70s memorabilia on the walls; downstairs is dedicated to the '80s.

Sting, 1015 Half St. SE, (202) 554-1500, features live performances by bands from techno, house, and Trance. Admission fee; must be over nineteen with valid I.D. to enter.

Zei Club, 1415 Zei Alley NW, (202) 842-2455; open 10:00 P.M.–3:00 A.M. Thurs.–Sat.

Brew Pubs

Capital City Brewing Company has two locations in downtown Washington—one right next door to Union Station (2 Massachusetts Ave. NE, 202-842-2337)—and the other in the heart of the downtown district (11th and H Sts. 202-628-2222). This bar offers a wide selection of the local microbrews, such as Foggy Bottom Ale, as well as burgers and bar food.

John Harvard's Brew House, 13th and E Sts, beside the Wagner Theater, (202) 783-2739. This bar offers its own homemade beers such as Imperial Russian Stout and Nut Brown Ale, as well as a wide selection of local beers. Hearty food is also on the menu such as chicken potpie and meatloaf.

Saloons, Pubs and Sports Bars

Brickseller, 1523 22nd St. NW, in Dupont Circle, (202) 293-1885. This saloon and restaurant offers a selection of more than 900 beers, as well as a menu that offers food from the fifty states.

Fado, 808 7th St. NW, within walking distance from the MCI Center, (202) 789-0066. This is an eclectic Irish bar, offering Irish themed rooms, as well as pints of beers on tap and in bottles. It's a interesting place to go after a sporting event.

Stoney's, 1307 L St. NW, (202) 347-9163. This is a Washington landmark of sorts, having served this downtown neighborhood for thirty years. It's a very basic, and very popular, Washington bar that is so well loved it doesn't have to take credit cards.

Velocity Grill, in the MCI Sports Center, 7th St. and F Sts. NW. This was closed for renovation when I was visiting, but if it is open when you are in town, you can watch the Washington basketball Wizards practice through a glass wall as you drink your beer or eat your burger, which is a must-do experience for any sports fan.

Art Galleries

Washington, D.C. has many art galleries, centered around 7th Street in the downtown area, in the Canal Sq. courtyard of the Shops at Georgetown, and along Connecticut Ave. in Dupont Circle. Each of these art centers has group opening nights, where you can see new shows at a number of galleries while sipping wine and eating cheese. For the Dupont Circle galleries, the first Friday of every month is the opening day; for the Georgetown Canal St. courtyard galleries, opening night is the third Thursday of every month.

Anna Maria Gambino-Colombo, a local lawyer with an art history degree, has painstakingly put together a comprehensive guide to all the galleries in the area, which you can find on her Web site at www.geocities.com/Paris/Musee/9650/index.html. Her wonderful Web site lists the top ten galleries, as well as the top ten local artists, with links to many of the galleries.

The following list of the top ten galleries in D.C. was put together by Ms. Gambino-Colombo.

Gallery K

2010 R St., NW. (202) 234-0339. In my opinion, the best gallery in Washington, D.C. with beautiful space in two levels. Shows mostly the cream of local artists. Owned and run by Mr. Komei Wachi, who seems to select the top notch local artists on a consistent basis. Good mix of abstraction and realism, with a leaning toward the latter. This gallery does everything right—good mix of artists, good openings, one to two group shows a year. Easily the best in town!

Troyer Gallery

701 Connecticut Ave. NW. (202) 328-7189. Considered one of the best galleries in the city, and I agree. The gallery has been run by three partners and has been around for over two decades. It was rumored to be closing soon, but one of the three former partners kept it going. Shows works by local and national artists with a good mixture of abstraction and realism. Shows many established artists and seems to be a hard place for new, emerging talent to "crack." Will be moving to a new location soon. Directed by Allan Troyer.

Fraser Gallery

1054 31st St. NW. (202) 298-6450. The best gallery in Georgetown! It consistently changes its shows on a monthly basis and exhibits works by many local artists as well as hosts an annual competition. Directed and owned by photographer Catriona Fraser. Routinely exhibits the most affordable topnotch fine art in Washington with a strong emphasis on contemporary realism and black-and-white photography. It has the cream of the youngest, fast-

A Night Out with the Kids

After a hard day of sight-seeing the monuments and the museums, your kids may not be ready to call it a night, but you might be tired. An easy dinner and a movie can be found at Union Station, where there's a nine-theater multiplex and a food court that offers everything from '50s-style diner burgers to quiche Lorraine or cannolis for dessert.

A night tour of the monuments by either Old Town Trolley or Greyhound is also a great way to continue seeing the sights without having to navigate the Metro or look for parking. The monuments are all lit up at night, which gives them a whole new look. The Greyhound tours deposit you at your hotel door, which is a nice plus when your energy runs out.

rising new stars in the Washington art scene. The best place to buy quality, affordable art in all of D.C.

Hemphill Fine Arts

1027 33rd St. NW. (202) 342-5610.

An elegant Georgetown gallery, it shows the cream of the abstract artists in both a regional and somewhat national context. In the last year or so it has been showing some new talent and exceptional group shows. All exhibitions rotated regularly. Directed and owned by George Hemphill.

The Art League

105 N. Union St., Alexandria VA, (703) 683-1780.

An open membership gallery, it has monthly juried shows in the main gallery and solo shows in the side galleries. The juried group shows are usually outstanding. Shows exclusively local artists. This huge space is the first stepping stone for most Washington-area artists and the best place to find emerging artists. Good mixture of all genres of modern art. Gallery director is Marsha Steiger.

Numark Gallery

406 Seventh St. NW, (202) 628-3810.

The best of the 7th Street galleries, this attractive gallery initially appeared to show mostly limited edition prints by big-name artists aimed at the corporate art market and personal collectors. However, in the last year or so it has included some brilliant work by Washington artists and now seems more focused on a mix of local artists and national names. Directed and owned by Cheryl Numark.

Gallery Okuda International

1054 31st St. NW, (202) 625-1054. Shows a mixture of local, national, and Japanese-ancestry artists. Chants show regularly on a monthly basis. A very nice gallery space, a wide range of art from contemporary abstraction to brilliant realism is featured. Directed and owned by Teruko Okuda, who also markets artists' work in Japan.

Maurine Littleton Gallery

1667 Wisconsin Ave. NW, (202) 333-9307. This gallery shows exclusively work by the top fine art glass artists in the world. Brilliant, beautiful work and equally brilliant catalogs are showcased, and has a long family history of glass. Shows are regularly rotated. Directed and owned by Maurine Littleton.

Anton Gallery

2108 R St. NW, (202) 328-0828. Shows many local artists and changes its shows on a regular monthly basis, offering a good mixture of abstract and new realists. Two floors of exhibition space are often shared by two artists. Directed and owned by Gail Evans.

Parish Gallery

1054 31st St. NW, (202) 944-2310. Shows mostly works by African-American artists and various racial and ethnic minority artists. Often shows works by local artists. Shows are changed on a monthly basis. Good mixture of art, with a leaning towards abstraction. Also does two to three group shows a year. Directed and owned by Norman Parish.

In addition to Anna Maria Gambino-Colombo's recommendations, there are four galleries that I liked immensely.

Connor Contemporary Art

1730 Connecticut Ave., (202) 588-8150. The Connor gallery shows many of the big names in pop art, but it is also the home of local artist Alan Simensky, whose large Lichtenstein-inspired banners were recently exhibited at the Corcoran and can be seen in the second floor gallery windows.

Late Night Shopping in Georgetown

If you want to just walk through the streets of the city and window shop (or even buy something), Georgetown is Washington's late night shopping area, where many of the stores are open until 11:00 P.M. From college gear such as The Gap and Banana Republic to fun youth-oriented clothing and housewares in a funky store like Urban Outfitters and Betsy Johnson's designs, Georgetown has an eclectic mix of stores and late night eateries too. The Shops at Georgetown, the three-story mall, are open until 9:00, as well.

Eklelitkos Gallery

1054 31st St. NW, (202) 342-1809. A friendly gallery, it is home to many new and emerging local artists with monthly shows. Hosts an annual juried show. Owned and operated by Michael Sprouse (cousin of '80s designer Stephen), a well-known painter.

Museum of Contemporary Art (MOCA)

1054 31st St. NW, (202) 342-6230. This nonprofit gallery is owned and operated by the affable Michael Clark and his wife Felicity Hogan, both well-known local artists. Their gallery has given many local artists their first exhibits, and it shows an extremely clever and eclectic mix of works.

Washington Printmakers Gallery

1732 Connecticut Ave. NW, (202) 332-1755. An artists co-operative, this gallery has a wonderful collection of almost entirely local artists work, most of which is very affordable.

Arts and Cultural Centers

Arts Club of Washington

2017 I St. NW, Washington, DC; (202)331-7282 Founded in 1916, the Arts Club of Washington considers promoting interest in the arts in the greater Washington area to be its sworn duty. Its location near the White House, in the historic Monroe House (after President James Monroe, whose inaugural reception was held here) is filled primarily with the work of local artists working in a wide variety of styles.

Paintings, drawings, and sculptures cover the top three floors of Monroe House, while special exhibitions appear in the first floor and cellar galleries—as well as in the adjacent Macfeely House. The Arts Club offers more than galleries; its activities also include a one act play festival, free concerts on Friday afternoons, and well known local authors reading from their works. The galleries are open from 10 A.M. to 5 P.M. Tuesdays through Fridays, until 2 P.M. Saturdays, and from 1 P.M. to 5 P.M. Sundays; admission is free.

Folger Shakespeare Library

201 East Capitol St. SE, Washington, DC; (202) 544-7077 The Folger Shakespeare Library has perhaps the world's finest collection of Shakespearean books and research materials. Scholars come from around the world to study and work here. Does this mean you have to *be* a scholar, dressed in full neck ruffle, to enjoy the place?

For starters, there are Folger's stage performances. Along with traditional productions of *Richard III* and *The Merchant of Venice*, you may also run across things like *The Complete History of America (Abridged)* by the hilarious Reduced Shakespeare Company. Musical offerings, meanwhile feature wold-renown artists playing works from the 15th and 16th centuries.

There are plenty of events for the kids and their parents, which bring the Elizabethan era to life through hands-on activities like authentic period feasts. These events take place on Saturday afternoons and cost just $8. Grownups, meanwhile, can enjoy the PEN/Faulkner literary series; according to the *Chicago Tribune*, This series is wonderful for "reminding Washingtonians (though they always forget) that there's more to life than government and politics." Recent guests have included Joseph Heller, Doris Lessing, Jane Siley, and Julia Alvarez. Tickets are generally $12.

Library of Congress

101 Independence Ave. SE, Washington, DC; (202) 707-8000 The Library of Congress is the largest library in the world. Over 100 million items in the library's collection stretch out along 532 *miles* of bookshelves! The library also sponsors some 350 public events each year. These include concerts, poetry readings, exhibitions, and lectures, and all are free of charge.

Many of these events are held at noontime, especially convenient for those who work in the Capitol Hill area. Lecturers of note have included author Herman Wouk, poet *laureate* consultant Rita Dove,

Gallery Openings Galore

Washington's art galleries have banded together and hold mutual gallery openings on certain days of the month when the galleries are open later, so that you can see new work and try a smorgasbord of wine and cheese all in one night.

In the Dupont Circle area, the first Fridays of every month the galleries along Connecticut Ave. hold opening night receptions. In Georgetown, the third Thursday of every month is the place to be along the Canal St. courtyard galleries, while the galleries along Georgetown's main drag hold their opening night on the third Friday of every month.

and Bruce Millken, CEO of Random Access. The library's American Folklife Center presents concerts that celebrate the diverse cultures of the United States. And, don't miss the free movies shown in the Mary Pickford Theater! Free tours of the library are also given regularly; call the Visitors Services Office at (202) 707-5458 for tour information. Call the number above for other general info.

College Performing Arts

The many college campuses of the Washington area offer a wealth of music, dance, theater, and films.

American University

4400 Massachusetts Ave. NW, Washington, DC; (202) 885-ARTS (2787) AU's Performing Arts Department produces four major performances a year, from the Greek drama *Medea* to dance concerts featuring faculty and students. General admission to these events is usually $10; there is a $2.50 discount if you order your tickets two weeks in advance.

The Kay Spiritual Life Center, AU's chapel, is the concert setting for the school's musical ensembles. The AU Symphony Orchestra, Concert Choir, and various chamber groups all perform here. Admission to these concerts is under $5. The aptly titled **American Music Festival** is an annual four-day extravaganza that unites the student groups, faculty, and visiting artists. Each performance features important works from "American" composers (the country *and* the college). Tickets to festival events ate usually $5.

AU also offers "Faculty Artist" and "Evening of Opera" series. The faculty series provides one concert a month while the opera series, which features young professionals from the community, offers five concerts a year. For more info on these, call (202) 885-3431.

Catholic University

620 Michigan Ave. NE, Washington, DC; (202) 319-5367 Hartke Theatre is the setting for CU's high-caliber theatrical productions. Generally performing six to eight plays a year, the department

draws upon works from both contemporary artists and classical writers. *Small Craft Warnings*, a rarely seen piece by Tennessee Williams, was one recent highlight. The admission price averages around $10 per production.

Although CU's music department focuses solely on classical music, the Benjamin T. Rome School of Music has much to offer: Half a dozen symphony concerts, two full-scale opera productions, and dozens of student and faculty recitals fill the academic calendar each year. Many of these events are free of charge; larger productions, such as the operas, range up to $15 a ticket. Call the concert info line at (202) 319-5416.

Gallaudet University

800 Florida Avenue NE, Washington, DC; (202) 651-5501 Gallaudet, a nationally acclaimed school for the deaf, offers a unique style of theatre performance. The theatre arts department assembles three productions a year, one in the fall, one in the winter, and a children's play in the spring. The productions range from comedies by Neil Simon to the dramatic *Firebugs* by Max Frisch. Student actors perform using sign language, while professional hearing actors provide vocal interpretations. Tickets cost $6 ($5 for the children's play). Discounts are available for students and kids, of course. Call (202) 651-5500 for reservations.

George Mason University

4400 University Dr., Fairfax, VA; Box Office, (703) 993-8888 The Center for the Arts organization brings major national and international artists to its new Concert Hall Building; you could spend a pretty penny for these, but there are some exceptions. Lesser-priced entertainment here and at other university hall is provided by local theatre groups (notably, artists-in-residence The Theatre of the First Amendment), along with various local music groups ranging from orchestras to military bands. Some of these performances are even free to all.

Ticket prices are only $5 for the GMU theater department's own plays and musicals. The dance program sponsors student ballet,

Catch Some Unique D.C. Entertainment

If you can get out at night, you can usually catch some good theater or performance in D.C. since many tourists are just too exhausted to go out at night. Many Broadway shows make their way to Washington, and you can often catch some really good theater on tour, often for half price by calling (202) TICKETS, which offers half-price tickets the day of the show. If there is a production at Ford's Theatre, it might be interesting to see a play in the same theater where Lincoln was assassinated.

The J.F.K. Center for the Performing Arts has free concerts every night, but check the *Washington Post* weekend section for other performances, as well as what's playing at the American Film Institute Theater, where there are often very intriguing film series and lectures.

jazz, and modern dance performances. "Informal" concerts cost only a $2 donation, while larger concerts with guest choreographers may go up to $8.

Many of the music department's concerts, including some faculty recitals, are free. Student groups such as the GMU Symphony Orchestra, Jazz Ensemble, Wind Ensemble (with its own recording contract), and Opera Workshop Project cover the spectrum of sound. Call this department at (703) 993-1380 for specifics.

Georgetown University

37th & O Sts. NW, Washington, DC; (202) 687-4422 Georgetown offers a treasure trove of inexpensive entertainment. **The Mask and Bauble Dramatic Society** (687-6783) produces two major plays each semester, like their recent *The Mystery of Edwin Drood*, a musical based on the Charles Dickens novel. **Nomadic Theatre** (687-8146), another on-campus troupe, brought the hit Broadway farce *Lend Me A Tenor* to G'town. Ticket prices range from $5, for the smaller Nomadic shows, up to $12 for those by M & B.

Black Movements Dance Theatre and the **Georgetown University Dance Company** both present modern dance performances. Admission prices range from absolutely free to about $7 for the GU Dance Company's biannual extravaganza of jazz, ballet and tap. Call (202) 687-1625 for info on dance doings.

GU's music department, meanwhile, showcases *a cappella* groups, a concert band and choir, and chamber ensembles—filling Gaston Hall with euphony all year 'round. Of particular note (pun intended) is the semi-professional **Georgetown Symphony Orchestra.** Music tickets range from $3 for band concerts up to $12 for the GSO.

George Washington University

600 22nd St. NW, Washington DC; (202) 994-6178 "The Lisner at Noon" series offers free, weekday lunchtime concerts to the public in the world-class Lisner Auditorium. It showcases local pianists, singers, and dance troupes; for upcoming shows, call the Lisner's 24-hour concert line at (202) 994-1500.

GW's music department presents both student and faculty artists: the GW University Singers, Symphonic Orchestra, Chamber Players, the *a cappella* Troubadours, and more. Most concerts are held at the Dorothy Betts Marvin Theatre, where tickets can be purchased in advance. General admission is usually $5, although subscription rates are available for the faculty artist series (which can bring season tix down to under $2 per concert!). Call the department at (202) 994-6245 for info.

The department of theatre and dance produces four major plays, including a musical, and two dance recitals. GW's modern dance troupe, the Dance Company, is often joined by guest artists. Most of these shows cost $8-$10; subscriber discounts again reduce the per-ticket price. For more info, call this department at (202) 994-6178.

Howard University

2400 Sixth St. NW, Washington, DC; (202) 806-0971 Howard University's department of theater and dance presents four plays and two dance concerts a year. General admission is usually around $10. The music department showcases most of its performing groups at free concerts held in the Andrew Rankin Chapel. Among those which regularly perform are the University Choir, the Gospel Choir, Concert Band, and Jazz Ensembles. Call the department at (202) 806-5862 for info on concert dates and times.

Mount Vernon College

2100 Foxhall Rd. NW, Washington, DC; (202) 625-4655 "The In Series" at Mount Vernon College will keep you in the know with all manner of dance, music, opera, performance art, and poetry events. Professional musicians, dancers, and actors from the national and even international circuit perform at Hand Chapel, a small and elegant hall perfect for intimate performances. Ticket prices average around $12.50, but can be as much as $21.50 for a Saturday night at the Opera. Discounts are available for students, of course; also for kids, who will most likely enjoy select dance and cabaret performances.

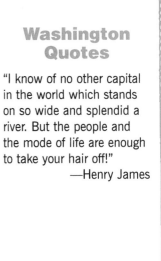

Washington Quotes

"I know of no other capital in the world which stands on so wide and splendid a river. But the people and the mode of life are enough to take your hair off!"
—Henry James

Trinity College

125 Michigan Ave. NE, Washington, DC; (202) 939-5277 Trinity features several free or inexpensively priced concerts throughout the school year. "Concerts in the Well" is a noontime student recital series held in Trinity's main building. Classical fare ranges from soloist to a group called the Chamber Players, whose makeup consists of different instrumental combinations every year. Other recitals, some in the evening, feature members of the faculty. All of these events are usually free and open to the public.

Recitals and concerts are also held at other campus performing spaces, such as O'Connor Auditorium or the Notre Dame Chapel. Here, you may catch *a cappella* faves The Belles (a student-run group), or the Pan American Symphony Orchestra (artists-in-residence). Performing four to five concerts a year, the orchestra show cases composers and artists from Latin America. Their concerts cost about $10—but are discounted for students.

In addition, Trinity's Drama Society produces two small-scale works a year, with tickets which won't cost more that $5. The number above is the school's public relations number; they'll give you info on the next production.

University of the District of Columbia

Van Ness Campus, 4200 Connecticut Ave. NW, Washington DC; (202) 274-7402 UDC's Department of Mass Media, Visual, and Performing Arts presents just that range of entertainment. The music department showcases about nine recitals each semester, most of which can be enjoyed for free. You can enjoy the jazz and gospel of the University Chorale, the Voices, and various instrumental jazz ensembles.

Less frequent, but every bit as enjoyable, are the stage works presented by the theatre program. They usually perform two plays each semester in the Little Theatre, a setting as intimate as it sounds. Recent years have produced a series of one-act plays, as well as larger works written by UDC theater majors. Culturally diverse themes dominate the scene at downright deviant ticket prices—ranging from free to $5 for larger works.

And, at no charge, interested patrons can attend photography exhibitions or sit in on related seminars on such topics as digital imaging. Call the office for an events calendar.

University of Maryland at College Park

University Blvd., College Park, MD; (301) 405-5548 U of M's University Theatre sponsors as many as a dozen plays throughout the year. Many are full-scale productions, such as Stephen Sondheim's musical *Into the Woods*. Tickets for these range from $7 to $12; but original plays, written and directed by students, are absolutely free. Call the theater line for more info at (301) 405-6693. Inexpensive professional shows are also presented by the National Players, a classical touring company in residence on campus.

The music department is "in tune" with presentations of its own. The bi-annual Handel Festival, at Memorial Chapel, features the UM chorus and the Smithsonian Chamber Orchestra, with top tickets priced around $20. However, tickets are under $10 if you don't mind sitting in the "C" sections of the chapel. Other concerts, held at the Stamp Student Union, include the "UM Bands Showcase" and the annual "Pops" concerts. Tix range from free up to around $7 or so. Call the music department at (301) 405-5568.

Back at the chapel is the "Monday Night Music Series," offering free concerts of high caliber. The series features everything from jazz to chamber music to the occasional sing-along session for those who'd like to join in. To inquire about Monday events, call (301) 314 - 9866.

Theater

Arena Stage

Sixth & Maine Ave. SW, Washington, DC; (202) 488-3300 Now in its fifth decade of operation, the Arena Stage is well-known as one of the country's leading regional theater operations. Its three-stage complex hosts nearly a quarter of a million patrons each season. Productions range from European classics by Voltaire, Lorca, and Noel Coward to contemporary American plays.

Washington Quotes

"I believe that the Prince of Darkness could start a branch of hell in the District of Columbia (if he has not already done it) and carry it on unimpeached by the Congress of the United States, even though the Constitution were bristling with articles forbidding hells in this country."

—MARK TWAIN

Another option is the Arena's "PlayQuest" series, which runs in December and January and offers two shows in the cabaret-style Old Vat theater—for free. It's a great chance to see new productions still in the development process. Seats for these plays go fast; call to see what's coming up.

Gala Hispanic Theatre

1625 Park Rd. NW, Washington, DC; (202) 234-7174 Nearing its twentieth anniversary, Gala Hispanic Theatre presents professional-quality Latino theater, dance, music, and poetry. Most performances are done in Spanish, but Gala also offers a simultaneous English translation. After many of the shows, the performers and directors come back out to discuss the work with the audience (again, in a bilingual format).

National Theatre

1321 Pennsylvania Ave. NW, Washington, DC; (202) 628-6161 D.C.'s famous National Theatre—opened in 1835, it's the Capital's oldest cultural institution—presents touring Broadway hits on a regular basis.

Once a week from September to April, both young and old can enjoy special events here that are absolutely free. Each of these Saturday mornings at 9:30 and 11 A.M. the National offers music and theater especially for children. A recent show demonstrated string instruments in performing "Peter and the Wolf" and "The William Tell Overture"; puppets, folk tales, and magic are also among the free offerings. And, on Monday nights at 7 and 8:30 P.M., the public is welcome to enjoy various one-act plays, music, readings, and dance performances.

Source Theatre Company

1835 14th St. NW (202) 462-1073 Calling itself "the face of provocative theatre in Washington," this has indeed been a prime source for exciting drama over the past two decades. STC is committed to innovative original plays, as well as modern interpretations of classical works. Moreover, it offers deals on tickets which belie the notion that quality theatre has to cost a fortune.

STC's month-long "Washington Theatre Festival" in July presents a remarkable seventy new plays and musicals of all kinds, at ten different area locations.

Warner Theatre

1299 Pennsylvania Ave. NW Washington, DC 20004-2405 Phone: (202) 628-1818 When the Warner Theatre opened in 1924 it was hailed as a building of beauty, featuring a spectacular marble and gold leaf lobby and large auditorium complete with gold leaf ceilings and chandeliers. Today, having undergone a $10 million restoration, the Warner is host to a variety of Broadway productions, comedy, dance, film, and music concerts. Hours and prices vary according to performance schedule. Accessible seating available. Metro: Metro Center.

The Washington Ballet

3515 Wisconsin Ave. NW Washington, DC 20016 Phone: (202) 362-3606 Annual repertory series of contemporary and classical ballet at the Kennedy Center and the holiday favorite, *The Nutcracker,* at the Warner Theatre. Performance times vary. Ticket prices at the Kennedy Center: $30; groups, $22.50- $25.50. *Nutcracker* tickets: $25-$34; groups $18.75-$28.90.

The Washington Opera

2600 Virginia Ave. NW #104 Washington, DC 20037 Phone: (202) 295-2400 Now entering its 44th season, The Washington Opera is one of the nation's leading opera companies and plays to standing room only audiences in the Kennedy Center Opera House and Eisenhower Theater.

Washington Stage Guild

924 G St. NW, (202)529-2084 Having recently celebrated its tenth year in show biz, the Washington Stage Guild presents four plays each season, running from October through May. "Neglected classics" are the focus here, according to someone from the theatre; he proudly cited an example from several years ago, when WSG produced Oscar Wilde's *An Ideal Husband* instead of the better-known *The Importance of Being Earnest.* More recently, *Husband* has seen a new popularity with many troupes.

George Bernard Shaw, T.S. Eliot, and other older playwrights have been given new life by the guild.

Antique Shops

Another popular entertainment on weekends is to stroll through Georgetown or Capitol Hill and window shop at the antique stores. There aren't very many bargains here, but there is some interesting stuff, especially in the newer stores that feature "antiques" from the '60s and '70s.

Antiques on the Hill, 701 N. Carolina Ave, SE, (202) 543-1819. This shop is a neighborhood institution, having been at this location for nearly 30 years. It features many small and lovely items, such as silver, jewelry, and tableware, as well as larger pieces such as lamps and furniture.

Cherub Antiques Gallery, 2918 M St. NW in Georgetown, (202) 337-2224. This gallery specializes in Art Nouveau and Art Deco antiques, as well as arts and crafts.

Geoffrey Diner, 1730 21st St. NW, (202) 483-5005. A very up-scale antiques shop, with some beautiful Tiffany lamps, as well as decorative and fine arts.

Millennium, 1528 U St. SW, (202) 483-1218. A little out of the way, but if you are in the neighborhood, this is worth the trip. This is a gallery featuring all the kitsch and culture from the '50s to the '70s, with an ever-changing assortment of stuff you wish your parents had never thrown away.

St. Luke's Gallery, 1715 Q St. NW in Georgetown, (202) 328-2424. A charming townhouse antiques store with Old master paintings, sixteenth–nineteenth century watercolors and many prints, etchings and line drawings.

Index

We Have EVERYTHING

More Bestselling Everything Titles Available From Your Local Bookseller:

Everything **After College Book**
Everything **Astrology Book**
Everything **Baby Names Book**
Everything **Baby Shower Book**
Everything **Barbeque Cookbook**
Everything® **Bartender's Book**
Everything **Bedtime Story Book**
Everything **Beer Book**
Everything **Bicycle Book**
Everything **Bird Book**
Everything **Build Your Own Home Page Book**
Everything **Casino Gambling Book**
Everything **Cat Book**
Everything® **Christmas Book**
Everything **College Survival Book**
Everything **Cover Letter Book**
Everything **Crossword and Puzzle Book**
Everything **Dating Book**
Everything **Dessert Book**
Everything **Dog Book**
Everything **Dreams Book**
Everything **Etiquette Book**
Everything **Family Tree Book**

Everything **Fly-Fishing Book**
Everything **Games Book**
Everything **Get-a-Job Book**
Everything **Get Published Book**
Everything **Get Ready For Baby Book**
Everything **Golf Book**
Everything **Guide to New York City**
Everything **Guide to Walt Disney World®, Universal Studios®, and Greater Orlando**
Everything **Guide to Washington D.C.**
Everything **Herbal Remedies Book**
Everything **Homeselling Book**
Everything **Homebuying Book**
Everything **Home Improvement Book**
Everything **Internet Book**
Everything **Investing Book**
Everything **Jewish Wedding Book**
Everything **Kids' Money Book**
Everything **Kids' Nature Book**
Everything **Kids' Puzzle Book**
Everything **Low-Fat High-Flavor Cookbook**
Everything **Microsoft® Word 2000 Book**

Everything **Money Book**
Everything **One-Pot Cookbook**
Everything **Online Business Book**
Everything **Online Investing Book**
Everything **Online Shopping Book**
Everything **Pasta Book**
Everything **Pregnancy Book**
Everything **Pregnancy Organizer**
Everything **Resume Book**
Everything **Sailing Book**
Everything **Selling Book**
Everything **Study Book**
Everything **Tarot Book**
Everything **Toasts Book**
Everything **Total Fitness Book**
Everything **Trivia Book**
Everything **Tropical Fish Book**
Everything® **Wedding Book, 2nd Edition**
Everything® **Wedding Checklist**
Everything® **Wedding Etiquette Book**
Everything® **Wedding Organizer**
Everything® **Wedding Shower Book**
Everything® **Wedding Vows Book**
Everything **Wine Book**